Jeremy Corbyn's Labour stands on the brink of power, promising a fundamental re-ordering of British politics. But what, in practice, will this entail? How can a radical government stand up to an establishment that is hostile to any significant redistribution of wealth and power? *People Get Ready!* dives into the nitty gritty of what's needed to bring about transformative change.

Unlike a decade ago, the left's problem is no longer a shortage of big ideas. Inside and outside the Labour Party, an agenda for new forms of public and community ownership is taking shape. Today the biggest danger facing the left is lack of *preparedness*—the absence of strategies that can make these ideas a reality.

People Get Ready! draws on previous attempts at radical change, from the election of Labour at the end of the Second World War and the progressive early days of Mitterrand's presidency in France, to Tony Benn's battles with Harold Wilson and Margaret Thatcher's icy insistence that there was no alternative to free markets. These stories highlight the importance of knowing your allies and, even more, your enemies, of being ready to deal with sabotage and resistance from the highest levels, of being bold enough to transform the structures of government, and of having a mass movement that can both support the leadership and hold it to its radical programme when the going gets tough.

Remarkably, democratic socialism in Britain is closer to government than in any other European country. The responsibilities this brings for those supporting the Corbyn project are as great as the opportunities it presents. But there isn't much time to get ready ...

PEOPLE GET READY!

PEOPLE GET READY!

PREPARING FOR A CORBYN GOVERNMENT

CHRISTINE BERRY AND JOE GUINAN

OR Books
New York · London

© 2019 Christine Berry and Joe Guinan

All rights information: rights@orbooks.com
Visit our website at www.orbooks.com

First printing 2019

Library of Congress Cataloging-in-Publication Data: A catalog record for this book is available from the Library of Congress.
British Library Cataloging in Publication Data: A catalog record for this book is available from the British Library.

Typeset by Lapiz Digital. Printed by BookMobile, USA, and CPI, UK.

paperback ISBN 978-1-68219-197-2 • ebook ISBN 978-1-68219-198-9

In loving memory of June Berry and Martin Guinan

CONTENTS

PREFACE AND ACKNOWLEDGMENTS

We both grew up in the monstrously elongated shadow of Thatcherism in Britain; consider this book our small revenge. The book was written at great speed over a couple of months in the late summer and early autumn of 2018. Our haste stemmed from our sense of hope at the historic opportunities being opened up by the Corbyn project, together with a growing foreboding that, collectively, we are not yet ready for the mammoth challenges ahead. We wanted urgently to help address what we perceived to be the lack of deep movement conversation around strategies for actually accomplishing transformative change. In writing this quick book we have thus taken many short cuts and turned away from the temptations of deeper investigations into areas we find interesting or compelling in favour of rapid intervention in Britain's constantly fluctuating and changing political-economic landscape. We are well aware of some shortcomings and omissions as a result.

We therefore offer up what follows as a conversation-starter rather than any claim to the last word. We are operating throughout at the level of broad-brush suggestion rather than definitive pronouncement or prediction. We certainly do not contend that we have everything right. Instead, we hope that we are asking some of the right questions at the right level for the development of the next phase of Corbynism: *preparedness*. To that end, we conclude with a Movement Discussion Guide, designed to facilitate ongoing conversation and debate about a number of the thorny strategic issues we have raised.

When explaining what we were setting out to accomplish with this short book, a colleague described it back to us as "an old-fashioned political pamphlet—like *Common Sense*". We are flattered by the comparison with Tom Paine (especially since one of us writes from voluntary exile in the United States) and embrace the characterisation of what follows as not a detached study but rather a sustained political argument or even a polemic. As will quickly become apparent, we are committed supporters of the Corbyn project—but also (we hope) critical friends, concerned at what we see as a missing strategic dimension to the current political conversation. While we've shared in the surging optimism and euphoria of the past couple of years, as the horizons of the possible in Britain have been radically expanded and the shimmering hope of a better future has reappeared miraculously ahead, we are also acutely aware of the tremendous challenges that remain and obstacles still to be overcome.

The purpose of our book—alerting the fledgling movement that is Corbynism to a number of dilemmas we see ahead at the level of politics, policy, and preparedness—means that it is aimed principally at the Corbyn base of Labour Party and Momentum members, political activists, trade unionists, campaigners, and community organisers, as well as assorted well-wishers and (with a bit of luck) a broader supportive public. We hope it will also be of interest to those of all progressive parties and none who wish to be part of transforming our economy and society beyond neoliberalism.

As such, what follows should be seen as an intervention for the particular moment we're in, not a tract for the ages. We were aware even as we wrote that the fast pace of current events could quickly supersede aspects of our argument or render it obsolete before it could appear in the world, even at the breakneck speed offered by O/R Books, our publisher. Such are the hazards of pamphleteering—especially in an era like the present that recalls the dictum, attributed to Lenin, of there being decades in which nothing happens and weeks in which decades happen.

As a collaboration between its authors, this book also contains compromises. Fortunately, we are substantially in agreement on the argument that follows, although there are some aspects that each of us might have put slightly differently. The tight timeline and division of labour on the manuscript has also required that we place a lot of trust in one another. On a couple of issues, most notably Brexit, we have larger differences, reflecting wider debates on the UK left. We have somewhat sidestepped these, not because we do not think they are important, but for the sake of the overall argument and because it seemed fruitless to attempt to speculate on the context into which this book will be published, on the other side of the 29 March 2019 date set for the UK's departure from the European Union. We do, however, share a view that the UK left—as divided over Brexit as the rest of the country—will need to come back together not merely around a different economic model domestically but also around a post-neoliberal vision for the international economy and a redefinition of the UK's role in the world. We applaud John McDonnell's recent leadership on these vital questions.

Our book starts from the premise that if we are serious about fundamental change then the movement around Corbynism needs to take itself seriously as an agent of historical transformation, and to begin laying some serious groundwork—not least because of the scale of the opposition we will face. Finance capital in particular is well aware that we are the enemy, and it is now time for us to return the favour. In late 2017, a client briefing note by Wall Street investment bank Morgan Stanley, as reported in the *Independent*, made the stakes abundantly clear. It expressed the view that Jeremy Corbyn becoming prime minister would be "worse for British business than Brexit", as it could usher in "the most significant political shift in the UK since the end of the 1970s". Such a shift is, of course, precisely what Britain so desperately needs, and why all those of us who support the Corbyn project must now get ready to fight for it against powerful and determined enemies. Hence our overall exhortation with this book, as Curtis Mayfield's beautiful gospel-inflected civil rights anthem had it—*People Get Ready*.

The book has been composed on the basis of desk research as well as a handful of interviews—some of them necessarily off the record and on deep background. Those people who generously agreed to talk with us but who must remain anonymous for political reasons know who they are, and we are deeply grateful for their insights and openness. We have also consulted, where we could, with allies and experts in our personal and professional networks, and portions of the manuscript have benefitted from the perceptive comments and reactions of friendly readers. We would like to thank Grace Blakeley, Charlie Clarke, Stephen Devlin, Deborah Hermanns, Michael Jacobs, Tasos Koronakis, Christos Katsioulis, Laurie Macfarlane, Laura Parker, Dave Powell, Annie Quick, Olivier Vardakoulias, and Dan Vockins for conversations that helped shape our thinking. Our gratitude also goes to Adrian Bua, Matthew Butcher, Catherine Charlwood, Sirio Canós Donnay, Mike Makin-Waite, and George Woods for reviewing draft chapters and providing insightful comments. Owen Jones graciously took time out from his unforgiving schedule to pen the Foreword, for which we thank him. We also want to give special mention to Thomas Hanna, who is an unfailing source of ideas and suggestions, to Sarah McKinley for maintaining high morale, and to Martin O'Neill for relentlessly promoting our ideas—and for patiently waiting his turn. All remaining faults are, of course, ours alone.

A seminar in London in June 2018, convened by the Real Democracy Movement around their pamphlet, *What If? Scenario Planning for a Corbyn-Led Government*, was helpful in clarifying our thinking, and we would like to thank the participants. The organisers of The World Transformed also generously made space for a high-level panel discussion of our themes at their annual festival of ideas in Liverpool in September 2018, shortly after the draft manuscript had been submitted. A number of publications, especially *Renewal* journal, *openDemocracy*, and *New Socialist*, have given us space to develop elements of the argument, and we are thankful to our editors there. We hope that these piecemeal discussions represent just the beginning of a wider movement conversation about strategy for transformative change.

"We must love one another or die", wrote W. H. Auden in his poem "September 1, 1939", as the "low dishonest decade" of the 1930s issued into the Second World War. Today, as our febrile politics gives rise to neo-fascism and the spectre of ecological collapse, the stakes are once again climbing—and solidarity and deep comradeship take on a renewed importance. We are fortunate to share in the love, support, and encouragement of a great many friends and colleagues, too numerous to mention, all of whom we would like to acknowledge here. They include: Tom Barker, Joe Bilsborough, Grace Blakeley, Fran Boait, Matthew Brown, Matthew Butcher, Lisa Calderwood, Aditya Chakrabortty, Andrew Clark, Maeve Cohen, Michaela Collord, Andy Cumbers, George Davies, James Doran, John Duda, Laura Flanders, Ronnie Galvin, Peter Gowan, Betty Grdina, Thomas Hanna, Jacqui Howard, Dan Hind, Simon Hooper, Michael Hudson, Emily Kenway, Mathew Lawrence, Laurie Laybourn-Langton, Mary Leng, Laurie Macfarlane, Neil McInroy, Sarah McKinley, Juliet Michaelson, George Morris, Tom Mills, Leo Murray, Martin O'Neill, Laura Parker, Annie Quick, Randeep Ramesh, Adam Ramsay, Linnie Rawlinson, Howard Reed, Duncan Robinson, Jessica Rose, Carla Santos Skandier, Bec Sanderson, Faiza Shaheen, Max Shanly, Clifford Singer, Andrew Small, Kristin Lipke Sparding, Peter Sparding, James Stafford, Beth Stratford, Amy Studdart, Florence Sutcliffe-Braithwaite, Sam Tarry, Fionn Travers-Smith, Ted Vallance, Dan Vockins, Hilary Wainwright, Adam White, Stuart White, Archie Woodrow, and George Woods.

At O/R Books, we are indebted to Alex Doherty, Colin Robinson, Emma Ingrisani, and their colleagues. The leadership, staff, trustees, fellows, and funders of The Democracy Collaborative and the Next System Project could not have been more supportive—in particular, Gar Alperovitz, Ted Howard, Marjorie Kelly, Gus Speth, and Allan Henderson have been sources of intellectual guidance and inspiration, while Dana Brown held the fort. Susan Sechler and Lloyd Timberlake, Hannah Wenzel Krieger and John Krieger, and Erin

Molnar Mains and Oliver Mains all provided sustenance and distraction, while Janie Koger LaPrairie provided emergency haircuts.

We would also like to thank our immediate families. Christine is especially grateful for the unfailing love and support of her father and parents-in-law, John Berry, Catherine Taylor and Chris Taylor, and her sister Ruth, without whom navigating book-writing and pregnancy at the same time would have been unimaginable; and for the bump, which has been a constant reminder of the important things in life. Joe would like to thank his mother, Patricia Harvey, from whom he gets half of his politics, and his sister, Lisa North, who works on the front lines of our failing system; as well as Peter Harvey, Barbara Harvey, Spencer Rhodes, James Rhodes, Marcia North, Shane North, Nancy Cenac, the late Dickie Robichaux, Estelle Robichaux, and Eugenie Rogers. Roux Robichaux has long proved the wisdom of Harry Truman's injunction that, if you want a friend in Washington, DC, you should get a dog. Last but definitely not least, nothing would be possible without the love, support, generosity, and patience of our partners, Mark Taylor and Emily Robichaux, to whom we are forever grateful.

Finally, it is a source of deep sadness that Christine's mother, June Berry, and Joe's father, Martin Guinan, are no longer with us. Recalling how they helped make us who we are, we dedicate this book to their memory, with love.

Christine Berry and Joe Guinan

November 2018

FOREWORD: OWEN JONES

Britain's social order is irretrievably broken. Workers have suffered the longest squeeze in wages since the Napoleonic Wars; the most severe of any industrialised nation other than Greece. Despite Conservative protestations that work is the route out of poverty, most people in poverty are in work, earning their poverty. Up to 10 million workers are in insecure work, from temporary contracts to bogus self-employment to the "gig" economy of Uber and Deliveroo.[1] With the mass sell-off of council houses—and four out of ten now owned by buy-to-let landlords charging twice the rent—and homeownership collapsing to 1980s levels, a generation is being driven into an unregulated private rented sector defined by insecurity and high rents.[2] Young people have been robbed of what might once have been thought of as a birthright—to have a better lot in life than their parents—as their youth services are decimated, they are saddled with debt, their living standards fall, and they are lumbered with both insecure jobs and rip-off rents. At the same time, a financial sector which had plunged the country into calamity was bailed out, continued to pay more bonuses than every other EU country put together, and carried on as though nothing had happened.

Privatisation, it was claimed, would usher in a new age of efficient, modernised, consumer-orientated services. Reality collided disastrously with dogma. As the *Financial Times* put it, the privatisation of water was "little more than an organised rip-off".[3] Household water bills soared by 40 per cent following the sell-off, with consumers spending an estimated £2.3 billion more than if water had remained nationalised.[4] The privatisation of the railways,

Conservative prime minister John Major had promised, would mean "a better, cheaper and more effective service for the commuter".[5] Instead, the result was a chaotic, costly mess, with a surge in public subsidies, some of Europe's most expensive fares, overcrowding, and those technological improvements that were made all being developed and underwritten by the state. Then there's energy. It has been estimated that electricity prices are up to 20 per cent higher than if the power companies had never been sold off.[6] No wonder that privatisation is rejected so overwhelmingly by the public. A poll commissioned by one think tank found that 83 per cent want water renationalised, and over three quarters favour the same for energy and rail. Half the public even back the nationalisation of the entire financial sector.[7]

Both Clement Attlee's post-war Labour government and Margaret Thatcher's Conservative government in the 1980s established a new political consensus. They overturned the underlying assumptions of the old order and forced their opponents to accept their fundamental principles. Britain today is ripe for another transformative government with the same mission—and it is within reach. The left's assumption of the Labour leadership—in the form of Jeremy Corbyn and his allies—and the Conservatives' loss of their majority in the 2017 general election have opened up the possibility of a radical rupture with the broken status quo.

But there remain many challenges ahead. Right-wing economist Milton Friedman once observed, rightly, that: "Only a crisis—actual or perceived—produces real change. When that crisis occurs, the actions that are taken depend on the ideas that are lying around". When the worst financial crisis since the Great Depression of the 1930s broke in 2008, some of the left's battered remnants had a sense of misplaced *schadenfreude*. Neoliberalism seemed self-evidently discredited; surely now an alternative would emerge from the rubble? But the "ideas lying around" did not, at that time, belong to the left. After Labour's turbulent civil wars and election defeats in the 1980s, the left had been vanquished and marginalised. The power of the trade union movement had been smashed by mass unemployment, repressive legislation, and industrial defeats. The rise of globalisation, it was said, meant that traditional social democratic governments were no longer possible. The end of the Cold War was portrayed not just as the final triumph of capitalism, but of a capitalism red in tooth and claw. It was in this context that New Labour—which surrendered to the hegemony of the market—became hegemonic. In the initial years after the crash, the left was in a defensive posture: defined by what it opposed, like cuts and privatisation, rather than united around a coherent vision of what society could look like.

Corbyn's leadership opened an intellectual and political space to lay the foundations for an alternative society. A once intellectually barren left is now in a state of ferment. There is ample evidence of it at The World Transformed, the annual event series of talks, forums and debates which takes place in parallel to Labour's Party Conference. Here, academics, economists, experts, campaigners, and politicians all debate issues ranging from climate change to housing, from workers' rights to feminism, from public ownership to taxation.

Now it's the Conservatives and the Labour right who are defined by what they are against, rather than what they are for. Perhaps one of the most exciting developments is a new vision of democratising the economy, rejecting the old style of nationalisation developed by Herbert Morrisson, a Labour right-winger in the post-war government, of top-down, bureaucratically run public corporations. Instead, democratic ownership by workers, consumers, and service users has become central to the project. From transforming finance to reducing the working week, it is the left that is winning the battle of ideas.

But we are still playing catch-up, and the debate and discussion over what a new economy and society will look like must continue in earnest. A socialist government in Britain will face exceptional challenges—not least concerted and determined opposition from finance, big business, and other vested interests, both domestically and internationally. The need to build a mass movement, one which crosses borders, particularly linking up with an ascendant U.S. left and leftist movements in countries such as Spain and France, is absolutely critical.

PEOPLE GET READY!

This book is as fascinating and politically stimulating as it is necessary. It is a vital contribution to a debate about how a radical government can assume power, backed by mass mobilisations within workplaces and communities, and successfully and irreversibly transform society in the twenty-first century. Struggle is not a linear process, and there will be victories and successes, as well as setbacks and defeats, in the coming years. But this book helps us prepare for an era of political opportunity as well as crisis—an era which will help determine the future of humanity for generations to come.

November 2018

INTRODUCTION

"It's far too late and things are far too bad for pessimism".
—Dee Ward Hock

Something extraordinary has been happening below the surface of British politics. The ground is shifting beneath an exhausted political and economic model. The resulting shocks—from Jeremy Corbyn's two leadership campaigns to the stunning outcomes of the 2016 EU referendum vote for Brexit and the 2017 general election—have shaken our politics to the point where it now feels as if anything could happen.

It is a moment both of great promise and of great peril. A decades-long political ice age appears finally to be coming to an end. Many hitherto fixed and long-established certainties are giving way to a world turned upside down. It is a terrifying but also an exhilarating prospect.

In a widely quoted observation that has become something of an epigraph for our times, the Italian Marxist theorist Antonio Gramsci, writing from one of Mussolini's prisons, famously warned of the dangers of crisis periods like the present in which "the old is dying and the new cannot be born". In such an "interregnum", Gramsci wrote, "a great variety of morbid symptoms appear".[1] This has been the experience of the past several years. The country has been caught in the wreckage of the 2008 financial crisis, which destroyed the legitimacy of the reigning economic paradigm without dethroning it. A decade on, politics—as Corbyn himself has noted—may finally be catching up.[2]

In *Forging Democracy*, his epic history of the European left, Geoff Eley has written compellingly of such moments, when the elusive prospect of transformative change suddenly heaves into view, and hope and history collide:

> Very occasionally, usually in the midst of a wider societal crisis, the apparently unbudgeable structures of normal political life become shaken. The expectations of a slow and unfolding habitual future get unlocked. Still more occasionally, collective agency materializes, sometimes explosively and with violent results … The present begins to move. These are times of extraordinary possibility and hope. New horizons shimmer. History's continuum shatters.[3]

The pundits have proven peculiarly ill equipped for the challenges of interpreting this surprising new era of flux and change, in which the recent past has become a poor predictor of future outcomes. The journalist Gary Younge, himself one of a small handful of honourable exceptions, has observed of his fellow commentators that they have largely spent their time "dismissing or lampooning one of the most interesting periods in recent political history, rather than trying to understand it".[4] As a result, they are continually wrong-footed by events, their monopoly on political wisdom increasingly called into question. This goes a long way to explaining the petulant tones of grievance and condescension with which the Corbyn phenomenon is most often discussed in the traditional media.[5]

A new era of politics

We are living through an "Age of Anger".[6] It is a time of "machine-breaking" politically, of boiling resentment amongst citizens and voters at an out-of-touch political class and an economic system they know is rotten to the core.[7] Those who fixate on how to protect a rhetorical "centre ground" from the bogey of populism are asking the wrong question. The old centre ground is already gone, having disappeared with the cratering of the economic model on which it rested. The real question is how to redirect the new mass popular anger into a force for change, for better or worse: who will break the machines of neoliberal extraction, and with what will they seek to replace them?

Already, across the world, terrifying answers to this question are being offered. A resurgent far right is everywhere on the march, from Poland to India, Italy to Brazil. In Germany, neo-Nazis once again rally openly in the streets. In the United States, the president orders immigrant children taken from their parents to be locked in cages. In the UK, racist attacks are on the rise. The emerging neo-fascist politics is even playing out on breakfast television: one day, millions of viewers can witness Piers Morgan shouting down a Muslim woman for being anti-Trump, the next they can watch a soft-pedal interview with Steve Bannon. Meanwhile, with the Conservative Party tearing itself apart, a new hard-right shock doctrine is emerging that seeks to shape a Brexit that would clamp down ruthlessly on workers' rights and put immigrants and people of colour in real physical danger—a renewal of "disaster capitalism".[8]

In the face of such popular anger, leafing through the centrist playbook to cycle in some new empty suit with a soundbite simply will not work. Clinging to the status quo for fear of something worse is a guaranteed losing strategy. After Brexit, after Trump, this much at least should be obvious.

Yet the left, and particularly the centre left, has an unfortunate tendency to be far too conservative in the face of unexpected and unstoppable change. Ed Miliband, reflecting on his time as Labour leader, seemingly now understands this. He openly admits that his leadership was too cautious, and that it is time his political generation, hidebound by their own increasingly out-of-date experience, learned to listen to a younger generation who know instinctively that things are changing and that the old ways no longer work. Intriguingly, this generational gulf has echoes in the experience of the 1930s, when an older cohort of senior left leaders, convinced that only they understood the political rulebook, clashed with younger activists—people shaped by the experience of war and depression, who understood that the rulebook needed to be ripped up in favour of a new politics more in step with the troubled times.[9]

Then, as now, attempts to preserve the status quo were doomed to failure, an invitation to catastrophe. We can and should be under no illusions: the challenge of a resurgent, racist far right will not be met by a bloodless centrism now firmly beached by history. Instead, it will fall to the radical left to forge a way out of this mess—one that transforms our economic model and addresses our social and environmental calamities without giving quarter to the dark forces of xenophobic nationalism to which they are giving rise. Our times require a response in tune with the spirit of the age: a politics whose boldness and radicalism matches the scale of the growing crisis. Developing such a politics is not merely our opportunity but our responsibility.

Corbyn's Labour is the only existing political force capable of channelling the rising energy for transformative change into formal politics in Britain. Within three years, the Labour Party's membership has tripled, making it the largest left-wing mass party in Europe. The chants of "Oh, Jeremy Corbyn!", heard at football matches and music festivals around the country, are an indication of Corbyn's appeal beyond his base to previously out-of-reach sections of the population—as is the spontaneous emergence of Grime4Corbyn.[10] "Corbyn gets what the ethnic minorities are going through", as Stormzy puts it—suggesting new possibilities around race and class for the new politics.[11] It is an extraordinary turn of events—but one that has rarely been recognized by the mainstream media and political establishment, ever inclined to dismiss young Corbyn activists as hard left entryists, cultish fanatics, or naïve dreamers.

In reality, what Corbynism has harnessed is the restless energy of a rising generation of activists deeply alienated from the status quo. This was most evident in the 2017 general election campaign, an event that shifted a whole generation's relationship with electoral politics. On canvassing outings, people who had never campaigned for a political party before rubbed shoulders with seasoned Labour activists and even supporters of other left parties, in a surge of grassroots mobilisation unlike anything else in our political lifetimes.

INTRODUCTION

Many experienced for the first time the euphoria, long absent from our official politics, that comes from collective agency and the democratic power of people in motion.

For many of these activists, gathered nervously on that June election night in 2017 to watch the results come in, the release of the shock exit poll was an extraordinary and unforgettable moment of vindication and hope. A left that had spent decades cultivating the habit of losing, that had been told repeatedly that it was headed for its most catastrophic defeat yet, suddenly dared to believe it could actually win. The movement's default setting switched almost overnight from a customary left-wing melancholy to one of determination, even of optimism.[12] Of course, this level of energy could not be sustained beyond the whirlwind of the snap election—and it has not. But, like the packed rooms and vibrant debates at the annual The World Transformed festival, it is a glimpse of the possibilities inherent in Corbynism, the most encouraging development in British politics in decades.

Across the world, this dynamic new political energy—evident in repeated outbursts from the Arab Spring and Occupy to the *indignados*, Syriza, and the Bernie Sanders campaign—has been searching for an outlet, attempting to find a path to the surface. In the UK, it has erupted (against all expectations) into the Labour Party, which now finds itself at the forefront of a global left urgently seeking answers and forging alternatives to a crisis-ridden but still aggressively destructive economic order increasingly on its deathbed. "It's been like being in a dark tunnel for a long period of time, and people are staggering into the light", as John McDonnell has put it. "There's been a constraint on hope and optimism, and what Jeremy Corbyn has brought is an optimism and a confidence that these policies can transform the world".[13] How fitting it would be if Britain, the first advanced industrial economy to provide a testing ground for neoliberal policies, were to be the first to fully re-emerge and seek to implement an alternative.

What holds a dying political-economic system in place, often, is a failure of imagination that things can fundamentally change—that there are real, viable alternatives for organizing something different and better. In such circumstances, an unapologetic left, one that is willing to advocate for a radical break with our failing system, might just be able to find a democratic exit from the Age of Anger—leading to a new, more equitable, inclusive, and ecologically sustainable politics. This is Corbynism's historic task.

Strategy and programme

The big question facing the UK left today, then, is this: are we ready? What would it take, truly, to meet this challenge? Certainly, it will require massive grassroots mobilisations and effective election strategies. We do not underestimate the difficulties of achieving a Labour general election victory, particularly in the context of relentless media onslaughts and establishment smears, right-wing MPs threatening to split and form a new centrist party, and the unpredictable, divisive, and often toxic politics of Brexit.

But what follows is addressed to a different question: what happens if and when we get there? As the left is just now beginning to realise, this achievement would be the start and not the end of the story. Relatively speaking, getting elected may prove the easy part. The task of transforming the UK economy beyond neoliberalism, in the teeth of powerful vested interests in what the historian R. H. Tawney once called "the oldest and toughest plutocracy in the world", will have only just begun.[14]

Since 2008, there has been a revival of interest on the left in political-economic change and in how big systemic shifts happen. In the aftermath of the financial crash, many were left feeling bruised and blindsided. How had a crisis of neoliberalism been turned into a pretext for intensifying existing economic arrangements, rather than an opening for change? How had the left allowed this to happen? What did we get wrong? Searching for answers, many looked to the last two crises that had occasioned major shifts in the political landscape: the Great Depression of the 1930s, which ultimately triggered the shift from laissez-faire liberalism to post-war Keynesianism, and the slow-burn economic crisis of the 1970s, which triggered the collapse of the post-war consensus and its replacement by neoliberalism.

A key lesson that was drawn from this history—one that has become something of a touchstone of left debate—was the way neoliberals had organised to keep their politics alive during their long stint in the political wilderness. The Mont Pelerin Society (MPS) has become a byword for the painstaking groundwork that was laid, allowing neoliberals to seize upon the 1970s crisis and control what happened next—and also for the UK left's failure to do the same during the long winter of Thatcherism. A powerful network of right-wing intellectuals, the MPS was convened by Friedrich Hayek, one of the founding fathers of neoliberalism, at a secretive ten-day summit at the Hôtel du Parc in the Swiss Alps near Lake Geneva in April 1947.[15] It became the centre of a web of well-funded think tanks—from the Atlas Foundation and American Enterprise Institute in the United States to the Centre for Policy Studies and Institute of Economic Affairs in Britain—able to reach influential business and political elites spanning the globe.[16] The "basic function" of this infrastructure, as Milton Friedman famously put it, was "to develop alternatives to existing policies, to keep them alive and available until the politically impossible becomes the politically inevitable".[17]

Five years ago, it seemed clear that this was the crux of the left's problem. Since the 1980s, the centre left had embraced neoliberalism, while the radical left had largely abandoned the terrain of big picture thinking and formal politics altogether. When the crisis hit, it found us trapped in an oppositional corner. We might rail against the banks' irresponsibility, or march against austerity, but we did not have a positive alternative vision—and still less a political vehicle capable of bringing it about. As a result, moments of political upheaval, like the 2010 student protests or the Occupy movement in 2011, could not be sustained.

But a lot has happened in the past five years, and we need to update our understanding of the task we face accordingly. The sea change we were holding out for in 2008 is now happening all around us. In Britain, we have a radical left political party with a real chance of taking power. An agenda for transformative change is taking shape, one that has been building up in social movements for some time and is now being embraced and further developed by the current Labour leadership.

Contrary to the claims often made by its opponents that it simply wants to revive a stale model of statist socialism, Corbynism is in fact embracing a new model: one that transforms ownership, but that eschews simply transferring economic control from private to public elites. Instead, this agenda is about putting power and resources in the hands of everyday people, through new forms of democratic public and community ownership at national, regional, and local levels. In doing so, it directly challenges the *extractive economy* built by neoliberalism—that is, an economy in which elites extract and monopolise wealth and power through their ownership of resources that should serve the common good, be they land, energy, or the money supply itself. Ultimately, the emerging *democratic economy* challenges the pre-eminence of the City of London, the engine of today's extractive economy.

Of course, much still needs to be done to fill out the details of this vision. The Labour Party is effectively trying to bridge a generational deficit in radical left thinking, with neither time nor—at least until recently—material resources on its side. It remains the case that only limited support is available from traditional think tanks and academia for Labour's policy development process. But the biggest danger facing the left today is no longer a shortage of ideas or a lack of positive vision. The biggest danger is lack of *preparedness*—that we are not yet ready for the hard work of turning that vision into reality. If the left has been unused to being propositional, it has been even less used to holding and wielding power. If we are serious about fundamentally transforming our economy, we must rapidly build our understanding of the scale of the challenge ahead. We must develop a clear strategy for carrying through this agenda for change. And we must build the social forces that can give it real power, buttressing it against the inevitable backlash from vested interests.

To do this, we will need four things. First, we need a clear understanding of the nature of the transformation we are trying to achieve, a power analysis of the political forces for and against it, and the levers we have available to tip that balance. Just as Thatcher's Conservatives drew up tough-minded battle plans for privatisation—identifying the industries where they were strong and those where they were weak, anticipating where they could press home their advantage and where they would need to make compromises in the service of their longer-term vision—so we must do the same for the democratisation of ownership and creation of a new economy. As part of this we must identify flagship measures—our own equivalents of Thatcher's "Right To Buy" policy of mass council house sales—that both carry a new story about ownership and give millions of people a stake in that new story.

Second, we must be ready for reaction from those who stand to lose from our political programme. A radical redistribution of ownership to the many and away from the few is unlikely to pass without challenge from the current owners, whose prosperity rests on their control of assets. And history tells us that global financial markets can and often do sink radical left governments. Capital flight, investment strikes, foreign exchange crises, trade retaliation—all are possible, whether as market reactions or deliberately administered punishment beatings.

Of course, there are aspects of Labour's agenda that are appealing to some of these interests—such as its commitment to public investment in infrastructure or a proactive industrial strategy to create new jobs and sectors. As we shall argue below, an unstated gamble at the heart of Labour's current approach is that this will be enough to secure tacit acceptance, or at least acquiescence, from the forces of capital. But it is essential to have contingency plans should this gamble fail. Some form of control on the cross-border movement of capital may well be necessary if we are to put the genie of footloose finance and hot money flows back into its bottle. And ultimately, new forms of international co-operation may well be needed to protect left governments at the national level from the genie's overwhelming global reach and power.

Thirdly, we must be ready to transform the institutions of government themselves so they are fit to deliver the project. The civil service is specifically designed to ensure continuity between governments. At times of radical discontinuity, when the new government is committed precisely to overturning the assumptions and orthodoxies that have shaped previous governments, this can become a major problem. An incoming Labour government will need to exorcise the "ghost in the machine" in Whitehall, or it will be operating with a set of tools that is simply not designed to serve a new agenda. This will require some bureaucratic changes, but it is not simply a matter of replacing a neoliberal technocracy with a progressive technocracy. The real prize is radical decentralisation and democratisation, breaking up the power relations of the old ways whilst also building the foundations for a new politics.

Finally, we must build a strong ecosystem of social movements and "organic intellectuals"—Gramsci's term for the thinkers who emerge from social movements and excluded classes and groups, and are capable of articulating their politics, culture, and concerns—both within and outside the Labour Party. Radical governments cannot succeed without a strong mass base of support—not just for their government but, crucially, for their *ideas.* This support must be independent, capable not only of defending the government when its agenda comes under attack, but also of keeping it on course when the pressures of governing push it away from radical change.

The institutional base of the UK left is not yet strong enough to sustain the kind of project we have outlined. It is therefore critical that we invest now. We must build collective popular power and agency through social movements and politically informed community organising. At the same time, we must build the practical economic alternatives from the ground up that will help form the backbone of the new economy, from public banks to worker co-operatives and community land trusts. We must also build new narratives, including by raising our game in media and communications, and new ideas, through new think tanks and popular education programmes. And, through all these things, we must begin to build the next cohorts of progressive political, intellectual, and community leaders.

Outline of the book

Throughout, we will need to look beyond the well-worn fable of the Mont Pelerin Society and seek new historical analogues and touchstones for the next phase of the left's development. In Chapter One, we will take the measure of our ambition in a radical transformative agenda for lasting change—a democratic economy to replace neoliberalism's extractive one. In Chapter Two, we will meet lesser-known characters like Nicholas Ridley and Lewis F. Powell, Jr, whose names deserve to become bywords for the neoliberals' development of hard-nosed strategy in the same way that Hayek and Friedman and Mont Pelerin have become bywords for their development of ideas. In Chapter Three, we will examine the painful experiences of past democratic socialist governments at home and abroad—and most especially of the Mitterrand government in France—to identify weaknesses and extract lessons for facing down reaction and avoiding defeat at the hands of capital. In Chapter Four, we will look at how Thatcher herself transformed the state after taking the reins of a government machine largely hostile to her worldview. And in Chapter Five, we will ask what can be learned from the recent experiences of Syriza in Greece and Podemos in Spain, where the opportunities and pitfalls of marrying party politics with social movements are being played out in real time.

This book is not about providing detailed blueprints, either for a future Labour government or for the social movements that will underpin it. It is about sketching the shape of the task ahead. More than anything, it is an invitation and a challenge to everyone supportive of the Corbyn project to play their part—and to recognise that our job extends much, much further than simply getting a radical Labour government elected and installed at Westminster and in Whitehall.

It is natural that we often look to the neoliberal revolution as the most recent historical precedent for achieving systemic change. And, as we explore throughout this book, it has much to teach us. But we cannot simply replicate the neoliberals' tactics. For all its attempts to don the rhetorical garb of democracy and popular freedom, neoliberalism was an elite political project in service of an elite economic project. In similar fashion, a truly democratic economic project can only be birthed by a democratic political project. Our methods must match our aims. This is about much more than one leader, one party, or even one government. It is about building a self-conscious, strong, and independent social movement, capable of achieving transformative economic change. Ultimately, the key question—the one to which this book hopes to make a contribution—is not how the movement behind Corbyn can help him succeed. Rather, it is about the far more radical question of how Corbyn's programme can help bring forth and empower a mass movement in Britain aimed at democratising our politics and economy—and how a transformative Labour government can help such a movement succeed.

CHAPTER ONE: PEOPLE GET READY

"At the heart of our programme is the greatest extension of economic democratic rights that this country has ever seen".
—John McDonnell MP, Speech to Labour Party Conference 2018

Change is coming. This has been Jeremy Corbyn's promise—and his prediction. The prospect of radical change, that things can and will get better, has driven the Corbyn project from the beginning. It is key to understanding Corbyn's improbable rise from obscure backbencher to Britain's prime minister in waiting, bringing the Labour Party back from demoralising defeat to the brink of power in a few short years despite constant sabotage from within. It is why he stands at the head of the largest and fastest-growing democratic movement in Europe, offering a transformative political programme—a historic opportunity, unmatched by the present position of the left in any other advanced industrial country, for the creation of a new economic model "for the many not the few".

This powerful promise of deep economic and social change is fundamental to the upheavals that are remaking Britain's political landscape. It is what drove a ragtag band of grassroots activists old and new to assemble in 2015 in support of his long-shot leadership bid—despite his coming from a wing of the Labour Party considered, just three years earlier, to be "absolutely without influence".[1] It is why those same activists suddenly found themselves part of what one describes, accurately, as "the biggest single campaign for an individual this country has ever seen".[2] It was the decisive factor when Corbyn's "people-powered campaign" went on to win the Labour leadership in a landslide, 40 points ahead of his nearest rival. It has been at the core of his unwavering commitment ever since, even as he has weathered an establishment and media onslaught of unprecedented ferocity.

Constantly ignored or discounted by his enemies, Corbyn's appeal to hope and change has allowed him to continually defy the odds. Theresa May called the June 2017 snap general election to annihilate him, only for Labour's vote to surge, as one shaken right-wing commentator put it, "in a way we've never seen during an election campaign before".[3] Starting more than twenty points behind in the polls, by the time the ballots were counted Labour had achieved its greatest vote share increase since Clement Attlee in 1945—ending up a mere 2,227 votes shy of a chance of becoming prime minister.[4] Along the way, Corbyn transformed Britain's national conversation, opening up more political space, and in a shorter time, than anyone in living memory.

Its detractors in the media frequently brand Corbynism "a cult". Ironically, Corbyn himself is both central and incidental to the movement that bears his name. Following a long period of technocratic rule by empty suits, it is no accident that radical movements in Britain, the United States, and France have been turning to an earlier generation of veteran political warhorses for their candidates. Jeremy Corbyn, Bernie Sanders, and Jean-Luc Mélenchon are all, each in their own way, representatives of a political "awkward squad" that was isolated by but somehow survived the neoliberal era intact. They have now been brought back in from the cold, untarnished due to their refusal to accommodate to neoliberalism, as figureheads and lightning rods for movements now intent upon its overthrow. Their authenticity and moral authority, accumulated over many years, as well as their belief in the power of the collective, allows them to function as "servant-leaders" and repositories for movement demands for economic and political transformation.

Corbyn's critics, inside and outside the Labour Party, have signally failed to appreciate the reasons for the immense power of his simple message of radical change based on a deep reading of the present moment.

The extractive economy

Powerful decades-long deteriorating social and economic trends—exploding inequality, poverty and hunger, wage stagnation, deindustrialisation, and community disinvestment—are driving the profound shifts we are now experiencing in our politics. For all but the richest few, the economy is flatlining. Corporate power dominates government decision-making through lobbying and political contributions. Income and wealth inequalities are spiralling to levels not seen in decades. Available jobs are ever more precarious. Housing and education appear increasingly out of reach. A generation of young people now expects to be less well off than their parents. The planet itself is threatened by climate change. Everywhere there is a sense of crisis and decay. At some point, something had to give.

Labour's radical new departure under Corbyn is a direct response to the scale of the political, economic, social, and ecological challenges that now confront us. Our deepening problems are not simply accidental or the result of poor policy choices but the predictable outcomes of the basic organisation of our economy. Our current system is programmed not to meet citizens' needs or respect ecological limits but rather to steadily concentrate the lion's share of economic gains in the hands of a tiny elite. More than half of all wealth in the United Kingdom is now held by the top 10 per cent with around 20 per cent held by the top 1 per cent—and inequality continues to grow.[5]

In a forthcoming book, Marjorie Kelly and Ted Howard name our current model of neoliberal capitalism "the extractive economy". They define the extractive economy as "an economy designed to benefit the wealthy, to enable the financial elite to extract maximum gain for themselves in every possible way, everywhere on the globe, heedless of collateral damage created for workers, communities, and the environment".[6] We can see this extractive economy operating all around us. The institutions and arrangements at the heart of today's British capitalism—concentrated private ownership, corporate dominance, the overweening might of London-based finance capital—together form a powerful engine for the extraction of wealth and its distribution upwards. It is this basic design that drives the outcomes we are seeing in terms of crumbling public infrastructure, social atomisation, environmental degradation, widening regional disparities, stalled social mobility, and a widespread sense of popular disempowerment.

How did we get into this position? The answer, in a word, is *neoliberalism*. There is a vast literature on neoliberalism, despite a small cottage industry of those still deeply invested in its nostrums churning out bad faith arguments that it doesn't in fact exist. Like every concept that has ever mattered, neoliberalism is messy, deeply contested, has evolved over time, and differs in theory and practice. There has been plenty of debate within the neoliberal movement itself about whether to self-identify as such (particularly given the associations of the word "liberal" in the United States), and about what the substantive content of its programme ought to be. And yes, it *has* also become a bit of a catchall term of abuse for things that the left doesn't like.

Despite all this, it is possible to determine some generally accepted core features of neoliberalism—which we are using here to denote the ideas, belief system, politics, and policies that came to dominate most of the world from a discernible point in the mid-1970s onwards. Neoliberalism, as far as it concerns the present argument, is the ideology and practice of a worldview in which the proper role of government is limited to the establishment and protection of "free markets" as the best means possible for organising the economy and society.[7] This is so as to permit rational, self-interested, individual actors (*homo economicus*, in the economic theory) to maximize their own utility—something that is measurable in terms of wealth, quantifiable through aggregate measures such as gross domestic product (GDP). Unlike classical liberalism, however, neoliberalism sees a strong role for the state in creating and maintaining open markets.[8] It has always been part of the neoliberal project to take over the state and transform it for its own ends, rather than simply to dismantle or disable it.

Neoliberalism is the ideology that, as we detail below, achieved broad international hegemony for the best part of the last four decades. At the moment of its greatest triumph, when the Berlin Wall came down and actually existing Communism collapsed in the East, neoliberalism was even proclaimed to be the ultimate destination point of human history.[9] No longer. To look around today, from the Capita and Carillion outsourcing débâcles to the grim shadow of Grenfell Tower and the travails of East Coast Mainline, is to see the entire edifice of the extractive economy in Britain coming apart at the seams. A decade after the 2008 financial crisis tore back the veil on the supposed superiority of deregulated capitalism, an exhausted neoliberal economic model seems finally to be running out of rope. The end of the long boom (or rather, "long bubble" as Saskia Sassen puts it) has shorn neoliberalism of no-longer-affordable public expenditures.[10] Its accompanying political strategy of buying off some of the "losers" from neoliberal policies by skimming the surplus for social spending has collapsed with the end of the growth on which it depended, ushering in a harsh new era of cuts and austerity.

The political backlash against the "stark utopia" of the universalisation of the market has now begun in earnest.[11] A key promise on the part of neoliberalism had been that unfettered markets would put ordinary individuals in control—albeit as consumers rather than as workers. But this promise of control was a fraud. Margaret Thatcher's "Right to Buy" policy of selling off council housing might have allowed some people to paint their own front doors, but it was also a *right to sell*. As the dynamic effects of the policy played out over time it produced the situation we are in today, with 40 per cent of former council homes now being rented back from private landlords.[12] Similarly, privatisation was supposed to produce a "share-owning democracy", whereas in fact most individual investors sold their shares within a relatively short period, reaping quick capital gains but re-concentrating ownership in the hands of a few big investors.[13] It is no coincidence that we have ended up in a new era of monopoly capitalism, with the "Big Six" energy firms, the "Big Five" banks, and the "Big Four" supermarkets—all of which have the power to rip off customers and suppliers with impunity. For ordinary people, the end result has been a toxic cocktail of stagnant wages, higher living costs, and rising household debt.

Everywhere, wealth and power have not flowed downwards to consumers but upwards to economic elites—and, crucially, to a very particular kind of elite. The new rulers of the world make their money not by producing goods and services that are useful to others, but by owning assets in an increasingly financialised economy.[14] Landlords and property developers control land, energy companies control our natural resources, banks control the money supply—even CEOs earn more from stock options than from their basic salary. Our economy is built around the battle to control assets, but this produces no new wealth. Instead, it *extracts* wealth from other people in the economy, whether through sky-high rents, rip-off energy bills, usurious bank charges, or share buybacks, bidding up existing asset values. The same logic can also be applied to the unsustainable extraction of natural resources, which is pushing us ever further towards ecological catastrophe. All of this means that the runaway success of today's elites is not part of a rising tide that lifts all boats, as the neoliberal doctrine of "trickle-down" has claimed.[15] Instead, it is achieved directly at our expense, the logical consequence of the extractive economy at work.

The good news is that the tide seems finally to be turning. Ordinary people up and down the country are way ahead of the politicians in understanding all this. They buy the argument that things are not working any more. They experience directly the growing inequality, the insecurity, the unfairness. They now want to hear, boldly and clearly, an authentic message about change that will make a difference.

The democratic economy

Embracing this challenge, and the magnitude of the historic opportunity it affords us, is one of the most urgent tasks before the growing movement behind Jeremy Corbyn's Labour. Collectively, this movement must now work with the leadership to create a transformational strategy capable of living up to the hopes and responding to the deep structural challenges of a fluid and rapidly changing political and economic landscape. What transformative change actually means in this context, and how we might possibly go about achieving it, is among the most pressing questions facing Corbynism (or, for that matter, any future left government confronting the same problems)—one that is insufficiently acknowledged and debated. Thankfully, we are not starting from zero. There is a great deal of experience to draw upon, with real-world examples of democratic, participatory economic alternatives in communities across the globe.

If we are serious about addressing the deep systemic challenges we are facing, then it is clear that merely tinkering around the edges of the extractive economy will not do. Instead, we need an altogether different set of economic institutions and arrangements capable of producing sustainable, lasting, and more democratic outcomes—an economy "for the many not the few".

When it comes to economic fundamentals, there has been a decades-long deficit of new thinking and ideas on the left. Where they have not capitulated totally to neoliberalism, most social democrats have been far downstream from where the real action is, seeking a way forward through "tax and spend" transfer policies and modest redistribution left behind by the high tide of postwar Keynesianism and the welfare state. They have largely avoided grappling with the deep structural determinants of who owns capital—and therefore with where the real power in the economy lies.

One of the most prominent features of the extractive economy in the neoliberal era is that returns to capital have increased at the expense of labour's share of national income—in other words, that more of the economic pie is going to capital owners rather than being taken home as wages by workers—while at the same time there has been an increase in income inequality *within* labour's share.[16] British workers have now experienced over a decade of wage stagnation—the longest squeeze on incomes since the end of the Napoleonic Wars over two hundred years ago. Moreover, increasing automation threatens to further accelerate these trends. Given all this, it is only natural that the left should begin looking at a more radical agenda of broadening and democratising ownership of the economy. Ultimately, as has become increasingly clear, a truly impactful alternative left strategy must go after capital itself.

Who owns and controls *capital*—productive wealth—is among the most fundamental questions of political economy, central to understanding the operations of any economic system. For socialists, responses to capitalist private ownership of the economy have traditionally divided along two main lines. In greatly simplified terms, *state socialism* placed ownership and control of capital with the state, whereas *social democracy* left it largely in private hands but sought to redistribute the returns through taxation and transfers. A somewhat neglected third tradition, however, is to be found in the long-running socialist commitment to *economic democracy*. The core idea of economic democracy is the notion of extending principles of popular sovereignty from the realm of politics into economics.

Such ideas are now making a significant comeback. In contrast to the extractive economy, Kelly and Howard posit as an alternative something they call "the democratic economy". They describe this as an economic model that "aims to meet the essential needs of all persons, to balance human consumption with the regenerative capacity of the earth, and to be responsive to the voices and concerns of ordinary people". Since the concept of the democratic economy may be unfamiliar to many, they offer a flavour of some defining characteristics that set it apart from both neoliberalism and traditional social democracy:

The aim isn't triumph for a few and passivity for the many, but economic empowerment for all—enduring empowerment, through broad-based asset ownership. It's a new concept of social change. It's less about regulations and social safety nets, and more about assets and institutions. It's about redesigning basic economic institutions and activities—companies, investments, economic development, employment, purchasing, banking—to serve the common good. And to serve the common good as the first, core, priority mission, not an add-on. Not lip service but real.[17]

The exciting thing about the democratic economy is that it is not some pipe dream but already emerging all around us—a spontaneous response to social pain by people in some of our poorest communities that have long suffered high levels of unemployment and deprivation. Traditional policies and approaches have demonstrably failed to alter deteriorating long-run trends on income inequality, concentrated wealth, community disinvestment and displacement, persistent place- and race-based poverty, and environmental destruction. As a consequence, more and more people are beginning to turn to genuine economic alternatives in which new wealth is built collectively and from the bottom up. Recent years have thus witnessed an explosion of interest in and practical experimentation with a variety of alternative economic institutions and models that are capable of fundamentally altering patterns of ownership—and of producing greatly improved distributional, environmental, and social outcomes as a matter of course.

Worker ownership, co-operatives, municipal enterprise, community land trusts, public banks, benefit corporations, social wealth funds, and a host of kindred institutional forms all represent ways in which capital can be *democratised* and held in common by small and large publics. They illuminate how practical new approaches can generate innovative solutions to deep underlying problems. They embody alternative design principles, relying not on regulatory fixes or "after the fact" redistribution but on deep structural changes in the economy and the nature of ownership and control over productive wealth that go right to the heart of our current difficulties. New hybrid forms are now emerging, as well as ideas as to how innovative combinations might produce still more powerful results. Taken as a whole, these institutions and approaches form the mosaic of a new democratic economy in the making, suggesting the contours of a next system beyond neoliberalism and the extractive economy and some pathways for getting there.[18]

In Britain, the basic institutions and principles of the democratic economy have a long and impressive lineage going back to the dawn of the industrial revolution—from Luddite insurrections to the Owenite movement, the Grand National Consolidated Trades Union, and popular movements for syndicalism and workers' control. The birth of the modern co-operative movement, which now boasts a billion members worldwide, can be traced back to the Rochdale Pioneers.[19] There have also been many overseas experiments, each providing important design and operational lessons. In Italy and Spain, both on the front lines of recent austerity struggles, there are prominent examples—Legacoop in Emilia-Romagna, Mondragón in the Basque region—that show the power of the institutions of the democratic economy when taken to scale in particular geographical locations.[20]

The Labour Party has now begun to take up these alternative ownership models as the building blocks for a very different kind of economic strategy. Largely unnoticed by its enemies within and without, the Corbyn leadership is already cohering around the core elements of a programme for transformative change that could form the basis for a new political-economic settlement—sometimes dubbed "Corbynomics". New institutional alternatives are at the heart of Labour's commitment to the democratisation of the economy.[21] *The Economist* offers a useful perspective:

> Economic programmes comprise three big things: monetary policy, fiscal policy and structural reforms ... In fact, fiscal and monetary policy turn out to be the least radical parts of Labour's economic plan ... The third plank of Corbynomics, therefore, involves structural reforms, proposals for which have been fleshed out since the general election. Here the most interesting ideas are to be found.[22]

Under Jeremy Corbyn and Shadow Chancellor John McDonnell, the Labour Party is now promising to deliver fundamental economic change via deep structural reforms—what the socialist theorist André Gorz termed "non-reformist reforms" or "revolutionary reforms", because they do not merely tinker around the edges of the system but instead seek to alter it in some fundamental way that helps "advance toward a radical transformation of society".[23] These structural reforms are intended to bring about new patterns of ownership and institutional relationships in the everyday operations of the economy. Instead of the extractive and concentrating forces of corporate capitalism, Labour's emerging "new economics" is circulatory and place-based, aimed at decentralising economic power, rebuilding and stabilising regions and local communities, allowing for the possibility of real democracy and participation in the workplace, and providing the long-run institutional and policy support for a new politics dedicated to achieving genuine social change.[24]

Labour's new economics

Building on popular elements of Labour's 2017 manifesto, *For the Many Not the Few*, and encompassing cutting edge thinking from the *Alternative Models of Ownership* report and beyond, the leadership is busy assembling the tools and strategies to enable a Corbyn government to pursue a bold transformation of the British economy organised around new ownership models and institutions in combination with democratic participation and control.[25] Rolled out across the entire economy, this could amount to a radical programme for dismantling and displacing corporate and financial power in Britain. It would undermine the social and economic basis of the neoliberal order just as Thatcher destroyed her opponents' strength by liquidating the public sector, shuttering entire industries, smashing the trade unions, and disinvesting in working class communities.[26]

Virtually alone amongst traditional left wing parties, Corbyn's Labour is now charting a course beyond neoliberalism, reanimating British politics through a vision of a more democratic economy. Widely described as a merely social democratic programme, *For the Many Not the Few* in fact contains the seeds of a radical transformation beyond social democracy. Policies such as taking the major utilities, railways, and postal service back into public hands, establishing a £250 billion national investment fund to help "rebuild communities ripped apart by globalisation", linking public sector procurement to a regionally balanced industrial strategy, creating a National Investment Bank and a network of new regional public banks in support of small- and medium-sized enterprises, and democratising ownership by supporting co-ops and worker-owned firms, all represent a break with tired neoliberal orthodoxies and a move in the direction of the democratic economy. In combination with a commitment to devolving and decentralising power and decision-making to local communities, and forming a constitutional convention that "will look at extending democracy locally, regionally and nationally, considering the option of a more federalised country", the contours of a very different pattern of political economy begin to appear.

To begin with, Labour is promising the biggest extension of public ownership in Britain since the mass nationalisation programme under the postwar Labour government of Clement Attlee. Rail, water, energy, and the postal service are all to be taken back into public hands.[27] This is proving to be very popular politics. A 2017 poll for the right-wing Legatum Institute found to their dismay something that had in fact always been true, even at the height of Thatcherism—namely, that there is massive and widespread popular support in Britain for public ownership.[28] The Legatum poll showed 83 per cent of the public supporting renationalisation of the water sector, 77 per cent for electricity and gas, and 76 per cent for railways. There was even 50 per cent support for nationalising the banks.[29]

Labour's public ownership policies have resulted in the usual lazy criticisms and horrified protests that the party is intent upon dragging the country back to the 1970s. In fact, even a moment's scrutiny would show that Corbyn and McDonnell have something very different and far more radical in mind. They are determined to pursue a programme of democratic public ownership that would seek to roll back not merely decades of neoliberalism but also the accretions of the preceding 30 years of top-down social democratic centralism by recovering and rediscovering some alternative economic forms.[30] The reasons for this can be found in their embrace of a powerful left-wing critique of past models of public ownership. Corbynism seeks to go far beyond a return to post-war social democracy by building something more democratic and participatory instead.

Under the Attlee government, nationalisation was conducted on the basis of Herbert Morrison's vision—that of large, top-down, centralised public corporations at arm's length from democratic control.[31] Morrison's public corporation model was based on his 1933 publication *Socialisation and Transport*, itself the product of his experience with London public transport in 1931. In the absence of credible alternatives, Morrison's vision for public ownership "held the field alone", bolstered by the fact that he was able to point to actually existing models, including the British Broadcasting Corporation, the London Passenger Transport Board, and the Central Electricity Board.[32] But there were major drawbacks to Labour's adoption of this form of public ownership, which stored up problems for the future and bequeathed a problematic legacy for the left.

To begin with, the centralisation it involved served to further concentrate power in London, working against regional rebalancing. At the same time, the boards of the new public corporations were deliberately techno-cratic and—purportedly—apolitical. Morrison emphasised the importance of expert control, in line with the arguments of *Socialisation and Transport*, which contained the claim that "the majority of workmen are ... more inter-ested in the organisation, conditions, and life of their own workshop than in those finer balances of financial, and commercial policy which are dis-cussed in the Board room".[33] There was thus a shocking degree of continuity in the membership and class composition of the governing bodies of indus-tries before and after nationalisation. Across the nationalised industries as a whole, some 80 per cent of the full-time board members were simply carry-overs from the era of private ownership.[34] To take a specific case, of the 14 members of the new Gas Council, nine had previously been associated with private undertakings, whilst none had experience with municipal gasworks.[35] The same pattern held throughout the newly expanded public sector.

In *Power at the Top*, his 1959 survey of persons appointed to the boards of public corporations, Clive Jenkins pointed out that, of 131 directors named by the Attlee government prior to December 1949, 61 also held directorships in private companies, 23 were knights, 9 were lords, and 3 were generals. For Jenkins, rather than serving as "popular instruments of social change" in line with the aspirations of Labour's activist base, the nationalised industries "can be seen to have become an instrument in maintaining the frozen class structure of British society".[36]

Top-down nationalisation also had the malign effect of supplanting older and more plural traditions of municipal and co-operative ownership.[37] Meanwhile, Morrison's dismal managerialism was a far cry from popular calls for workers' self-management and economic democracy. Long-running dis-cussions of workers' control within the Labour Party in the 1930s and 1940s were shut down by arguments about the impracticability of workers assuming management responsibilities, epitomised by Stafford Cripps' intervention during the 1946 debates over nationalisation:

> There is not yet a very large number of workers in Britain capable of taking over large enterprises. I have on many occasions tried to get representatives of the workers on all sorts of bodies and working parties. It has always been extremely difficult to get enough people who are qualified to do that sort of job, and, until there has been more experience by workers of the managerial side of industry, I think it would be almost impossible to have worker-controlled industry in Britain, even if it were on the whole desirable.[38]

The failure to incorporate industrial democracy into public ownership was to have a particularly debilitating effect upon political support for the nationalised industries among workers, as Raymond Williams pointed out, with public firms reproducing, "sometimes with appalling accuracy, the human patterns, in management and working relationships, of industries based on quite different social principles".[39]

It didn't have to be this way. Other collective public models, based on extensive real-world experience with the history and practice of co-operativism and municipal socialism, were available to draw upon—if only ministers had been prepared to look. This could be seen when Nye Bevan launched the National Health Service in 1948. For inspiration he was able to turn to the Tredegar Medical Aid Society, a small community-based model in his hometown in South Wales, where workers had banded together in a friendly society "to provide for themselves and their families medical aid beyond the bare facilities available".[40] Begun in 1890, this small Welsh experiment had grown to serve the vast majority of the town's population, encompassing the services of five general practitioners, a surgeon, two pharmacists, a dentist, a physiotherapist, and a domiciliary nurse—all free at the point of use.[41] It was taken up by Bevan and scaled into one of the world's truly great national public health systems, testament to the power of what is known in the American political science literature as the "laboratories of democracy".

Corbynism is now excavating and updating this alternative tradition as well as applying it to other spheres of the economy. Here Jeremy Corbyn has been clear from the beginning:

> I believe in public ownership, but I have never favoured the remote nationalised model that prevailed in the post-war era. Like a majority of the population and a majority of even Tory voters, I want the railways back in public ownership. But public control should mean just that, not simply state control: so we should have passengers, rail workers and government too, co-operatively running the railways to ensure they are run in our interests and not for private profit. This model should replace both the old Labour model of top-down operation by central diktat and the Tories' favoured model of unaccountable privatised operators running our public services for their own ends.[42]

As it goes about returning the railways, Royal Mail, and major utilities to public hands, Corbyn's team has pledged to avoid a simple resurrection of the post-war model of centralised public corporations run by civil service mandarins and private sector directors. McDonnell has spoken of the limitations of such bureaucracies, stating: "The old, Morrisonian model of nationalisation centralised too much power in a few hands in Whitehall. It had much in common with the new model of multinational corporations, in which power is centralised in a few hands in Silicon Valley, or the City of London". The alternative, he argues, is plural forms of democratised and decentralised common ownership at a variety of scales: "Decentralisation and social entrepreneurship are part of the left ... Democracy and decentralisation are the watchwords of our socialism".[43] This dual emphasis on democratised ownership and radical political decentralisation is truly remarkable coming from the national leadership

Distr. dutced
energy

of a major political party. True to their word, work is already underway to consult on and flesh out the detailed design of more democratic forms of governance for public ownership, so they are ready for implementation by an incoming radical Labour government.[44]

Labour's proposals for taking energy back into public ownership are an example of the new thinking at work. They show both how far the terms of debate have shifted—with energy price caps, denounced as a Marxist outrage when first proposed by Ed Miliband, having become the "moderate" Tory alternative—and lend support to the contention that Corbynism won't be a reprise of pre-1970s nationalisation. Instead, Labour is developing a sophisticated plan for an energy ecosystem that is publicly owned from top to bottom but has democratic participation and local control baked in.

Some parts of the system, like the National Grid and large-scale offshore wind, are to be publicly owned outright at the national level. But beyond this, the transition to renewables will make highly centralised energy systems increasingly out of date. Below will sit a layer of city-level public energy companies—like the pioneering Robin Hood Energy in Nottingham, Our Power in Scotland, and Bristol Energy in the South West—committed to providing affordable, green energy to people in their areas. These municipal companies in turn will be supplied in part by community-owned renewable energy co-operatives. Successful energy transitions in Germany and Denmark have been built on such an ecosystem of mutually supportive public and community ownership—thereby building a culture of "energy citizenship" and giving people the experience of co-owning and participating in a piece of the economy that directly affects their lives.[45]

New models of ownership

Further radical policy development is also in the pipeline. For Corbyn, McDonnell, and their aides, the 2017 manifesto is clearly a jumping off point and not the last word on economic change. A few days before the June 2017 election Labour released *Alternative Models of Ownership*, a report to McDonnell and Shadow Secretary of State for Business, Energy and Industrial Strategy Rebecca Long-Bailey, by a group of radical theorists and practitioners, including Andy Cumbers of Glasgow University, Neil McInroy of the Centre for Local Economic Strategies (CLES), Preston City Council Leader Matthew Brown, and others. This report represents the outlines of the most exciting economic programme to be developed for the Labour Party in many years. It heralds the way in which the wider left should now be rolling up its sleeves and getting to work, going beyond rhetoric to detailed institutional design and policy formulation. In particular, the authors of the report call on Labour to "push issues of economic ownership and control to the front of the political agenda" and "commence work on a strategy to win support" for such ideas.[46] A well-attended conference in London in February 2018 began to give these ideas, from new forms of public ownership to energy democracy and beyond, a serious airing in the wider movement.

Since then, further detailed policy work has been commissioned, including on the design of a new public banking system and the creation of profit-sharing schemes that will give workers an expanding ownership stake in some of Britain's largest companies. There is also a significant push from the Corbyn leadership around "community wealth building", drawing upon the pioneering work of Councillor Matthew Brown and the flagship Labour council of Preston in Lancashire, with technical support from CLES and others.[47] Corbyn's office now contains a Community Wealth Building Unit dedicated to rolling out the approach to Labour councils and local authorities across the country, without having to wait for a radical Labour government at the national level.

The widely discussed "Preston Model"—itself derived from the "Cleveland Model" in Ohio and the work of the Evergreen Cooperatives—is indicative of the untapped potential power of local government and associated public institutions in the creation of a new democratic economy in Britain.[48] Hailed by *The Economist* as "an unlikely laboratory for Corbynomics", in a few short years Preston has gone from being one of the most deprived parts of the country to a poster child for radical innovation in local government, in part through its embrace of community wealth-building approaches.[49]

Community wealth building is a local economic development strategy focused on building collaborative, inclusive, sustainable, and democratically controlled local economies. In recent years economic development has relied on public-private partnerships and private finance initiatives, which waste billions to subsidise the extraction of profits by footloose corporations, often registered offshore with no loyalty to local communities. Instead, community wealth building supports democratic collective ownership of—and participation in—the economy through a range of institutional forms and initiatives. These include worker co-ops, community land trusts, municipal and local public enterprise, participatory planning and budgeting, and—increasingly, it is to be hoped—public and community banking. Community wealth building is economic system change, but starting at the local level.[50]

Preston is already seeing the payoffs from its strategy, which includes a radical repatriation of its local government spending into the city economy and surrounding Lancashire. The city has been named by PricewaterhouseCoopers and the Demos think tank as the UK's most improved urban area. As George Eaton has noted in the *New Statesman*, "the share of the public procurement budget spent in the city has risen from 5 per cent in 2013 to 18 per cent (a gain of £75m), while across Lancashire it has risen from 39 per cent to 79 per cent (a gain of £200m). Unemployment has fallen from 6.5 per cent in 2014 to 3.1 per cent and ... Preston has also achieved above-average improvements for health, transport, work-life balance, and youth and adult skills".[51]

There is already a growing movement for community wealth building at the local and city level across the United Kingdom. This reflects the recognition that local government's economic footprint and associated spending (by so-called "anchor institutions" stewarding public funds) is sufficiently large that, used more intentionally, it could help stabilise local economies on the basis of "sticky capital" and rooted jobs. This in turn would reduce corporate leverage and restore the capacity for real democratic local economic decision-making.

Finally, Corbyn's Labour is developing the elements of a major push on worker co-operatives and associated forms of democratic ownership of enterprise. There are huge potential benefits to pursuing a massive expansion of worker ownership in Britain. The opportunity presented by the coming "silver tsunami" of retiring baby boomer business owners, and the succession question this raises for large numbers of firms that might otherwise be wound down or gobbled up by private equity, means that the time for such an expansion is already upon us.

For the Many Not the Few calls for a "Right to Own", which would give workers the right of first refusal when their companies are up for sale. *Alternative Models of Ownership* takes this further, urging among other things that local public authorities should be actively supporting and funding the incubation and expansion of worker co-ops and other social enterprises as part of their local economic development strategies, as Preston is already doing. It also suggests that Labour should investigate the benefits and limitations of Employee Stock Ownership Plans (ESOPs), for-profit entities in which employees own part or all of the businesses for which they work via a trust, which—again as in the United States—could dramatically increase worker ownership with little risk or cost to workers.

McDonnell's team is looking at how to help bring about such a large-scale transformation in the form of "Inclusive Ownership Funds" (IOF). This was one of the recommendations of a recent New Economics Foundation report authored by Mathew Lawrence, Andrew Pendleton, and Sara Mahmoud, based on an adaptation of the key elements of the visionary "Meidner Plan" developed by trade union economists in Sweden in the late 1970s.[52] The core mechanism is a compulsory share levy on all companies above a certain size, based on number of employees (currently 250)—an annual disbursement of new company stock equivalent to 1 per cent of corporate equity per annum for ten years that would accrue to purposely created, collectively owned worker funds.[53] The effect would be to gradually dilute existing holdings and create a significant ownership stake for workers in their companies. Individual workers would receive an annual dividend up to a proposed cap, with returns above that amount being passed along in the form of a social dividend to be put to wider public purposes. The radical beauty of such a scheme is its ability to bring about this transfer without negatively impacting investment or liquidity within the firm — no money is removed or taxed away, with no effect on capital formation, but there is a gradual shift in beneficial ownership.[54]

The NEF paper calls for such a policy in order to "create a deep economic heartbeat that consistently and over time transfers the ownership and control of businesses to workers and other key stakeholders".[55] Mathew Lawrence, one of the principal architects of the policy, calculates that in its current form the IOF policy would cover roughly 10.7 million employees, or 40 per cent of the private sector workforce, and almost half of the UK's economic output. At the same time, it would impact less than 0.1 per cent of firms, roughly five thousand companies. On average, a 10 per cent stake would generate a £1,000 dividend per worker, as well as establishing powerful control rights. The more aggressive versions of the scheme could socialise upwards of half a trillion pounds in the course of a couple of decades.

While the full potential impact of Labour's IOF policy will obviously depend on the yet to be finalized details, the Meidner Plan from which it draws inspiration represented one of the most radical proposals for democratising the economy in the second half of the twentieth century. Had it been adopted in full, it would have progressively diluted the shares of the existing capitalist owners of Swedish enterprise to the point of tipping the entire economy into full worker-public ownership.[56] Nothing quite so radical is yet on Labour's agenda. But, as Peter Gowan indicates, the IOF policy "shouldn't be viewed exclusively through the lens of 1970s Sweden, but instead as a key pillar of a growing edifice of radical economic policies designed to shift power, ownership, and control to working-class people. Labour is hoping to push toward socialism not with a single policy, but rather with a broad-based strategy that makes progress on multiple fronts".[57]

* * *

The elements of the new political economy already under development will go a long way towards the creation of a new economic model in Britain—one that can be made to work "for the many not the few". That said, much more remains to be done. And in areas where the vision is well developed, the technical and practical details of implementation often still need to be worked out. And there are whole areas ripe for the democratising approach where the left simply has not yet done much thinking—from private pensions to big data and the digital monopolies. As John McDonnell has indicated, there are also clearly unanswered questions on such overarching issues as trade and globalisation, which are likely to take on increased importance in the contexts of Brexit and climate change. We return to questions of policy development capacity in Chapter Five.

Taken as a whole, the essence of Labour's "new economics" is to bring about a radical egalitarian rebalancing of power through a reordering and democratisation of the basic institutions of Britain's economy. It is an ambitious agenda—but one commensurate with the scale of the crisis we are facing.

CHAPTER TWO: GET READY FOR CHANGE

"Attlee and Thatcher worked hard to cement their political legacy, so it proved politically difficult to repeal. Labour must think hard about how it does the same".

—*Owen Jones*

How can a Corbyn government hope to bring about a sea of change in our political economy? There are two precedents that can help us think through what it actually takes for a government to enact transformative change in Britain. "I want us to surpass even the Attlee government for radical reform", John McDonnell has said. "The situation demands nothing less".[1] The historical comparison is apt. Twice before in the post-war period, radical reforming governments of the left and then the right were able to navigate major crises in order to impose new settlements on British politics that brought about real and lasting change.

There are important lessons from the manner in which the 1945–51 Labour government of Clement Attlee and the 1979–90 Conservative government of Margaret Thatcher each accomplished fundamental transformations of Britain's political economy. These governments were able to set the terms for succeeding decades because they enacted deep structural changes in ownership and control. To differing degrees, they did this by developing hard-headed power analyses and deeply thought-out strategies for advancing their agenda that simultaneously built up new institutions and sources of political strength whilst undermining the position of their enemies. This included liquidating the economic bases of their opponents' support—the most obstreperous and disruptive of the interwar capitalist industrialists, in the case of Attlee; the trade unions and working class communities around the nationalised industries, in the case of Thatcher. In both instances, new social strata and formations were created and incorporated into the newly emergent economic order, helping ensure its consolidation and endurance.

The post-war settlement

In the first instance, the nationalisations of the 1945–51 Labour government brought the Bank of England, coal, steel, civil aviation, the railways, and all the major utilities (electricity, water, and gas) into public hands. The Attlee government was able to take advantage of the unique circumstances of the period, with the end of the Second World War, the prestige of the left following its role in the defeat of fascism, and the mass influx of workers into unions and politics. The stage was set for an extended period of economic reconstruction on the back of broad-based economic growth that could accommodate both increased profit rates for capital and higher real living standards for labour. In a few short years the Attlee government laid the foundations for a decades-long political-economic settlement around a mixed economy with a significantly expanded state sector.

By 1951, Labour had reorganised large sections of British industry and assembled a public sector workforce of four million, around 18 per cent of the total. A fifth of the economy was in public ownership, with the government sector responsible for half of annual capital expenditure as it operated industries with a capital stock greater than the entirety of UK manufacturing. Taken as a whole, the 1945–51 nationalisations accounted for more than 80 per cent of the total transfers of private industry into public hands in the British economy in the twentieth century.[2] These dramatic shifts in ownership were conducted in the teeth of vehement political opposition, including interventions on behalf of the UK private sector by the United States government. For all its shortcomings, this remains the most radical economic programme ever implemented in Britain.

Acknowledging the success of the Attlee government does not require exaggerating its ambition or turning a blind eye to its limitations. From strike-breaking at home (including government action against dockers, postal workers, miners, and power workers) to colonialism abroad (brutal campaigns were waged from Kenya to Malaya), the overall record is mixed at best.[3] Even on its domestic economic programme, justifiably regarded as the capstone of its accomplishments, it is important to be clear about intent. For while the nationalisation of the "commanding heights" of the British economy evidently posed "a serious challenge to the private ownership of capital", it is also clear that it was not envisioned as a fully fledged attempt to bring about a transition from capitalism to socialism.[4] Instead, the Attlee government saw itself as being involved in "a complicated social project that included both the setting up of a comprehensive welfare programme and the creation of a mixed economy".[5]

Nonetheless, in terms of transforming the British economy by changing the underlying institutions and ownership patterns, the Attlee government's achievements in creating the post-war settlement are quite remarkable. Willie Thompson's verdict seems reasonable:

> Political and social affairs at every level proceeded under an accepted wisdom that the advances of the 1940s were permanent and irreversible and that the substance of political debate was about further advance within that framework. It would not be fanciful to claim that labourism at that point had attained hegemony within British public life.[6]

There are valuable political lessons from this experience regarding strategy and effectiveness. Critically, in addition to transforming the underlying patterns of ownership in the economy, the Attlee government also operated on the basis of a power analysis. To the disappointment of the left, the national-isation programme was *not* intended to be a socialist transformation beyond capitalism but rather sought to socialise those sectors of the economy where private owners had proved to be incompetent in running an industry either for their own benefit or that of the community. As such, nationalisation had the deliberate effect of liquidating sections of private capital that had been destabilising forces in Britain's political economy.

This was true to varying degrees in coal, iron, steel, energy, and trans-port. The private coal owners, in particular, had—through short-sightedness and long-term underinvestment—produced recurring crises of competitive-ness and profitability in their industry that in turn caused contractions and strikes, and led to political setbacks for the labour movement—the most nota-ble example being, of course, the 1926 General Strike. By bringing the mines into public hands, the Attlee government neutralised this source of difficulty and instability whilst also incorporating their workforces into the ranks of an expanded public sector that formed the basis of a new mixed national economy.

The case of coal is emblematic. Britain's coalfields had been plagued by discord and industrial conflict since the turn of the century, culminating in the 1926 lockout and General Strike.[7] Repeated official reports and commissions and governmental interventions—including the Sankey Commission (1919), the Samuel Commission (1925), the Coal Mines Act (1930) establishing the Coal Mines Reorganization Commission, and the Reid Report (1945)—under-scored the unsatisfactory position of the industry, including its technological backwardness and fragmentation. Moreover, coal had had a "bad war", with deep-mining output falling from 231 to 192 million tons between 1939 and 1944.[8] The findings of the Reid Report were scathing, effectively spelling the end of private ownership:

> Much of the industry was out of date. Methods of coal-getting and haulage had to be modernised. Coal leases were not adapted to the

requirements of coal-getting. There was an acute shortage of technical ability and an acute shortage of finance. The industry required
reorganisation into larger units which would enjoy the benefits of
large-scale production.[9]

By the time the Attlee government was elected in a landslide, the political
groundwork for coal nationalisation had already been laid well in advance.
A generation of bitter political controversy had influenced public opinion
as to the poor wages, dangerous working conditions, and blatant profiteer-
ing of the industry, and the lack of prospects for regeneration as long as it
remained in private hands.[10] The trade unions in particular were clamour-
ing for public ownership, and 35 Labour MPs had been elected in 1945 with
sponsorship from the mining unions.[11] Coal was thus a prime candidate for
summary nationalisation. For Corbynism today, the best parallel is perhaps
the railways, whose private operators are obviously incompetent and widely
despised even by the wealthy, and whose franchise system makes them relatively easy to take back into public ownership. Like coal, railways might be
regarded as a wedge to prise open the wider agenda on public ownership.

Another lesson of the Attlee experience is that a big picture agenda for
transforming ownership is one thing, but the practicalities of implementing it
are quite another. In practical terms, the post-war nationalisations turned out
to be no straightforward matter, even with much of the politics squared away
in advance. As Emanuel Shinwell, Labour's minister of Fuel and Power, artic-
ulated in November 1945: "We are about to take over the mining industry. It
is not so easy as it looks. I have been talking about nationalisation for forty
years but the implications of the transfer of property have never occurred
to me".[12] With the exception of a small handful of publications by the Fabian
Society and the Labour Research Department, "few detailed blueprints" for
public ownership were available to government ministers.[13] One contemporary story—apocryphal perhaps, but revealing nonetheless—recounted that,
when Shinwell went rummaging for ideas in the archives of Transport House,

all he could find was a single pamphlet by James Griffiths entitled *Glo* ("Coal"), written in Welsh.[14] Shinwell later confirmed the general point in his memoirs:

> For the whole of my political life I had listened to the Party speakers advocating state ownership and control of the coal mines, and I had myself spoken of it as a primary task once the Labour Party was in power. I had believed, as other members had, that in the Party archives a blue-print was ready. Now, as Minister of Fuel and Power, I found that nothing practical and tangible existed. There were some pamphlets, some memoranda produced for private circulation, and nothing else. I had to start on a clear desk.[15]

What was true of coal was also the case in steel, transport, energy, and the other industries targeted for public ownership. What it amounted to, as Kenneth Morgan suggests, was something of an "intellectual void at the heart of Labour's proposals for nationalization".[16] The unfortunate result was an immediate gap between theory and practice, in which there were "insufficient attempts to relate the organisation structure and the operational rules of the nationalised industries to the socialist ideas that are held by many supporters of public ownership".[17]

Just as significantly, the policy framework within which nationalisation took place compromised the profitability of public firms from the outset. Government policy dictated the subordination of the nationalised industries to the needs of the private sector. They were placed under constraints regarding borrowing for investment, vertical integration, and pricing—especially the mandating of unrealistically low prices for their outputs. This meant that, far from being a drain on the economy, they actually *subsidised* the private sector, making them in effect "sinks" that disguised the poor performance of the British economy overall while reinforcing existing power relations.[18] The result was low profitability—an altogether inadequate

measure of their true performance, but one that fed into widespread per-
ceptions of inefficiency and bureaucratisation, and eventually made them
sitting ducks for privatisation.

In truth, despite a great deal of mythology to the contrary, the nationalised industries were actually quite efficient, outperforming both the British
economy as a whole and their privately owned U.S. counterparts when
measured for total factor productivity (the portion of total output of a firm,
industry, or national economy that cannot be explained by the inputs used,
such as labour and capital).[19] For all their problems, the data simply does not
bear out the negative verdicts by ideological opponents that have seeped
into the nation's collective folk memory. Even so, there were major drawbacks to the form of public ownership adopted, which stored up problems
for the future.

The experience of post-war nationalisation underscores the importance
of ensuring that new policies are not inadvertently weakened by simply pro-
ceeding down the path of least resistance but are instead prepared carefully
in advance, with particular attention to their role in the wider transformation
we are seeking. The role of each new approach should be carefully examined
for its ability to help embed a wider political and economic transformation,
and potential conflicts and contradictions ironed out and resolved. Moreover,
the underlying process of social and economic change must be thought of as a
democratic and not a technocratic one. The changes a radical Corbyn government rings in must be ones in which ordinary citizens are able to participate
as well as experience the resulting gains.

This, in a nutshell, was the Achilles' heel of post-war Labourism, the strategic weakness that eventually led to its downfall. As Robin Blackburn put
it, "the social democratic and Keynesian policies of the post-war era failed
to enlist the mass of working people in the consolidation of a new pattern of
political economy ... [They] failed to find a route to the socialisation of the
accumulation process, or to engage the mass of working people in the new

social dispensation".[20] It was a weakness of the post-war model that was to be ruthlessly exploited by its successor.

Thatcher's offensive

The second precedent for bringing about fundamental change of Britain's political economy took the form of a counterrevolution. It was launched by Margaret Thatcher and her supporters, and it successfully overthrew the post-war order that had fallen into crisis, replacing it with neoliberalism. The victory of social democracy in its heyday was to have successfully convinced its conservative opponents of the merits of working within its formula. Now the opposing pattern set in.[21]

The Thatcher government set about substantially reversing the earlier transformation of ownership. It did this through a massive programme of "privatisation"—a new term, attributed to American management theorist Peter Drucker, adopted to give a more positive ring to "denationalisation".[22] One commentator called the coining and circulation of the term "a master-stroke of public relations".[23] For Ernst & Young, the consultancy firm that produced a global guide for clients eager to get in on the action, privatisation was "the great economic transformation process of our time".[24]

In a 2002 ode to privatisation, the Treasury calculated that, all told, between 1980 and 1996 Britain racked up fully 40 per cent of the total value of all assets privatised across the OECD.[25] This is an astounding figure, denoting a massive transfer of wealth from public to private interests. It took place through a process described by David Parker, author of the UK government's official history of privatisation, as "a complex set of interacting policy initiatives including public flotations and trade sales of nationalised industries, divestments and asset sales, and competitive tendering and contracting out in central and local government and the National Health Service".[26]

Just as Labour is not now seeking to return to the earlier political economy of the post-war era, so Thatcherism was not merely an attempt to turn back the clock to the laissez-faire of the pre-war era. Instead, it was an

un thinkable
privatisce

offensive new political project, which rather than shrinking the state sought to use state power for its own purposes—"the free economy and the strong state".[27] In effect, Britain was leading the way in the creation of a new economic model—one that, by changing the economy's underlying institutions and installing a neoliberal policy framework, intervened to shift the balance of forces between public and private, and between labour and capital, decisively in favour of the latter.

It is easy to forget just how radical a break all this was at the time, as Thatcher herself noted in her autobiography: "Now that almost universal lip service is paid to the case for privatization it is difficult to recall just how revolutionary—how all but unthinkable—it seemed at the end of the 1970s".[28] Richard Heffernan confirms this, recounting the reception with which ministerial instructions to identify government assets for disposal were greeted at a meeting of senior civil servants at the Department of Energy in 1981: "Scepticism turned to outright amusement as gas, electricity and, finally, coal itself were solemnly presented as possible candidates; civil servants literally fell about with laughter as the list was read out".[29] As it turned out, ministers would have the last laugh.

It is hard to avoid a sneaking admiration for the ruthlessness, strategic discipline, and political élan with which with the Thatcherites set about their devastating work. All memory of capitalist mismanagement of factories and mines in the interwar years was erased, as the commanding heights—telecoms, civil aviation, gas, water, electricity, and railways—were sold off one after another. Nothing quite like it had been done before, requiring ingenuity, quick learning, and a high degree of flexibility. From the first hesitant steps, success was used to create more success, gathering a head of steam that carried the privatisation programme far beyond what had been planned at the outset.

Decades of underinvestment were offset by "sweeteners", with a torrent of public money flowing into state-owned firms right before they were delivered up for auction at discounted prices. It was a rip-off of giant proportions, but the public outcry was muffled at best, perhaps because people were lulled by the promise that a golden dawn of "property-owning democracy" was upon them. Henceforth everyone would own their own house, while the privatised industries, freed from bureaucratic state management, would become models of capitalist efficiency in the smooth delivery of goods and services under conditions of open market competition. This at least was the litany from the conservative think tanks set up to proclaim the gospel of privatisation.

Having presided over the transfer of state assets, many directors of public firms were nimble enough to skip across into well-remunerated positions with the newly private companies. The City itself was transformed and modernised in the process, with the abolition of exchange controls and the liberalisation and deregulation of financial markets opening up London's genteel world of banking and trading to the icy winds of global competition. The London Stock Exchange went from being "a closed-entry market with restricted competition run by an oligopoly of traditional London gentlemanly capitalists", as Alexander Gallas puts it, to "an open, internationalised, competitive market run by international financial corporations".[30] Old establishment elites gave way to a new corporate and financial business class—a new power elite that has itself been "denationalised", according to business scholar Stephen Wilks, in that it "is no longer committed to the British national interest or even to continued location in Britain".[31] Above and beyond the plentiful commissions and other earnings, privatisation drove the process of financial innovation itself, creating new forms of flotation and debt financing that were later adapted for private offerings.[32]

One important lesson in terms of how to go about large-order political-economic change is the manner in which different aspects of Thatcherism were made to reinforce and strengthen each other. For the Thatcher project, privatisation served a dual function—at once breaking up the institutional sources of its opponents' strength while at the same time providing the building blocks for the construction of the new neoliberal economic order. Privatisation not only allowed for attacks on the trade unions and a restoration of capital's "right to manage" but was also—together with "Big Bang" financial deregulation—instrumental in the build-out of London-based capital markets.

There was a symbiotic relationship between privatisation and the increasing "financialisation" of British capitalism as the new era unfolded. Once underway, the privatisation programme began to require "flotation on a scale never seen before", with initial questions as to whether it was even feasible. At a dinner in the City, Chancellor Nigel Lawson was told by all but one of the leading merchant bankers present that privatisation of British Telecom would be "impossible" because "the capital market was simply not large enough to absorb it". Warburg & Co., the London-based investment bank, had also warned the government that there was no way BT could be floated in its entirety, estimating the capacity of the market for *all new issues* to be no more than £2 billion per year.[33]

Unwilling to accept that it couldn't be done, the Thatcherites pressed on regardless, turning obstacles into opportunities to deepen and extend their project. The initial public offering (IPO) for BT went ahead in 1984. At £3.9 billion, the rollout of shares was *six times* larger than any previous UK stock offering (the prior record, itself a privatisation, was held by the flotation of BP in 1983), while dwarfing the world's previous largest equity share offer—a secondary offering by AT&T in America valued at a little over $1 billion. In the first fortnight of trading, more than 700 million BT shares passed through the London Stock Exchange, with a further 280 million being traded in New York.[34] The pattern was set for subsequent flotations. In this way, the serial privatisations of the 1980s and 1990s helped to secure the ascendancy of finance capital and guarantee the City's future as a world financial centre, while at the same time incorporating more and more people, even if in a small way, into the regime of shareholder capitalism.

Most momentous of all was the aforementioned "Right to Buy" policy by which local authorities were forced to sell council housing to any sitting tenant able to purchase their homes, at discounts of up to 50 per cent. By far the biggest of the Thatcher privatisations, 2.5 million council homes were sold after 1980, for a total value of £86 billion—more than all other sell-offs combined. In terms of the wider political economy, mass council house sales helped generate the UK real estate boom while ultimately feeding into the property credit bubble.[35]

The "Right to Buy" policy explicitly targeted swing voters in order to create a mass constituency for the new right-wing politics—what social historian John Boughton calls "the fifth column of Mrs Thatcher's housing revolution".[36] Meanwhile, revenues from these plus the sale of other public assets—the latter totalling £68.6 billion between 1979 and 1997—allowed successive Tory governments to maintain public spending while cutting taxes for short-term electoral gain.[37] Leon Brittan once insisted that "people always overestimated Mrs Thatcher's grasp of economics while underestimating her grasp of politics".[38]

The strategic use made by the Thatcherites of flagship policies like "Right to Buy" was impressive, simultaneously giving millions of people an immediate stake in the project while at the same time shifting the underlying ownership patterns and carrying a symbolic narrative regarding the new politics of private ownership in Britain. Thatcher herself famously said: "Economics are the method; the object is to change the heart and soul".[39] She clearly understood the manner in which economic conditions shape the outlooks and interests that fix the boundaries and horizons of political possibility. This lesson should be at the forefront of left thinking as part of any effort to bring about a systematic institutional overthrow and replacement of neoliberalism.

Both the Attlee and Thatcher governments were game-changers in that they created durable political settlements that subsequent governments had to accept and work within. In the same way, we should see our task today as not simply the election of a Corbyn government that can wield power for a couple of terms, but as the use of that power—and the power of the movement underpinning it—to reshape the boundaries of the political and economic settlement for a generation or more. We need a strategic conversation about what it takes to achieve this kind of lasting transformation—and what this means in practice for the movement's role today.

Battle plans: Ridley and Powell

We also need to discuss the importance of moving beyond the contest of ideas to the development of concrete political-economic strategies and battle plans. This is one of the most important but under-discussed lessons of the success of the neoliberals. Their rise to global dominance in the last quarter of the twentieth century was a remarkable political achievement. But how exactly did they pull it off? And what lessons does their success offer for a left seeking to achieve a similarly ambitious transformation of today's political economy?

The outlines of the neoliberals' decades-long project of preparation for power, by which they moved their ideas from the margins to the mainstream, are by now a familiar story—at least as far as they concern broad ideology.

The Mont Pelerin Society led with *ideas*.[40] As the effort gathered steam, business interests bankrolled a supportive "intellectual infrastructure" in the form of a well-funded network of think tanks like the Atlas Foundation, the American Enterprise Institute (AEI), the Centre for Policy Studies (CPS), and the Institute of Economic Affairs (IEA), as we discuss further in Chapter Five. These think tanks represented "a new type of political organization" and were critical to the wider dissemination of the movement's ideas.[41] The ideas themselves were therefore the work of a deep transatlantic network of scholars, businesspeople, lawyers, lobbyists, politicians, and journalists who invested a massive amount of time, energy, and financial resources over decades into their creation. It is testament to what can be done against seemingly long odds. This much is by now fairly well understood.

Less appreciated is the long-range institution building and strategizing that made them so effective, issuing in concrete battle plans at just the points at which they were needed. Key historical documents reveal the disciplined rigour with which the New Right undertook the re-conquest of power on both sides of the Atlantic as the post-war Keynesian orthodoxy ran into increasing difficulties.

Perhaps the best known of these battle plans is the infamous 1971 "Powell Memorandum" to the U.S. Chamber of Commerce, entitled *Attack on the American Free Enterprise System*. At the time it was written, Lewis F. Powell, Jr, was a former president of the American Bar Association and partner in a leading Richmond, Virginia law firm—although he would shortly be nominated by Richard Nixon and confirmed by the U.S. Senate to serve as an associate justice on the United States Supreme Court. Powell's Richmond friend and neighbour, Eugene B. Sydnor, Jr, was intent upon awakening the sleepy U.S. Chamber and transforming it into "a powerful force capable of defending business in the new and uncertain political world". At some point in the course of the summer of 1971, Sydnor asked Powell to craft a memorandum for the organisation outlining "a thoroughgoing political strategy that the business community could use to confront the new threats it faced".[42]

Powell's response was a tightly focused document aimed at organising the right around a strategy, laid out briefly in the memorandum, by which they could turn around the early 1970s malaise facing American capital. "No thoughtful person", the memo began, "can question that the American economic system is under broad attack", with the "attackers" being identified as including not merely the usual suspects on the left but also consumer rights advocates, environmentalists, and the liberal intelligentsia. Powell argued that business leaders were for the most part taking this deadly assault lying down, an altogether unwarranted display of "apathy" in the face of mortal danger: "The overriding first need is for businessmen to recognize that the ultimate issue may be *survival*—survival of what we call the free enterprise system".[43]

Powell's memo recommended what amounted to a coordinated counteroffensive by American corporate interests across a broad front of American society, "aggressively" advancing a pro-business agenda in the universities, the media, the courts, and the political arena. "Strength lies in organization", he wrote, "in careful long-range planning and implementation, in consistency of action over an indefinite period of years, in the scale of financing available only through a joint effort, and in the political power available only through united action and national organizations".[44]

The strategy encompassed support for conservative scholars, a speakers' bureau, efforts to shape the content of academic textbooks, monitoring of television networks for "balance", paid advertising, attention to the opportunities represented by radio, mobilisation of the latent power of shareholders, and—perhaps most significantly—an unabashedly proactive strategy in the neglected arenas of electoral politics and the legal system. All this was required to turn around the dire situation in which "the American business executive", in Powell's maudlin assessment, had become "truly the 'forgotten man'".[45]

Sydnor and the U.S. Chamber wholeheartedly embraced the memo's argument for an offensive strategy by American business. Although Powell ceased to promote it once his Supreme Court nomination was underway, it circulated in private until receiving widespread public attention when a *Washington Post* journalist obtained a copy and wrote about it in 1972. At that point, the Chamber published the memo in their *Washington Report* newsletter and made printed copies available upon request.

One particularly effective aspect of Powell's proposed strategy was its focus on playing to the strengths of the business community whilst also learning from the left in applying these strengths to areas they had not been used to contesting. One example of this was the notion of applying skills in advertising and the manipulation of consumers' desires—a core business function—to the political arena. This involved utilising the most effective capacities of the right while also exploiting their opponents' weaknesses. And for all that it was the work of an ideological warrior for free enterprise, the Powell Memorandum also contained a very pragmatic strategy, designed to build the broadest possible base of support for business' demands—as can be seen in the demand for "balance" in education, which they knew could achieve wider support than an overtly propagandistic pro-enterprise platform.

Powell's suggested strategy of investment in the law—borrowing a leaf from the left's book, given its successes in civil rights, environment, and other areas—was particularly inspired. It had a direct influence on the thinking of important actors on the right, and was cited as such by wealthy conservative benefactor John M. Olin, who founded the right-wing Olin Foundation that went on to support the law-and-economics movement and the "campaign for the courts". How much of this can be straightforwardly attributed to Powell's influence is a matter of some debate; but many of the strategies he identified did in fact get taken up. Among those pulled into the broader effort was Charles G. Koch.[46] Together with his brother David, with whom he is co-owner of Koch Industries, the second largest private company in the United States, Koch would later become synonymous with the influence of corporate special interest "dark money" in American politics.[47]

Despite its outsized influence, the Powell Memorandum must share the title of world's most successful neoliberal strategy paper with another document, produced in Britain by right-wing Conservative MP Nicholas Ridley. Ridley had developed an "ideological opposition" to public ownership while a student at Oxford, when his wealthy family's coal and steel interests in North East England had been nationalised under Attlee. "I wanted to see the nation's industry and economy properly run", he recalled in his memoir: "I wanted socialism defeated for ever".[48] The 1977 *Final Report of the Nationalised Industries Policy Group*—the so-called "Ridley Plan"—was a far-sighted internal report that set out a proposed strategy by which the Conservatives could launch an assault upon the economic underpinnings of working class power in Britain through "denationalisation", based on the hiving off of profitable parts of public sector companies.[49]

The objective of the Thatcherites was to restore the discipline of the market by eliminating key political and economic obstacles to its operations: "First of all the monopolies enjoyed by the trade unions, second the 'monopoly' of the state in the economy".[50] Ridley's group took up the task with surgical precision, codifying these goals into a careful but proactive political strategy for an incoming Thatcher government determined to fundamentally reshape Britain's economy. The resulting report was a short document, divided into two sections: one concerning the running of nationalised industries, the other on the favoured policy of denationalisation.

The first section recommended the deployment, as far as was possible, of market measures in the nationalised industries, including setting strict targets for the rate of return on capital, removal of price controls, recruitment of politically sympathetic leadership, and introducing clearer objectives and greater rewards and penalties for managers. The second section suggested ending statutory monopolies and "fragmenting" the public sector industries into independent units, which could eventually be sold to private buyers—and perhaps even to the public via share offerings at discounted prices.[51] This latter proposal anticipated the later approach of "popular capitalism", holding out the "possibility of a 'coup de theatre' ... a positive act of giving public assets to the public, as well as making every man a capitalist".[52]

In terms of immediate political strategy regarding the trade unions, the report recommended against "a frontal attack", urging instead "a policy of preparing the industries for partial return to the private sector, more or less by stealth".[53] This implied "a cautious 'salami' approach—one thin slice at a time, but by the end the whole lot has still gone".[54] A final section contained a confidential annex on "Countering the Political Threat", the most controversial part of the report—later leaked to *The Economist*, which ran a piece on it in May 1978.[55] This set out the plans by which a Conservative government would be able "to hold the fort until the long term strategy of fragmentation can begin to work". It included provoking battles in "non-vulnerable industry, where we can win", identifying as possible candidates "the Railways, B.L.M.C., the Civil Service and Steel".[56]

Regarding the existence of "state monopoly industrial unions", Ridley was bluntly emphatic: "Since they have the nation by the jugular vein, the only feasible option is to pay up". At the same time, however, this did not mean capitulation but eventual showdown: "We must take every precaution possible to strengthen our defences against all out attack in a highly vulnerable industry".[57] The report named coal as "the most likely area" for such a strike, and sketched a political battle plan to win it. This included building up coal stocks at power stations; making contingency plans for coal and oil imports; encouraging the recruitment of non-union lorry drivers by haulage companies that could move coal; and the introduction of dual coal/oil firing in power stations as quickly as was practicable. Lastly, there should be "a large, mobile squad of police who are equipped and prepared to uphold the law" against violent picketing.[58]

Altogether, the Ridley Plan is an extraordinary document, amounting to a hard-headed analysis of the realities of the political-economic balance of power in Britain at the time. In particular, Ridley had clearly been scarred by his experience of the blundering government of Ted Heath, which had ended up nationalising more than it privatised, only to become the first government in Western Europe to be brought down by an industrial dispute.[59] He pushed the Thatcherites to ask themselves the really tough questions. In which industries were the Tories in a strong position to privatise, and in which were they weak? Which battles should they pick now, and which should they leave for later? For areas in which they were weak, were there ways to prepare the ground to win later? What and who would be the key obstacles and opposing forces, and how might their power be weakened and undermined? For all the inclusiveness and compassion of our vision, these are the kinds of questions today's left must ask if it is really serious about fundamentally transforming the patterns of ownership and control in the British economy.

In the same vein, the Ridley Plan set out the balance and trade-offs between strategy and tactics. Ridley appreciated that everything could not be achieved all at once, and that Thatcherism must be a long-term project. This is something that will be particularly important for the grassroots movement around Labour to remember. We must balance pressing a Corbyn government to stick to its radical promises with strategic patience and an awareness of the realities of delivering this kind of transformation—which is to say, it is not going to happen overnight. Strategic compromises will have to be made, and we must not immediately lose heart or desert the project altogether at the first sign of difficulty.

Armed with the Ridley Plan, together with three other important publications—the Carrington Report on the "Authority of Government", the *Stepping Stones* report by John Hoskyns and Norman Strauss on strategic communications, and the *Right Approach to the Economy* report on economic policy by a group of Conservative frontbenchers led by Keith Joseph—the Thatcherites had the backbone of their strategy. (Significantly, the *Stepping Stones* report urged in Ridleyesque fashion that the Conservatives "must ensure that the preparation of policy includes plans for the removal of political obstacles to its implementation".)[60] With these documents, as Alexander Gallas has noted, "the new right around Thatcher and Joseph now possessed a fairly coherent and comprehensive political agenda", including "detailed strategic considerations concerning its communication to the general public".[61] They went on to deploy this agenda to great effect. While it was certainly not "a master plan to which Thatcher and her associates stuck slavishly", the existence of an underlying strategy meant that, unlike previous governments, they weren't simply muddling through. On the contrary, they were in a position to make sober and careful decisions, including tactical compromises, in pursuit of consistent overarching objectives.[62]

The Ridley Plan, in particular, "was followed almost to the letter once Thatcherism gained power in 1979".[63] This can be seen in the manner in which the Thatcher government prosecuted an offensive against organised workers whenever they were able—in the steel industry in 1980, in the civil service in 1981, and with health and railway workers in 1982—whilst at the same time avoiding being drawn into decisive conflicts with stronger unions for which they were as yet unprepared.

It was a form of Gramscian "war of manoeuvre".[64] In her autobiography, *The Downing Street Years*, Thatcher described the deliberation with which decisions were made in the early days of her government, with short-term tactical retreats in the service of long-run strategy and preparedness. The 1981 "coal strike which never was", in which the government backed down and awarded the National Union of Mineworkers (NUM) a higher-than-agreed pay increase, is explained thus:

> There had been no forward thinking in the Department of Energy about what would happen in the case of a strike. The coal stocks piled at the pit heads were largely irrelevant to the question of whether the country could endure a strike: it was the stocks at the power stations which were important, and these were simply not sufficient ... It became very clear that all we could do was to cut our losses and live to fight another day, when—with adequate preparation—we might be in a position to win. When my attitude became clear one official could not prevent himself from expressing disappointment and surprise. My reply was simple: there is no point in embarking on a battle unless you are reasonably confident you can win. Defeat in a coal strike would have been disastrous.[65]

By the time of the next confrontation with the NUM, much more adequate preparations had been made. To begin with, labour law had been changed, via the 1980 and 1982 Employment Acts and the 1984 Trade Union Act, to add more coercive provisions, such as outlawing flying pickets—a significant factor in the miners' 1972 victory—as well as secondary action.[66] Coal stocks were increased from 37 million tonnes in 1981 to 57 million tonnes in 1984. On the day after her 1983 re-election, Thatcher reportedly said: "We're going to have a miners' strike". The full administrative functions of the British state were then brought to bear on planning, and a secret Cabinet committee was established to conduct detailed technical preparatory work in anticipation of the coming contest.[67] This committee had in its remit, in the words of Cabinet Secretary Robert Armstrong, "all aspects of the situation which may be of concern to Ministers: industrial relations, law and order, power station endurance, the effect on the economy, the scope for mitigating action by the Government, and the handling of the media".[68] So much for the government's public claim that it was uninvolved in what was formally a dispute between the National Coal Board and the NUM!

Even with all this, when the strike came in 1984 it was a close-run thing—testimony to the enormous grit and determination of the miners:

> For a while, the stoppage brought the government close to defeat—a result that would have weakened the hold of the Thatcherites over the political scene and would have derailed their attempt to undermine organised labour. In other words, the stakes were high in this conflict, and the strategy sketched out in the Ridley Plan was by no means invincible.[69]

Invincible or not, in the event it was enough—not least because of the spinelessness of the then Labour leadership under Neil Kinnock and Roy Hattersley. Thatcher defeated the miners and then, flush with victory, went on to roll out a privatisation programme that would turn out to be beyond even Nicholas Ridley's wildest ambitions.

Reverse Ridley?

Just as the Mont Pelerin Society has become a byword for the way in which neoliberals moved their ideas from the margins to the mainstream, these landmark strategic documents that laid the political foundations for Thatcherism and Reaganism must now become bywords for the way they moved from broad visions to concrete *battle plans*. And just as the British left sought to learn from the Mont Pelerin Society after the crash, it must now learn from the Ridley Report and the Powell Memorandum. We need not mimic the exact manner in which the right organised for power—we lack the material resources available to copy them, for one thing, and we ought also to be much more democratic in our processes. But we cannot afford to arrive in government without such plans, and thus find ourselves once again "in office but not in power".

In that spirit, it is worth asking how today's left can learn these lessons and build its own battle plans for change. What might be some key elements of Corbynism's "Reverse Ridley"?

To begin with, we should "know our enemy"—in just the way that the Thatcherites understood their real opponent to be the trade unions, particularly the public sector unions. From our own vantage point, there is an obvious candidate—the City of London, and the stranglehold of finance capital over both our economy and our politics. Naming our principal enemy as extractive finance capital would be clarifying, bringing the elements of a transformative strategy for fundamental change increasingly into focus. As Aditya Chakraborrty has said, "Britain either shrinks the City of London, or the City of London will swallow Britain".[70] This is something the leadership has flirted with but is understandably yet to say outright—but which we in the wider movement should be able to discuss much more freely. In the same way that Thatcherism had, as two sides of the same coin, *denationalisation* and *financialisation*, with the one serving as fuel for the other, perhaps we might think of flipping that around, and pursuing a strategy of *de-financialisation* and *democratisation*?

What would that mean, practically speaking? On the one hand, new institutions would be needed in support of a new industrial strategy and regional rebalancing away from speculative finance and in favour of the real economy. These include the National Investment Bank already in Labour's plans, supported by a network of regional and local public banks, combined with proper support for co-operative and mutual sources of finance. On the other hand, measures would be taken to cut big banks' power down to size—especially full separation of retail and investment banking, tougher capital requirements and restrictions on their most damaging activities, and eventually their displacement altogether by the institutions of the democratic economy.

This in turn could allow us to think of two vectors of activity—a "levelling up" of the new democratic economy and a "levelling down" of the extractive one. "Levelling up" would consist of many of the policies for democratisation indicated in Chapter One. Democratic public ownership and insourcing would push out sources of financial extraction, while new banking arrangements, the "Right to Own", and the Inclusive Ownership Funds would help grow the new economy. This would be flanked by increasing social control over investment through a new top-to-bottom public banking system, and the growth of local economic resilience through economic development strategies like community wealth building. "Levelling down" would consist of displacing the old through de-privatisation, insourcing, breaking up the big commercial banks, and pushing out speculative financial activity through regulation, taxes, and levies. It would also mean unpicking the structures which make ordinary citizens dependent on the whims of financial markets—for instance, through outsize mortgages (which demands a carefully designed package of measures to gradually bring down house prices) and private pensions (which requires work to transition these pension pots into new, more democratic, and less financialised savings funds, as well as a more generous state pension). Should another massive financial crisis occur we should also be ready to seize the moment and bring the UK's big banks into full democratic ownership.

In rolling out such a strategy we must be ready to take steps to minimise economic disruption, and to protect the most vulnerable from the impacts of economic change. For example, deflating the property bubble in a controlled way is far easier said than done. The imposition of rent controls could trigger an uncontrolled fall in prices that might hit poorer homeowners as well as destabilising the wider economy. As Beth Stratford has argued, we need to be prepared to find ways of avoiding these effects if we are serious about transforming our broken housing market.

The real prize here is to identify the kind of Gorzian non-reformist reforms mentioned earlier, which both mitigate short-term effects (for example, by providing a soft landing for the housing market) whilst also moving us towards the longer-term goal (in this case, of transforming the ownership of land). In this instance, Stratford proposes a People's Land Trust, which would buy up the land from underneath people's houses and lease it back to them, as a way of managing this difficult transition.[71] Such a policy would simultaneously support people struggling as a result of falling house prices, cushion the impact of falling prices on the wider economy, and begin the process of bringing land into common ownership. Just as Thatcher's huge privatisations demanded that capital markets be built out to absorb them, it would transform a potential economic obstacle into a means of furthering the project.

We will also need to be ready for more orchestrated reaction, given that finance will understandably dislike much of the programme set out above. We will take up some of these difficult matters in Chapter Three, including the question of timing—which we must choose carefully, a key lesson from the Thatcherites.

Otherwise, it is possible to identify some of the pieces that could form a potential politics for such a strategy. Labour's emerging approach to public investment, for example, could mobilise significant new sources of political support. Capital is far from a monolithic bloc, and it should be possible to develop policies capable of appealing to many of the genuinely productive sections of the business community—the "makers" rather than the "takers".[72] Pragmatic policies aimed at benefitting small businesses, such as taking more robust action against their exploitation by big banks and providing them with low-cost growth capital, could allow for cross-class alliances against the dominance of big multinationals and monopolies, serving to divide the opposition and create unlikely allies and bedfellows.

Similarly, the Right To Own and the Inclusive Ownership Funds could function in a manner similar to Thatcher's flagship Right to Buy policy, giving millions of people an immediate stake in the new democratic economy, meaningfully shifting relationships of ownership and power whilst also carrying a new story about who we are and the values upon which our society should be based. As Mathew Lawrence argues, "By offering real, substantive material benefits to a broad mass of the electorate, while reshaping how power and wealth flow through society, Inclusive Ownership Funds could be the left's 'Right to Buy'—a proposal that can bind in expanded social constituencies to a new economic model and embed a sentiment of feeling that supports that paradigm shift—solidaristic, collective, and democratic in practice".[73]

A large worker-owned and co-operative sector could form an important institutional base for a new place-based economics and politics in Britain. This would be a politics capable of overturning simplistic notions of "pro- or anti-business" and replacing them with new alignments around democratic local and regional economies in opposition to footloose, extractive multinational corporations. In a political landscape fractured and divided by Brexit, decentralised collective ownership and control of the economy in this manner could reconstitute the basis for democratic participation by giving people real decision-making power over the forces that affect their lives—a chance to actually "take back control".

We also need to make strategic use of the assets we already have to build the foundations of this new economy before extending it into more challenging areas. For example, the "anchor institution" approach that underpins the Preston Model, leveraging the massive purchasing power of large public and non-profit place-based institutions such as hospitals and universities in support of community-based economic development, could be applied on a national scale, including through the National Health Service. Given its enormous economic footprint, the NHS has the potential to become the backbone of an industrial strategy around the production of goods and services for health and community well-being. This would represent the very opposite of neoliberal extraction, keeping public funds in circulation, anchoring jobs and building community wealth, reversing long-term economic decline in disinvested regions.

Labour is already working on an agenda to hit the ground running through preparations in Shadow Cabinet for a first Queen's Speech. Franklin Delano Roosevelt's first "Hundred Days"—deftly packaged as such for the first time, in one of his legendary "fireside chats"—blitzed his opponents with one of the most rapid and audacious legislative reform packages in history, and remains a model for how a radical reforming government can roll out its programme. The Hundred Days encompassed legislation on everything from agricultural relief (the Emergency Farm Mortgage Act and the Farm Credit Act) and industrial regeneration (the National Industrial Recovery Act) to transport (the Emergency Railroad Transportation Act), energy (creation of the Tennessee Valley Authority), and banking and monetary reform (the Glass-Steagall Banking Act and abandonment of the gold standard).[74] Moreover, all this took place at the lowest point of the Great Depression, with a quarter of the workforce (upwards of 15 million people) unemployed, and the American banking system on the brink of collapse. And yet it still managed to lay the foundations for the New Deal.[75]

* * *

As we have seen, Attlee and Thatcher, each in their own way, set the terms for what followed over the next several decades. The significance of what was accomplished can be seen in the fact that, even today, ordinary people are still benefitting from the Attlee government's programme—and still paying the price for Thatcher's. Our ambition should be lasting change on the scale of these two powerful precedents.

In this regard, Corbyn and McDonnell have created a hugely important opening for the British left. Already, the leadership has opened up space for a far broader political conversation on the economy than has been possible in decades. Not since the 1970s and early 1980s—when Labour was committed to bringing about what Tony Benn termed "a fundamental and irreversible shift in the balance of power and wealth in favour of working people and their families"—has the party put forward as bold a plan for the transformation of Britain.

Like the Attlee and Thatcher programmes before it, Corbynism contains the possibility of conjuring up the conditions for its own political success and consolidation. But making this a reality will require that we move beyond broad visions and into the terrain of strategy and planning, learning the lessons of Powell and of Ridley. This is about more than just a programme for government—it is about deep and lasting transformation. Such a shift is, of course, precisely what Britain desperately needs—and why all those of us who want to see radical change must now get ready to fight for it.

CHAPTER THREE: GET READY FOR REACTION

"The roof will fall in".

—Ray MacAnally as prime minister
Harry Perkins in A Very British Coup

Speaking to a capacity audience at The World Transformed on the Labour Party Conference fringe in Brighton in September 2017, Shadow Chancellor John McDonnell tackled a sensitive subject head on, touching upon some of the left's deepest fears and suspicions about the fate that awaits a radical Labour government as it enters office. "What happens when, when or if, they come for us?" he asked—*they* in this instance being the capital markets, high finance, the power of big money. McDonnell sought to reassure the activists crowded into the room that he and his team were on top of such concerns:

> We're not going to be a traditional government, we're going to be a radical government. And we're going to face all the challenges that I'm sure you've discussed before I got here ... and we've got to scenario plan for those, and that's exactly what we're doing at the moment, bringing the relevant expertise together at every level to talk through what happens if, what happens if there's such and such a reaction, what happens if there is a run on the pound, what happens

if there is this concept of capital flight. I don't think there will be, but you never know, so we've got to scenario plan for that.[1]

McDonnell's words prompted a small firestorm of criticism in the media, leading the Labour Party to put out a clarifying statement to the effect that such scenario planning was "an exercise not done by us but by members ... to deal with numerous events such as national disasters and acts of terror that could occur under any government".[2]

But McDonnell wasn't speaking out of turn. If Corbynism is not to join the dismal litany of failed attempts at democratic socialism, it is imperative that the fledgling movement at its back quickly absorb the lessons of previous radical governments around the world as to what it will really take to institute transformative change—and how to prepare for, and respond to, the inevitable challenges and opposing forces that will arise in reaction. Getting a Corbyn government elected will in all likelihood prove to be the easy part—at least relatively speaking. The real challenge is to be ready for power with a pro-active agenda, complete with contingency plans in the event that financial markets do in fact "come for us".

Labour pains

The historical record in this regard is not particularly encouraging, either at home or abroad. In Britain, the incoming Labour governments of 1964 and 1974—the latter elected on a radical left-wing manifesto—were quickly blown off course, their carefully laid plans for economic modernisation falling victim to what one sympathetic observer described as "a combination of bad luck, rigid expectations and early loss of nerve".[3] In both instances, Labour entered office with promising medium-term plans for structural reforms aimed at restoring investment and productivity growth to the UK economy and installing a degree of economic planning—the Department of Economic Affairs (intended to counterbalance the power of the Treasury) in 1964, and the National Enterprise Board in 1974. In both instances, these ambitions were "defeated comprehensively" as a result of short term policy decisions taken "very early in the life of the governments" in response to macrocco nomic pressures.[4] Each time, a newly elected Labour government faced immediate economic crises; and each time, it took the conservative, orthodox policy route in response—closing off rather than extending future possibilities for socialist advance.

In 1964, Harold Wilson's incoming government inherited an £800 million trade deficit due to rising imports. At the same time, international investors were offloading sterling in the aftermath of Labour's election victory, threatening a disastrous fall in the value of the pound. These were problems for which "only sketch plans were available".[5] Within the Bretton Woods regime of fixed exchange rates operating at the time, two paths were open to the government—either an early devaluation of the pound, thereby allowing for adjustment and continued expansionary measures; or a defence of sterling, requiring an interest rate hike and limits on spending to dampen demand for goods from abroad, together with other restrictive policy measures.

The choice of the second course—"taken within a day or two of the formation of the new government and taken largely on political grounds", according to contemporary accounts, then subsequently regarded as "irrevocable" within Wilson's inner circle—locked in a deflationary path for the lifetime of the 1964–70 Labour government.[6] This meant interest rate increases, contracting public expenditure, rising unemployment, reduced growth, and further deflationary budgets—a cycle both savage and depressingly familiar. It included cuts in public investment programmes that had been central to Labour's economic strategy, effectively marking the government's abandonment of its own National Plan. Gone were ambitious promises about harnessing the "white heat" of the technological revolution to accelerate industrial development. Instead came what was at the time the most severe set of austerity measures since the war, prompting one observer to remark acidly that the economy was "being sacrificed on the altar of the pound sterling, but this time it is a Labour high priest who is performing the ceremony".[7]

Wilson himself offered a window into the intensity of the pressures in an arresting account of the early days of his government in late November 1964:

> That night we had our most desperate meeting with the Governor of the Bank [of England]. Claiming that our failure to act in accordance with his advice had precipitated the crisis, he was now demanding all-round cuts in expenditure, regardless of social or even economic priorities, and fundamental changes in some of the Chancellor's economic announcements. Not for the first time, I said that we had now reached the situation where a newly-elected Government with a mandate from the people was being told, not so much by the Governor of the Bank of England but by international speculators, that the policies on which we had fought the election could not be implemented; that the Government was to be forced into the adoption of Tory policies to which it was fundamentally opposed. The Governor ... had to admit that was what his argument meant, because of the sheer compulsion of the economic dictation of those who exercised decisive economic power.[8]

As it turned out, the Wilson government was eventually forced to devalue anyway—but "at the worst possible time internationally, when resources not only of foreign exchange, but of confidence, patience and credibility had all been nearly exhausted".[9] Ironically, Wilson was against a devaluation of sterling because he viewed the difficulties facing the British economy as primarily "structural"—and therefore immune to a monetary fix. "There is *no solution* to our problems", he had said at the outset of the 1964 campaign, "except on the basis of expanding output, expanding investment and rising productivity".[10] But while he was surely correct to see devaluation as "no substitute for fundamental adjustments" to an ailing economy, the problem was that the struggle over the former came to preclude the latter, with "a refusal to devalue, and a determination to deflate, effectively destroy[ing] the opportunity to set about making the fundamental adjustments required".[11]

In the same vein, the Labour governments of 1974 faced a similarly deteriorating balance of payments, coupled with world recession and the after-effects of the OPEC oil shocks. This led to the disastrous decision to honour the restrictive incomes policy (an economy-wide effort to keep the lid on wage increases to combat inflation) initiated by the previous Conservative government of Ted Heath—sold within the Labour Party as a short term political expedient, but setting the pattern for all that was to follow. After the second election in 1974 returned a slim Labour majority of just three in October, the radical Alternative Economic Strategy (AES) developed by the Labour left in opposition was summarily abandoned after perfunctory consideration by the Treasury and the economic sub-committee of the Cabinet, with a deflationary strategy adopted in its stead.[12]

Tony Benn complained of a "systematic social democratic betrayal of socialist policy".[13] He argued in Cabinet that "the price we must pay for borrowing to finance a free trade policy is too high because it involves unacceptable levels of unemployment, unacceptably low levels of investment and a progressive deterioration of our manufacturing capacity", urging instead a five-point plan for national recovery, consisting of import quotas, controls on currency exchange, targeting of investment, active monetary policy, and an industrial strategy based on expanded planning agreements.[14] For a moment, more than just the Labour government's economic policy hung in the balance. U.S. Secretary of State William P. Rodgers described the decision as "a choice between Britain remaining in the liberal financial system of the West as opposed to a radical change of course", recounting American concerns about Benn "precipitating a policy decision by Britain to turn its back on the IMF". Viewed from Washington, the stakes were enormous: "I think, if that had happened the whole system would have come apart ... So we tended to see it in cosmic terms".[15]

In the event the Cabinet rejected Benn's proposals, the "IMF Road" was taken, and disaster ensued.[16] "Monetarism"—the restrictive new doctrine that argued that changes in the economy could be traced back to changes in the money supply—was first installed in Britain by Jim Callaghan and Denis Healey, through the IMF-compliant austerity budget of 1976.[17] Workers seeking to protect their living standards through wage claims in line with cost of living increases then took action that issued in the Winter of Discontent, itself a factor in the subsequent defeat of the government in the 1979 general election. Once Margaret Thatcher entered Downing Street, the terms for exiting the crisis could be set by the labour movement's class enemies, through what was christened "sado-monetarism".

It is easy to forget the willingness of the Thatcherites to countenance wrenching economic dislocations in pursuit of deep political change. In Thatcher's first term alone, UK industrial production fell by nearly 20 per cent, manufacturing capacity declined by a third, unemployment rose above three million, and inflation reached double digits.[18] Nicholas Ridley, then a Treasury minister, openly declared the pain to be necessary: "Bringing down the rate of inflation can only be done by restricting the money supply; and doing that inevitably causes difficulties for business and rising unemployment. The high level of unemployment is evidence of the progress we are making".[19] Thatcher adviser Alan Budd later admitted that the unemployment resulting from anti-inflationary policy was a deliberate part of the strategy. "What was engineered in Marxist terms", Budd confessed, "was a crisis in capitalism which re-created a reserve army of labour, and has allowed the capitalists to make high profits ever since".[20]

French lessons

If the capitulations and betrayals of previous Labour governments in Britain provide a cautionary tale, then the story of the fate of left-wing governments elsewhere is if anything bleaker still. That is true in the case of France under François Mitterrand, Spain under Felipe González, Greece under Andreas Papandreou in the 1980s and then again under Alexis Tsipras of Syriza after 2015, and—most disastrously of all—Chile under Salvador Allende. Of these, the example of the Mitterrand government in France is perhaps the one that cuts closest to the bone for Corbynism, and is therefore worth considering in some detail. Unlike the Wilson and Callaghan governments, Mitterrand actually sought to implement his radical agenda. It is what happened next that should give the movement serious pause for thought.

It began with a moment of triumph. At eight o'clock in the evening on Sunday, 10 May 1981, France learned that for the first time it had elected a Socialist as president of the Republic through universal suffrage. François Mitterrand had begun his long journey to the Élysée Palace in 1972, when the French Communist and Socialist parties agreed their *Programme commun*, which sought to "break the domination of big capital and implement a new economic and social policy". Now Mitterrand had swept into power at the head of a united left, with 15.6 million votes, 52.2 per cent of the total.[21] The promise was of *la rupture*, a break with capitalism—and the election result was greeted with "an explosion" of joy among millions.[22] The young in particular flocked to the Place de la Bastille in Paris to dance and celebrate through the night; when there was a sudden cloudburst at midnight, a hundred thousand people "caroused in the rain".[23] Mitterrand swiftly followed up his presidential victory with a landslide in the subsequent parliamentary elections, obtaining an unprecedented share of the vote—55.2 per cent—in the first ballot on Sunday, 14 June 1981, which translated into a commanding left majority in the National Assembly.[24]

True to his word, Mitterrand set about implementing his radical policies and pledges, drawing up a vast legislative agenda to enact the famous "110 Propositions" into law—including higher wages, increased social benefits and legal protections, and large-scale nationalisation of industry and finance. His government, Mitterrand repeatedly promised, would enact "nothing but its program, but the whole of its program".[25]

Huge public spending increases underpinned a programme of economic reflation. Old age pensions were increased by 20 per cent, family allowances by 30 per cent, and the legal minimum wage by 10 per cent—the latter boosting the wages of a million and a half workers.[26] With unemployment at 7.4 per cent, the working week was cut to 39 hours (with the goal of 35 hours by 1985), while the government created 61,000 new public sector jobs.[27] The "Auroux laws" extended trade union and employee rights in the workplace, while political decision-making power was decentralised to 29 regional assemblies in order to boost local autonomy. The death penalty was also abolished as part of the democratisation agenda, thereby doing away with what Minister of Justice Robert Badinter denounced as "a totalitarian concept of the relationship between the citizen and the state".[28]

The other pillar of Mitterrand's economic policy was a massive extension of state ownership. The expansion of the public sector encompassed the takeover (with compensation) of a dozen giant industrial conglomerates (seven of which numbered among France's 20 largest firms), two flagship merchant banks—Paribas and Suez—and over 30 smaller banks.[29] This gave the government control over virtually the entire financial sector, including 74 per cent of all deposits and 69 per cent of loans.[30] In industry, where private capital had been "pre-occupied with quick financial gain" and "did not invest and modernize enough to be able to stand up to foreign competition", nationalisation resulted in a state sector that accounted for as much as 29 per cent of sales, 22 per cent of employment, and 52 per cent of all investment.[31]

Altogether, in the words of one historian, it amounted to "an attempt to repeat the Attlee experience in far less conducive economic and political circumstances".[32] Those challenging conditions included worldwide economic tightening as a result of higher U.S. interest rates (the "Volcker Shock"), the constraints of France's position within the European Monetary System (EMS), and the liberal framework of the European Economic Community's trade regime, which did not sit easily with a radical left programme.[33] Attempts to boost the economy through state action were rendered increasingly difficult and costly, as attacks from international speculators, growing trade deficits, and rapidly increasing inflation combined to pile pressure on the value of the French franc.[34]

The eventual resolution of these difficulties took a spectacularly awful form. Within two years Mitterrand's whole programme had been abandoned, a moment of "utter ideological and political bankruptcy" culminating in his government's infamous *tournant de la rigueur* ("turn to austerity") in 1983.[35] As ambitions for radical change gave way to stagnation and mass unemployment, the policy reversal was almost complete—and the French example set the European left back for a generation.

How did this happen? For the most part, it was because France's exposure to international trade and finance caused Mitterrand to quickly run into a wall of capitalist opposition, with large-scale capital flight, trade and currency crises, and a rapid increase in inflation. Unwilling to break with the orthodoxy embodied in the EEC and EMS, there was little choice but to capitulate and throw overboard the principal elements of his economic agenda—a chilling warning for Jeremy Corbyn and John McDonnell, given the family resemblances between Mitterrand's programme and the one they are busy setting out for Britain. Although the particular challenges and constraints imposed on Mitterrand by the EMS do not apply to a Corbyn government, the destabilising power of global capital markets most certainly does. History may not repeat itself, but it often rhymes.

For Mitterrand, the difficulties had begun even before he took office. Capital flight—the movement of financial assets abroad—intensified steadily in the run up to the election, with $5 billion estimated to have left the country between February and 10 May 1981. From 11 May to 15 May, another $3 billion absconded, climbing to daily losses of $1.5 billion by inauguration day on 21 May. On 11 May, trading in the Bourse—the Paris stock exchange—had to be suspended, because there were only sellers and no buyers, and so could be no quotation. There was also intense speculation against the franc, which plummeted to its floor level within the EMS.[36] In the ten days between Mitterrand's election and his investiture, the Banque de France lost $5 billion, a third of the country's reserves, in "a fruitless effort to stop the haemorrhaging of capital".[37]

At first, the Socialist government fought back with the tools it had available, tightening exchange controls on the movement of currency in and out of the country and raising the bank rate of interest. All prices and incomes were frozen by decree, over the objections of Communist ministers. But the government quickly came up against the constraints of interdependence, both regarding the trade deficit and the value of the currency. After two decades of European integration, France was a relatively open economy, with exports and imports each representing about 20 per cent of GDP and trade barriers lowered both against other EEC countries and the rest of the world. Measures to boost the economy therefore served principally to increase imports through consumer spending, while a depressed world economy did not respond by increasing the purchase of French exports. Within the EMS, a significant portion of foreign reserves was expended defending the overvalued franc— dubbed the *franc fort* policy. Despite this, France was forced to devalue three times between October 1981 and March 1983.[38]

What else could the Socialist government have done? Several close advisors to Mitterrand—including the industrialist Jean Riboud and Pierre Bérégovoy, secretary general of the presidency and then minister of social affairs—urged withdrawal from the EMS to permit a more radical devaluation, estimated at as much as 20 per cent. There was precedent in the fact that Valéry Giscard d'Estaing, Mitterrand's conservative predecessor, had briefly taken France out of the so-called "snake" of European currencies. But Mitterrand betrayed a common weakness on the left in his determination to appear more orthodox than the orthodoxy. While floating the franc might have provided more latitude, the government rejected this option "in order to show its orthodoxy, its respect for bourgeois niceties, and the international rules of the game".[39] Mitterrand's own comment was: "You do not devalue the money of a country when that country has just placed confidence in you".[40] He opted for deflation instead. "To do otherwise", as one academic observed, "would have entailed adopting a radical and long-term strategy of the sort that governments can rarely develop in the midst of an economic crisis".[41]

Economically, staying the course would likely have required strict capital controls, a breach with international markets, continuing curbs on wages and prices, trade protection, and an all-out effort at import substitution. Politically, this would have meant hand-to-hand combat with speculators and an explicit showdown with the power of the international financial establishment—a confrontation of precisely the kind Mitterrand's government was "making frantic efforts to avoid".[42] This would have necessitated a clear articulation of the reasons for the economic difficulties the country was experiencing and a mass mobilisation of the left's base in defence of the government's programme. Instead, Mitterrand chose capitulation—at least in part because he felt bound to remain within the European currency regime and EEC.

The about face was dramatic. There were savage public spending cuts, and swingeing tax increases. France's European partners assented to a steep devaluation of the franc within the EMS—but only in exchange for agreement to limit the French public sector deficit to 3 per cent of GDP. It was a definitive resort to capitalism's "classic methods for a cure"—in other words, brutal "restructuring" to destroy "excess capacity", thereby "throwing millions out of their jobs" in the process, and deflation.[43] In other words: austerity.

Corbynism against capital?

How can Corbynism avoid a re-run of the disasters of Mitterrand and of other left-wing governments of the past, brought to heel by the power of international capital? There would seem to be both political and economic lessons, as well as at least one deeply challenging unresolved question sitting at the heart of the Corbyn project. Speaking at The World Transformed in Liverpool in September 2018, pro-Corbyn economist Grace Blakeley argued that "Labour should think about the banks the way Thatcher thought about the unions ... You can't build a new economy if the power relations that sustained the old one still exist".

Our financial system is the UK's most potent lever for change—but also the most ominous potential obstacle to change. As the Bank of England pointed out in a widely discussed 2014 *Quarterly Bulletin*, banks do not simply mediate between savers and borrowers, but in fact create money "out of thin air" each time they make a loan.[44] This gives banks enormous power to determine the size and shape of the economy.

The chronic skewing of the economy towards financial services both heightens this power and holds back the rest of the country. For decades, our financial system has been treated not as a utility serving the real economy but as our major export sector—not as the oil lubricating the engine, but the petrol on which it runs. Politicians have been too afraid to take on the City of London. The 2008 financial crisis ought to have exposed the folly of this approach, but little has really changed. Both the complexity of the issues involved and the lack of readily available alternatives from progressive forces have thus far allowed the City to escape largely unscathed.

The City of London therefore remains the pinnacle of the extractive economy discussed in Chapter One, and is simply incompatible with the attempt to construct a democratic economy. The City sits atop one of the most highly financialised economies in the world. It has long been more focused on finding new ways to extract "rent" from the rest of the economy than on productive investment or social need. Richard Roberts and David Kynaston, who have written extensively on the history and practices of the City, even suggest that we think of it as "a foreign country"—but one whose activities have inordinately "big implications for government and industry" in Britain.[45]

Although estimates vary (between 3 per cent and 14 per cent depending on the measurement used), it is clear that only a small percentage of UK bank lending is used to finance productive investment—with even less being directed to sustainable and socially useful activities.[46] Even the Bank of England acknowledges that loans to small businesses account for just 4 per cent of domestic lending.[47] By far the lion's share (around two-thirds) is absorbed by mortgage lending—serving mainly to push up house prices and destabilise the economy.[48] The explosion of speculative activity since the "Big Bang" of the 1980s has also allowed the City to grow to a size that dwarfs the UK's real economy. For instance, London remains the largest foreign exchange market in the world, with around $1.2 trillion per day in spot transactions and derivatives trades. At two hundred times UK GDP, these flows are clearly not financing domestic production. Nor are they financing U.S.-European trade, which they exceed by a factor of four hundred.[49] The UK's status as a highly open international financial centre, together with our economic dependence on this status, could render a future radical government particularly vulnerable to the kinds of speculative international capital flows that so effectively undid the Wilson and Mitterrand programmes.

It is also bad for the rest of the economy. Far from the City being the "goose that lays the golden eggs", critics are increasingly pointing to a debilitating "finance curse" from this large and over-mighty financial sector—akin to the infamous "resource curse" afflicting economies endowed with too many valuable natural resources. Campaigning journalist Nicholas Shaxson offers a useful summation of the finance curse in his recent book:

> Once a financial sector grows above a certain optimal size and beyond its useful roles, it begins to harm the country that hosts it. Finance turns away from its traditional role serving society and creating wealth, and towards often more profitable activities to extract wealth from other parts of the economy. It also becomes politically powerful, shaping laws and rules and even society to suit it. The results include lower economic growth, steeper inequality, inefficient markets, damage to public services, worse corruption, the

hollowing-out of alternative economic sectors, and widespread damage to democracy and society.[50]

Nor are such concerns confined to a fringe on the left. Back in November 1989, in the wake of "Big Bang" deregulation of UK financial markets, the Bank of England itself noted the potential downsides of playing host to a major financial centre:

Salaries and wages may be forced up, thus driving up rents and house prices, with undesirable social consequences. Regional disparities may be exacerbated and the congestion of local transport systems may be aggravated. The economy may face risks due to over-dependence on a single sector. The operation of monetary policy may become complicated by the need to nurture the financial sector. Regulation may need to be more complex than otherwise. Finally, it has sometimes been argued that the financial sector merely preys on the rest of the economy, adding to costs and distorting other markets—by, for instance, attracting able individuals who might be more socially productive in other areas such as manufacturing.[51]

The experience of recent decades has almost entirely borne out these warnings, and international research confirms it. A study by the IMF found that, when bank lending exceeds the size of the real economy (measured by GDP), it acts as a drag on economic activity rather than enabling it.[52] The Bank of England and European Central Bank have also found that large financial systems are associated with financial instability, perhaps because they indicate a high volume of unsustainable speculative activity.[53] When banking systems do fail, the costs to taxpayers are unsurprisingly greater the bigger the financial system.[54] An analogy might be that of a person needing to obtain electricity to run their home, but who is then confronted with a nuclear reactor in their living room. Its capacity to generate energy far exceeds their needs, and its physical presence is massively distorting of everyday life—but at the same time this overkill is also dangerous and potentially a source of catastrophic destruction were something to go wrong.

All of this means that Labour needs a strategy to neutralise and down-size the City of London. This doesn't necessarily mean a full-frontal assault on the City from Day One of a radical Labour government. Learning the lessons of the Thatcherites, we must choose our timing extremely carefully. As Thatcher herself argued, "There is no point in embarking on a battle unless you are reasonably confident you can win".[55] A premature confrontation with the City, particularly in the context of Brexit and before industrial strategy has had a chance to take effect and reduce the economy's dependence on the financial sector, could easily be fatal to a Corbyn government. For the time being, the City has the economy "by the jugular vein" in just the same way that Ridley argued the public sector unions did in the 1970s.

The implicit strategy of the current leadership is consistent with this realisation. Their current priority is to build up the power of the democratic economy through public ownership and public investment. This may well be necessary before taking on the enormous power of London-based finance capital. The trade-off, however, is that such a confrontation would likely only be politically feasible in the very earliest days of an incoming radical government, when its political capital is at its highest—that is, barring another financial crisis that turns public opinion sharply against the banks. The risk is that such a confrontation is effectively postponed indefinitely. In the meantime, the nuclear reactor is still in the living room. And, if the confrontation comes to us, we are less likely to be prepared enough and strong enough to respond. For this strategy to pay off in the longer run, then, we need a plan to erode the City's power over time, as well as building up new sources of democratic finance to replace it.

What might such a strategy look like? There are a host of possibilities for more democratic finance, from public and postal banking systems to mutuals, credit unions, community banking, and fintech innovations that support peer-to-peer lending. Building up these sources of finance is an implicit part of Labour's platform. The 2017 Labour manifesto promised "to transform how our financial system operates" through increased regulation of financial firms and creating a "more diverse banking system" to drive investment to localities and regions. This includes the creation of the National Investment Bank (supported by regional development banks), a Post Bank under the auspices of the Post Office, and the possible breakup of RBS into a network of local public banks.

The question is how easy it will be to grow these new sources of finance without actively taking on the existing players' overwhelming market power. Getting new banks off the ground is notoriously difficult, especially given that most people are not prone to switching banks. In terms of retail banking, at least, "growing the new" without reducing the dominance of the existing big players may be like trying to grow plants between the cracks of paving slabs. Yet there has been relatively little serious thinking on the left about how we might go about this.

Labour is committed to a Financial Transactions Tax (or "Robin Hood Tax") to discourage speculative activity. It has also floated (via an independent report commissioned from economist Graham Turner) the idea of giving the Bank of England a mandate to promote productivity, which would entail new powers to direct bank lending away from speculative activity and towards productive investment.[56] Beyond this, though, it has had little in the way of detailed policy work to draw on. Possible options include breaking up the big banks by forcing them to split their retail from their investment banking operations, forcing banks to hold much more capital, imposing a "too big to fail tax" on the largest banks, or imposing outright bans on their most damaging speculative activities (such as certain kinds of derivatives trading). More work is needed on all these ideas, though, to turn them into implementable policy.

Labour's position: playing it straight?

How is Labour currently thinking about these strategic challenges? At the time of writing, the picture was somewhat ambiguous—perhaps necessarily so. Corbyn has certainly been more than willing to take on the bankers rhetorically. When Morgan Stanley declared him a bigger threat to British business than Brexit, he seized upon the opportunity to hit back with a short video riposte that quickly went viral, reaching more than a million people:

> These are the same speculators and gamblers who crashed our economy in 2008 and then we had to bail them out. Their greed plunged the world into crisis and we're still paying the price, because the Tories used the aftermath of the financial crisis to push through unnecessary and deeply damaging austerity. That's meant a crisis in our public services, falling wages, and the longest decline in living standards for over sixty years. Nurses, teachers, shop-workers, builders—well, just about everyone is finding it harder to get by, while Morgan Stanley's CEO paid himself £21.5 million last year and UK banks paid out £15 billion in bonuses. Labour is a growing movement of well over half a million members and a government in waiting that will work for the many. So when they say we're a threat: They're right. We're a threat to a damaging and failed system that's rigged for the few.

However, it is less clear whether taking on the City will be a genuine strategic priority should Labour enter government. There are also signs pointing in the opposite direction, towards what might be called a strategy of accommodation, at least in the short term. Recalling the actions of previous shadow chancellors like John Smith with his prawn cocktails, John McDonnell has reportedly been on a "cup of tea offensive" in the City, aimed at providing "absolute clarity" as to how a Corbyn government would run the economy, and promising financiers that he has "no tricks up [his] sleeve".[57]

Some aspects of Labour's policy platform also suggest a desire to bolster the party's orthodox credentials in order to reassure the financial markets that it can be trusted. Like the Wilson and Callaghan and Mitterrand governments, Corbyn's Labour currently combines a commitment to deep structural reform with a relatively orthodox monetary and fiscal approach. This can be seen in the so-called "Fiscal Credibility Rule", adopted in conjunction with the careful costing of the 2017 manifesto. The Fiscal Credibility Rule states that:

> Labour believe that, in the medium to long term, governments should not need to borrow to fund their day-to-day spending. While there are exceptional times when shocks from the private sector mean that government has to step in to help, everybody knows that if you're putting the rent on the credit card month after month, things need to change. And that is why we would commit to always eliminating the deficit on current spending in five years, as part of a strategy to target balance on current spending after a rolling, five-year period.[58]

Effectively, this means that Labour can only increase "day to day" spending—for instance, on more generous pensions and benefits or on teachers' and nurses' salaries—if it can pay for this by raising taxes and not by borrowing. It should be acknowledged that this rule is qualified in two important ways, both of which loosen somewhat the straitjacket it represents. First, it excludes public borrowing for investment in capital projects, which pay for themselves over time. Second, it contains a trigger, in the manner of a "get-out-of-jail-free" clause, that suspends the rule when monetary policy is at the "zero-lower bound"—that is, when lowering interest rates can no longer stimulate the economy—allowing fiscal policy to step in.

That said, this rule remains a striking piece of economic orthodoxy—especially when considered in combination with the apparent intention to leave untouched the much-vaunted "independence" of the Bank of England, and the further extension of policy making "independence" through legislation to make the Office for Budget Responsibility report to Parliament and not the Treasury. The Bank's Monetary Policy Committee is given sole authority over the trigger for suspending the rule, leaving critical tools for managing the economy in the hands of unaccountable technocrats rather than the democratically elected government itself (we return to this point in Chapter Four).

To this extent, the Fiscal Credibility Rule amounts to a self-denying ordinance on the part of a future Corbyn government, voluntarily surrendering important powers in order to secure its credibility with financial markets and mainstream opinion. Although a political masterstroke at the time (and still tactically advantageous at times, as could be seen in Theresa May's misfiring attempt to paint Labour as "fiscally irresponsible" using the book John McDonnell edited, *Economics for the Many*, at Prime Minister's Questions in October 2018), this may be a somewhat less clever strategic move for a radical Labour government should the gloves come off in financial markets.

At the same time, Labour has backed away from more radical options on monetary policy. In the early days of the Corbyn leadership, much was made of the idea of "People's Quantitative Easing" (PQE). This policy effectively involves the Bank of England creating new money to stimulate the economy—as it has already done since the financial crisis, to the tune of £435 billion.[59] The difference is that, instead of being released into the economy via an effective subsidy to big banks as has been the case under recent QE, under PQE the money would be spent directly into the economy by the government—for instance, on green jobs programmes. The PQE policy was widely used as a stick with which to beat Corbyn in the mainstream media. Robert Peston wrote that it could be "stupendously dangerous", as an uncontrolled power to create new money would trigger a collapse in the pound and rampant inflation. "This is not same-old, same-old socialism", he added: "it is new, radical thinking".[60] The leadership has since quietly buried this policy—perhaps because it was deemed too much of a political liability, perhaps because some of Labour's advisors genuinely share these concerns. It has also distanced itself from other proposals involving government-backed money creation, such as so-called "helicopter money", whereby new money is created and distributed to citizens (as advocated by Adair Turner, former chair of the Financial Services Authority) or used to write off their debts (as suggested by the economist Steve Keen).[61]

Thus far, what public debate there has been over these issues has mostly involved a rather unhelpful (to non-economists) theoretical war of words between New Keynesians who support Labour's position and Modern Monetary Theorists who oppose it—a debate that can often appear as an overly personalized exercise in talking past each other. Certainly, we do not intend to get into that controversy here, and it will doubtless continue to rage. From the perspective of the wider movement, the question as to whose economic theory is "correct" is less interesting than the matter of what all this says about the wider political and economic strategy of a Corbyn-led radical Labour government—especially how it might be expected to behave under particular crisis conditions and circumstances.

Overall, the orthodox fiscal and monetary position at the heart of current Labour policy underscores the leadership's position that this is not really where the action is in Corbynism's transformative agenda—which can instead be found in proposals concerning decentralised public ownership, economic democracy, and an investment strategy focused on productivity, competitiveness, and technological innovation. The strategic calculation appears to be that Labour must be "more orthodox than the orthodoxy" in other areas in order to build the stability and credibility to push through this latter programme—and that, by treading this path, it will be able to avoid major financial disruption or backlash, including limiting the danger of currency crises or troubles in the bond market. And time may yet prove this calculation to be correct. But there are legitimate questions over whether this is the right strategy, whether it will succeed in its aim of preventing a backlash, and—if it does not—whether it will unduly limit a Corbyn government's ability to respond. For this reason, it is vital for the wider movement to understand the stakes that are in play, to be able to engage in the debate—and, ultimately, if the bet does not in fact pay off, to advocate the tough measures that could insulate a Corbyn government from the pressures of international financial markets enough to keep its radical agenda alive.

Expect the unexpected

To understand this, we need to consider the headwinds for which a Corbyn government might have to prepare. It is impossible to predict exactly how future financial difficulties, currency crises, or economic shocks might play out. For one thing, a Corbyn government would differ from the historical precedents we have looked at above in various important ways. For instance, unlike Wilson or Mitterrand, the UK today does not have to defend a fixed exchange rate. This means the government is less vulnerable if the value of the pound falls—although there are of course limits to this, and a concern for the value of the pound even under a floating exchange rate regime will still affect any government's room for manoeuvre. But, even if the past cannot provide a precise guide to the future, it can help us to think about the *kinds* of difficulties a radical Labour government might face.

The lessons of history suggest that, given the deeply challenging nature of its agenda to the status quo, a Corbyn government would be highly likely to encounter various forms of economic warfare against its policies from powerful vested interests—especially the current owners of capital whose long-term position will be under threat. We should say that this concern is far from universal. Some—such as Simon Wren-Lewis and Ann Pettifor, two economists who have advised the Labour leadership—argue that Corbyn's economic programme would be on balance beneficial to business, and therefore question whether we should really expect such dramatic resistance and retaliation.[62]

But there are a number of reasons for thinking that such sanguine views might be missing an important part of the picture. The first is what investors and businesspeople are themselves saying about a prospective Corbyn government. The second concerns other potential sources of market instability, above and beyond reactions to Corbyn's programme—notably, the potential

93

economic dislocations of Brexit, and the ongoing fragility of a still largely unreformed and insufficiently regulated crisis-prone global financial sector.

First, it is worth being sceptical as to how tolerant markets will actually be of a Corbyn government, no matter how carefully costed and presented its programme. Even though Corbyn's programme may be economically expansionary, it still threatens to shift the balance of power in the UK economy, posing a direct challenge to capital owners, especially the *rentier* interests of the City—which is why they are highly likely to oppose it.

We can already detect some of this in the infamous November 2017 research note prepared for their clients by a team of economists at the Wall Street investment bank Morgan Stanley. This note, which ended up being widely reported in the British press, made the stakes abundantly clear, warning that, "For the UK market, domestic politics may be perceived as a bigger risk than Brexit":

> For much of the past 30 years and more, a change of government ultimately had a relatively limited impact on the UK equity market, as policy settings didn't change too dramatically. However, this may not be the case if we see a Labour government take power under its current leadership, given its very different policy approach. It is certainly plausible that the Labour Party could ultimately moderate some of its more radical policy ideas; the alternative could be the most significant political shift in the UK since the end of the 1970s.[63]

Among the expected impacts, nationalisation of utilities and infrastructure-related assets, higher corporate taxes, and a shift in government spending priorities "in favour of low-income households and the public sector and away from outsourcers and defence companies" were seen as potentially damaging to company valuations. A more recent poll of over a hundred British corporate executives told a similar story, reporting that the prospect of a Corbyn-led Labour government was second only to Brexit as the greatest challenge "keeping business leaders awake at night".[64] One in three believed a Labour government would be in power within the next five years, with nearly 70 per cent expecting an early election before May 2022.

Should this mood persist, among the weapons that are available to capital owners are *capital flight*—both from investment in financial assets and from direct investing in plant and machinery—and a *capital strike*, the withholding of new investment when the return on investment is perceived to be too low. There are live questions as to the vulnerability of the UK economy to each of these, as well as how a Corbyn government could prepare and respond.

There are already early reports from UK tax lawyers and accountants of a "Corbyn effect" among the uber-wealthy, who are making contingency plans to move their wealth offshore. Indeed, capital flight has already begun, at least in terms of portfolio investment. Iain Tait, director of private clients at London & Capital, a wealth management firm, told the *Financial Times* in October 2018 that many rich people "want to make sure their investment accounts are Channel Islands–based or Switzerland–based so their money would not be subject to capital controls. It is activity we have seen from real live clients in direct response to the threat of a Corbyn-led government".[65]

But there is more than one way to neutralise a radical government. It may not be necessary to take aggressive measures to bring a government down, if the *fear* of such measures is enough to muzzle that government's radicalism. Wren-Lewis and Pettifor may well be right that there are aspects of Labour's agenda, such as its commitment to invest in infrastructure and innovation, that are compatible with the interests of sections of capital. Another strategy open to economic elites may therefore be to attempt to box a Labour government into this narrower political space of "acceptable Corbynism", whilst tying their hands in ways that prevent them from going any further. Arguably, hysterical scare stories about the likely reactions of business to a Corbyn government serve this purpose in and of themselves, apparently justifying the leadership's calculation that it must self-censor in order to appease these interests. Ex-Tory minister and former Goldman Sachs economist Jim O'Neill, in a widely noticed *Guardian* piece cosying up to Corbynism for having "caught the mood of the country", reserved his criticisms for monetary and fiscal policy, insisting that the Labour Party still lacks credibility and calling for "some version of Gordon Brown's golden rule that couldn't be fiddled". As Corbyn and McDonnell get ever closer to power, a combination of siren songs and threats from the City are only likely to intensify.

Secondly, beyond reactions to Corbyn's programme *per se*, there is the matter of economic crises as a result of more general volatility—the hallmark condition of our present era of unpredictability and political instability. There is a strong possibility that Corbyn could take power in the midst of the greatest crisis of confidence in the British economy since the end of the Second World War—namely, Britain's exit from the European Union (the shape of which is still radically uncertain at the time of writing, but will likely have been determined by the time this book appears). Depending when the next general election occurs, a Corbyn government may need to quickly intervene across a range of fronts in order to stabilize the economy and manage any pain and dislocation that will occur as a result of Brexit. Similarly, there is the question of another global financial crisis, whenever it comes. Ten years after the collapse of Lehman Brothers, the onset of such a crisis is widely considered "all but inevitable":

> While its exact timing and severity cannot be predicted, both the accelerating frequency of crises in recent decades and the continued consolidation of the banking sector in an increasingly financialized economy suggest that we should be prepared for a crisis sooner rather than later ... During the next crisis, a robust policy response can and should convert failed banks to permanent public ownership.[66]

There are good questions as to whether Labour's adherence to a fairly conventional macroeconomic framework unduly constrains the range of responses available to it in the above scenarios, or in the event of other "black swans". The Fiscal Credibility Rule may well make it harder to increase government borrowing to boost demand in a downturn, despite Labour's efforts to provide a safety valve in this respect. Meanwhile, holding to Bank of England independence and ruling out unconventional monetary policy options would deny the government an alternative route to stimulate and shape the economy. In this sense, such compromises amount to a double gamble: if they fail to prevent economic and financial disruption, the government may find itself trying to deal with this disruption with one hand tied behind its back.

By way of historical analogy, otherwise progressive figures in the Labour governments of the 1920s could not conceive of abandoning the gold standard—"Nobody told us we could do this", Sidney Webb famously said, when the National Government that replaced Labour did eventually come off gold. The result was that they became "supplicants of international finance, seeking a transfusion of foreign funds for which the predictable condition was implementation of a deflationary package ... favoured, anyway, by the Treasury, the Bank of England, and the City of London".[67] The current Labour leadership may be trapping itself into a similar orthodoxy—more orthodox than the orthodoxy itself—regarding today's monetary and banking system.

Greek tragedy

Although the situation is clearly very different, there are potential parallels here with the fate of the radical left Syriza government that took power in Greece in 2015 in the midst of that country's sovereign debt crisis. At an early stage, the Syriza government ruled out the option of exiting the euro and adopted a strategy of trying to negotiate with the "Troika"—the name given to the negotiating team of the European Commission, European Central Bank, and International Monetary Fund—in good faith. As Stathis Kouvelakis puts it, "for the Syriza leadership, exit was unthinkable—a black hole. It was outside their cognitive mapping, alien to their strategy which had already ruled out the possibility of an all-out confrontation".[68]

Key to this strategy was demonstrating to the domestic and European establishment that Syriza could be trusted—that they were not the dangerous radicals the elites had been led to believe. Kouvelakis characterises Tsipras' position as, "I'm ready to be a nice boy, much more reasonable than you think—but I should get something in return".[69] The problem with this was that the Troika was evidently never very interested in good-faith negotiations with Syriza. Indeed, it soon became apparent that the main interest of the European establishment was to make an example of Greece—both as a debtor nation and as a country with a radical left government—by crushing Syriza *pour encourager les autres*.[70] With no viable alternative government waiting in the wings, its strategy became one of trying to "destabilise and demoralise" Syriza, isolating its left wing and forcing the government into the mould of acceptable neoliberal governance.[71] One week into the Syriza government, Greek banks were excluded from normal European financing mechanisms, in what one person we spoke to described as a clear "declaration of war". At this point, he argued, it was obvious that Syriza needed a Plan B. Persisting with their strategy of ruling out more radical options in order to demonstrate their credibility amounted to unilateral disarmament.

Of course, any government in Syriza's position would have found itself in an impossible bind. The Syriza leadership was making a strategic calculation, not seeking deliberately to sell out the movement. Its actions deserve to be looked at in that light.[72] Nobody pretends that leaving the euro would have been painless or easy, nor had public support for such a move been adequately cultivated. But those who advocated a harder line *were* developing practical plans in this period for an alternative course. Left figures like Costas Lapavitsas argued at an early stage that the government needed to impose capital controls to prevent the flight of capital out of the country, and begin preparing a parallel currency so the economy could survive outside the euro.[73] And the huge *Oxi* ("No") vote in the referendum on the bailout deal—in a context of economic warfare against the government, where banks were shuttered and Greeks could not take money out of the country—proved that the people preferred to accept some economic pain in the service of a democratic project rather than continue to have a different kind of pain imposed on them by an undemocratic project. By stifling debate in the party, the leadership closed down these possibilities and left itself without options when it became clear that its strategic gamble had failed. The forces of neoliberalism succeeded in "domesticating" the government, while the mass movement was left dispirited and demobilised, its hopes for radical change dashed for another generation.

At first sight, these experiences might seem so extreme and so specific to the politics of the euro that they have little relevance for a Corbyn-led government in the UK. But, as one former senior Syriza figure to whom we spoke emphasised, whether in or out of the euro, radical left governments still need to find a way to face down the might of the global financial markets. Just like the Troika, the City is "extremely powerful, highly mobilised and well armed".[74] And, just as the European establishment was not motivated to find a mutually beneficial solution but rather to make an example out of Syriza, so high finance—hardly motivated by the best interests of the UK economy—will surely be eager to find a way to crush Corbynism rather than risk it becoming a beacon for a new socialist politics that threatens their power, including in the United States in the form of the Bernie Sanders movement.

If Labour's strategy does indeed rest on self-denying ordinances and artificially constraining its policy options in order to make a Corbyn government acceptable to the City, it is imperative that it has contingency plans in its back pocket if confrontation is forced upon it in spite of its best efforts. And it must also welcome internal debate about whether, when, and how to move to those contingency plans in the event of destabilising capital flight, a run on the pound, another financial crisis, a global trade war, or a crisis in the bond market.

Radical responses

What tools might be necessary to react to financial market disruption—or, indeed, to other negative economic headwinds capable of blowing a transformative Labour government off course? Depending on the circumstances, there are two broad types of tools that might be useful: first, tools that allow the government to inject demand into the economy while sidestepping the financial markets; and second, tools to limit speculative flows of "hot money" in and out of the country.

In the face of capital flight or an investment strike, Labour's banking policy, and especially the strategic use of its new public banking institutions, could become a way of injecting new demand into the economy and directing investment to where it is needed. This would mean that the government would not be wholly reliant on taxation or on borrowing from bond markets—both of which are vulnerable to economic countermeasures and market shocks—to support the economy and pursue its full programme. It is not clear whether Labour is viewing the creation of new public banks in this strategic light, as a tool of money creation which provides a potential source of resilience against shocks to the economy, rather than simply as the instrument of its industrial strategy. Direct money creation tools such as "helicopter money" or new forms of QE could potentially fulfil a similar role (although Labour insiders argue that these policies are not completely insulated from the vagaries of global financial markets—for instance, if investors worried about excess money creation start betting against the pound, they could trigger a fall in its value and a currency crisis).

Another potential response, already inching back onto the agenda in the wake of the financial crisis, is the possible reintroduction of *capital controls*, should they be required to relieve a Corbyn government under pressure from international financial markets.[75] Interestingly, these seem to be among the greatest fears of City types who are otherwise seeking to take the measure of Corbyn's programme. Jim O'Neill's *Guardian* piece declared in darkly threatening tones: "If ideas such as capital controls are thrown around by the party then it may never be in a position to deliver on any of its manifesto ideas".[76] *The Economist*, too, has fretted that "The party's leftward march is not over" and that "Further radical ideas are being discussed in Labour circles, such as introducing capital controls".[77]

Capital controls are government-enforced limits on the cross-border movement of financial assets in and out of a national economy, and they can be economy-wide or specific to an industry or sector. Gerald Epstein offers a concise summary:

> Controls, first of all, are simply types of government regulations or taxes that affect inflows or outflows of capital or the effects of the latter on the domestic economy. Types of capital flows that are affected are most easily thought of as the buying by domestic residents of foreign assets (outflows) or the selling of assets by domestic residents to foreigners (inflows).[78]

Once a core structural feature of the Bretton Woods system of global economic governance put in place after the Second World War, capital controls have been largely out of favour in recent decades, progressively abandoned by developed country governments as part of the advent of neoliberalism.[79] For example, the surprise abolition of *exchange controls* (a subset of capital controls governing currency transactions) was one of the Thatcher government's earliest acts, laying off overnight a quarter of the Bank of England's staff who were responsible for monitoring them. In Paris, the official in charge of enforcing the OECD's *Code of Liberalisation of Capital Movements* was taken aback: "Nothing like this had ever happened before in the history of the Code. At one stroke, all United Kingdom reservations were removed, all controls wiped out".[80] It later transpired that the Thatcher government, in a calculated act of ideological sabotage, also destroyed the Bank of England's files on the controls to prevent their re-imposition by any future government.[81] They have since been done away with altogether across the European Union, where they are illegal except on a temporary basis in emergency situations— as was the case with their deployment during recent crises in Greece and Cyprus.

A great deal of neoliberal mythology has been built up as to the impossibility of closing down cross-border financial flows—particularly on a national basis. However, as Andrew Glyn has argued persuasively, "despite its utterly devastating consequences, the belief that it is not possible to stand up to international financial pressure is not based on any serious review of the evidence".[82] In part, the neoliberal story of "no alternative" to liberalised capital flows depends on deliberately ignoring the previously widespread and still continuing use of capital controls around the world. Today, even the IMF endorses capital controls in certain circumstances—and they have been used to good effect by a diverse array of countries seeking to stabilize their economies during periods of severe financial crisis.

Both Malaysia and Iceland, for example, have implemented varying forms of capital controls in order to stem outflows of capital. In September 1998, Malaysia implemented a yearlong waiting period for the repatriation of money from liquidated investments as part of its capital control measures during the Asian Financial Crisis. It also deployed a graduated system of exit levies in order to stop capital fleeing as soon as the 12 months had expired.[83] A study of this experience undertaken by Ethan Kaplan and Dani Rodrik concluded that "the Malaysian controls produced better results than the alternative in almost all dimensions. On the real side, the economic recovery was faster, and employment and real wages did not suffer as much. On the financial side, the stock market performed better, interest rates fell more, and inflation was lower".[84] Iceland implemented similar measures during the 2008 financial crisis, when it faced total banking collapse but was able to engineer a recovery—in this instance, with an added twist in the form of a "stability tax", effectively a capital levy of 39 per cent on all creditors' assets as a condition of exemption from strict capital controls. The results were impressive, with the Icelandic Treasury receiving assets worth 27 per cent of GDP after reaching a settlement with the country's creditors.[85]

More generally, a series of studies on the use of capital controls during financial crises have shown that, in the words of a team of IMF economists, capital controls "are associated with greater economic resilience (smaller output declines) during the crisis".[86] An even larger country sample, encompassing capital controls utilised in Chile, Colombia, Taiwan, Singapore, Malaysia, India, and China, concluded that "dynamic capital management techniques have been successfully utilized across a range of countries ... in our sample we have seen examples of policy success in both dimensions [inflows and outflows]".[87] In 2008, Brazil introduced capital controls to keep excessive flows of global hot money *out* during the financial crisis, as a means of avoiding domestic overheating and the risk of rapidly increasing inflation.

The first rule of capital controls, of course, is that *you don't talk about capital controls*—understandably so. John McDonnell will have learned his lesson from the backlash surrounding his remarks about scenario planning for economic crisis management. But it is imperative that a Corbyn government does in fact have something readied in this regard. As indicated above, capital controls are not just a theoretical possibility—they are a living reality in many parts of the world. But neoliberal ideology runs deep, even on the left—which is also not used to having to reach for practical economic alternatives. As well as drawing from successful examples overseas, we may need to look back at the UK's own history of capitalist crisis management, including the contingency plans for trade and capital controls drawn up for deployment by the civil service in the face of the sterling crises of the 1960s and 1970s—plans that can be excavated from the archives, with names like Hecuba, Brutus 1, 2, and 3, and "the Unmentionable".[88] At the end of the day, we must be ready to withstand the full oppositional force of financial markets. Our prepared responses must be adequate to the scale and seriousness of the challenge.

A new Bretton Woods?

These measures amount to a strategy of operating a "siege economy", at least for a time, to insulate a radical government from attacks by global capital markets. While this may be necessary in adverse circumstances, it is not particularly desirable as a long term solution. Ultimately, as John McDonnell said in his speech to the 2018 Labour Party Conference, we may need new forms of economic governance at the international level to really tame the power of global capital. (A few days later, in a speech at the Marx Memorial Library, he put things more bluntly: "Socialism in one country won't work".)[89] Although it is certainly possible to implement measures like capital controls and financial transaction taxes on a national scale, there is no denying that it is more difficult than doing so internationally. There will always be limits to what a single left government can achieve at the national level in the context of a highly neoliberalised, financialised international order. Whether it is protecting governments from the vagaries of the currency markets, taming the activities of global banks, or tackling climate change, a serious left agenda for hegemony must ultimately be an international agenda.

Paradoxically, moving beyond neoliberal globalisation does not mean retreating inside national borders: rather, it hinges precisely on our ability to forge a new vision for the governance of the global economy. A key challenge here is to go beyond unhelpful binaries about "open versus closed economies", or "pro versus anti globalisation", which too often amount to a Hobson's choice between neoliberal internationalism and xenophobic, anti-immigrant nationalism. Instead, we need to build a politics that is open to people but closed to extractive capital flows.[90]

In the same way that neoliberalism moulded the IMF, WTO, and World Bank around the Washington Consensus, so we will need to imagine new democratic forms of global governance. This means a new left politics on trade— rejecting trade deals that give corporations the power to veto labour legislation and WTO rules that stop local governments from protecting local jobs.[91] It means international action to tackle tax avoidance, and to rein in the financial centres that enable it. It means breaking up global mega-banks, forcing them to hold more capital and regulating their financial weapons of mass destruction. It means relegitimising capital controls and other tools of economic management at the international level.

It may eventually demand a new international currency regime. The dire experience of Greece has focused attention on the need for this at the level of the eurozone, with figures such as Yanis Varoufakis putting forward proposals for radical reform to rebalance power between countries with big trade surpluses (like Germany) and those with deficits (like Greece).[92] But the need for such thinking does not depend on the fate of the euro, nor is it limited to countries that share a currency. Varoufakis' proposals are based on those John Maynard Keynes put forward at Bretton Woods in 1944, for what he envisaged as a global solution.[93] A radically new system governing global exchange rates could both help to redress global economic imbalances and create more policy space for domestic left governments fearful of triggering a currency crisis.

Just as the Mont Pelerin Society did in the post-war era, we also need to be building the international alliances that can eventually make this a reality. As McDonnell's recent speech acknowledged, the prospects for that might seem bleak with Trump in the White House—but that only makes it all the more imperative that the left start forging its own international connections. It is to be hoped that Labour's planned international forum in 2019 marks the start of this endeavour. In doing so, it is important to be crystal clear that blaming globalised capital for undermining democracy and driving down wages is not the same as blaming immigrants, and that restricting flows of capital does not entail restricting flows of people. It may well be possible that the left could make common cause with the new populist far right on some of the above issues: but that emphatically does not mean that it *should*. Instead, a new global economic settlement must be built on solidarity with the global south, and it must go hand in hand with anti-racist, anti-fascist politics.

At present, these complicated issues are under-discussed on the left. But they are an essential piece of the puzzle if we are serious about promoting radical domestic governments that not only survive but thrive as the creators of a new democratic economic world order.

Voice of the movement

In all of this there is an obvious need for much wider movement discussion, so that make-or-break decisions do not remain the reserve of technocratic insider policy making or top-down leadership judgment calls, but are subject to broad democratic debate. As we explore further in Chapter Five, the movement must be ready both to defend the government when necessary and also to hold it to account.

In this regard, there are eerie resonances for Corbynism in other aspects of the Mitterrand experience. Unlike in 1936, when the Popular Front government won election in France as a coalition of radicals, socialists, and communists on the back of factory occupations and an upsurge in worker militancy, Mitterrand's "miracle at the polls" came somewhat "out of the blue"—an electoral victory "neither preceded nor accompanied by a vast social movement".[94] To make matters worse, Pierre Mauroy, Mitterrand's prime minister, having written a *Le Monde* article entitled "To Govern Differently", went on to do no such thing.[95] Operating in what was inevitably a hostile environment, it was as if "it did not cross their minds that a Socialist government must govern differently from a capitalist one, must mobilize, because it has no chance of success unless it is carried by a wave of popular support".[96] When Mitterrand subsequently ran into difficulties, retreat was the only option. A more radical posture was needed, but he was unprepared to assume it—and there was no resolute movement at his back committed to defending the programme and insisting upon the radical decisions necessary to stay the course.

A Corbyn government, too, could face a challenge along these lines, as it contains within it a similar vulnerability. The paradox of Corbynism is that the left finally won power in the Labour Party at precisely the point when it appeared at its weakest historically. We are thus having to do a lot of things back to front—like using the leadership to reverse engineer a movement, or the adoption of a radical policy agenda to drive popular education at the grassroots and community levels.

Daniel Singer, one of the most astute left-wing observers of the Mitterrand débâcle, underscored the critical role of mass political education and mobilisation in any drive for transformative change. Despite the odds, he insisted, there was no predestination at work, and a different strategy on the part of a determined Socialist government could have produced a different political dynamic and a different outcome. Singer imagined a radical government engaged in a pedagogical campaign of "open discussion and debate at all levels—in factories and offices, in local and ministerial councils" over the economic challenges the country was facing, pledging to stick to its programme while being honest about the costs ("the situation is even worse than we thought"), and making a direct appeal to the electorate concerning the way forward:

> A Socialist government may then have been in a position to ask people for sacrifices. The workers were probably ready to tighten their belts for a time, if told for how long and for what purpose and shown the road ahead. A vision and a project were probably the only means for splitting the middle classes.[97]

There are clear lessons here for Corbyn's Labour. A hostile media will inevitably blame any economic problems or disruption on Labour's "failed economic programme" even if it is nothing of the sort. Attlee's government faced similar criticism: as it struggled with the domestic and international legacy of war, journalists on both sides of the Atlantic were eager to point to its woes as proof that socialism didn't work. Although the government was remarkably successful at boosting production for exports, this inevitably took time, and in the interim the UK economy suffered recurrent problems with trade deficits and dwindling currency reserves. In 1948, the *Wall Street Journal* ran a long article on "The education of Mr Attlee", claiming that these problems proved the folly of a socialist planned economy.[98] A future Labour government will need to control the narrative about why economic disruption is happening, perhaps learning from the way the 2010–15 coalition government—remarkably successfully—pinned the blame for a stuttering UK economy on the legacy left by New Labour. We return to these themes in Chapter Five.

Encouragingly, Corbynism has already demonstrated a powerful ability to speak over the heads of the establishment pundits and mainstream media to address the electorate directly. As Ben Sellers, one of the original Corbyn campaign volunteers, puts it, "Social media now needs to be seen as an integral part of what happens next … We need to launch the biggest ever social media counter-narrative to the storm that is coming our way".[99] This is where Corbynism's hybrid status as both party-political programme and mass movement may prove invaluable. Unable to rely fully on the Parliamentary Labour Party, Corbyn nevertheless has a half-million-strong party membership to turn to, amounting to in effect a spokesperson on practically every street in practically every community in the country. Suitably empowered and mobilised, the social weight of this movement could prove decisive in swinging the balance of public opinion for the government, should tough economic interventions in troubled markets—up to and including capital controls, and beyond—become necessary.

On the other hand, as we explore further in Chapter Five, this is not simply a case of mobilising foot soldiers to defend the government. If the leadership is to be effectively held to account for these critical strategic decisions, then its popular base must be independent minded and capable of developing its own ideas about the right way forward. We must therefore develop a far higher degree of economic literacy in the movement, concerning both the details of the Corbyn programme and the challenges it may encounter—no easy matter, given the technical complexity and arcane nature of the knowledge involved. Again, there are potential parallels with the experience of Syriza: Kouvelakis acknowledges that the politics of the euro were extremely technical, and that his own faction (which favoured leaving the euro) "failed to provide a properly elaborated alternative vision and a counter-programme that would have triggered a broader public debate".[100] Having been granted an unexpected afterlife, the Labour left cannot now be allowed to fall into reprising failed strategies from the past, already tested to their limits and found wanting. If and when the crunch comes, we must make absolutely certain that a Corbyn government has been sufficiently steeled in advance to push ahead with its programme rather than turn back. Much will hinge on such readiness to press on.

***

None of this is going to be easy, as the difficult history of every previous left government has demonstrated, one way or another. "There is simply no historical model anywhere in the world for what we want to do which has been successful", as an unnamed senior Corbynite told George Eaton of the *New Statesman*. "A left government being elected in a post-industrial society and then successfully managing to transition into a major new settlement, whether a new form of capitalism or socialism".[101] It is imperative that both the movement and the leadership are prepared for the scale of the challenge.

Nor are these problems confined to external attacks from the forces of capital. As a Corbyn government reaches for the levers at its disposal to meet such attacks, it will encounter another pillar of the neoliberal establishment— namely, the British state.

CHAPTER FOUR: GET READY TO GOVERN

*"When [senior officials] are united they can be devastating, particu-
larly when arguing against a proposition".*
—*Joel Barnett, Treasury minister under
the Callaghan government*

In 1974, newly appointed secretary of state for industry Tony Benn met with his top civil servant, Permanent Secretary Anthony Part. Part said casually, as if it were a statement of the obvious: "I take it you are not going to implement the manifesto". Benn was taken aback. "You must be joking", he replied: he had every intention of implementing it. He circulated the manifesto to all civil servants in the department and told them, "That's what we have been elected to do".[1]

This, to put it mildly, did not go down well. It was the start of a long and unhappy relationship between Benn and his officials, who are said to have routinely resisted his plans and even briefed other Cabinet ministers behind his back. A Treasury advisor later went so far as to talk of a "Whitehall-wide conspiracy to stop Benn doing anything ... they had an obsession about defeating Bennery".[2] Benn appointed two political advisors and began sharing his official briefs with them (this was an era before special advisors became a fixture of government life). One official later admitted, "It didn't do him any good, because we immediately started writing different kinds of briefs".[3] Benn was to remain an embattled figure for the rest of his time in government.

A decade later, Sir John Hoskyns, the former head of Thatcher's Downing Street Policy Unit, was equally vexed. Reflecting on the limited achievements of Thatcher's first term in a speech to the Institute of Directors, he argued that the task facing her in the second term was much greater: nothing less than a "transformation of our entire political economy". He fretted that the government machine was simply not equipped to bring about this sea change:

> Where are the thinking and planning for all this going on? The answer is "nowhere". The reason why the thinking is not done is that Whitehall is not organised to do it. Ministers cannot do this sort of thing in the odd day at Chequers.[4]

If the Conservatives were serious about rewriting the rules of the British economy, he argued, they first needed to rewrite the rules of policymaking itself. They could not transform society without transforming government. If they proved unable or unwilling to do so, he feared that the Thatcher project would fail.

These stories both tell us something important about the challenge facing an incoming transformative administration. On the one hand, it will depend on the civil service for advice on the practical implementation of its programme: no opposition, however well resourced, can prepare for everything. On the other hand, as Benn knew all too well, such advice is never neutral: it is shaped by the assumptions of the person giving it. During times of major transformation, where the assumptions that structure Whitehall's thinking may not align with those of their new political bosses, this can become a serious problem. Hoskyns understood that the civil service was specifically designed to maintain continuity, and that this was a major obstacle for a government specifically committed to radical change.

This is not to say that the civil service will be uniformly or implacably hostile to a Corbyn government. Current and former insiders we spoke to emphasised that most civil servants do genuinely try to serve the government of the day, and that junior officials in particular sometimes have progressive inclinations and can be as ready as anyone to criticise the rules under which they have to work. Ministers can control the machine, but only if they have a strong sense of mission, a clear grasp of strategy, the support of experienced political advisors, and a healthy dose of diplomatic skill. At times of transformative change, they also need to be ready to repurpose the machine itself, changing the way policy is made and not just the individuals making it. There is no direct precedent in post-war political history for the challenge a Corbyn government would face on this front.

Untried and untested

The Attlee government of 1945–51 had two key advantages which today's Labour Party does not. First, it had experience of governing: most of the key figures in the 1945 Cabinet had also served in the wartime coalition government. Not only were they familiar with the workings of the bureaucracy, they had also been directly involved in planning post-war economic policy from the inside, where a consensus was gradually emerging on many of Labour's key social democratic ideas.[5] They did not have to make the abrupt transition from insurgent opposition to governing party that has proved so difficult for radical left parties like Syriza. (Paul Mason recounts: "I've seen, from the inside, ministries run with only politicians and political advisors, the civil servants sidelined because they were suspected of acting for the opposition ... Syriza at times felt like prisoners in these ministries".)[6]

By contrast, today's Labour Shadow Cabinet has no collective experience of government, and includes many relatively young and inexperienced MPs. In this respect, the Blair government offers a better parallel than the Attlee years, coming as it did after decades in the political wilderness—but of course, Blair's was not a transformative project.[7] He also had access to a much deeper bench of political talent. The decades-long marginalisation of the radical left means that parliament is not filled with dozens of capable and experienced potential Corbynite ministers. The Parliamentary Labour Party's outright refusal to accept and embrace Corbynism has exacerbated this problem: successive rebellions, coup attempts, and the reshuffles that followed have shrunk the pool of candidates for Shadow Cabinet positions to the degree that at times Corbyn has struggled to field a whole team.

John McDonnell has joked that this was in fact "one of the best things that happened to us", since it forced the leadership to bring forward a new generation of young, working-class frontbenchers who have since been lauded as rising stars: people like Rebecca Long-Bailey, Angela Rayner, and Laura Pidcock.[8] There is no doubt that this new generation is a breath of fresh air in British politics. But their inexperience remains a challenge. Most are relatively new to parliament, let alone government, and the hostile attitude of Labour's former ruling factions has meant the leadership has very little institutional knowledge it can draw upon. (We have heard tales of incoming frontbenchers being left to start from scratch on complex parliamentary bills after their hostile predecessors erased their files rather than pass them on.)[9] Nor do they have advisors with deep experience of how to run departments—a completely different skill set from being an effective opposition spokesperson.

Sympathetic ex-officials and special advisors have been running sessions for the party to help prepare this cadre of potential future ministers for the realities of government: effectively, a crash course in the nuts and bolts of how departments work and how to get things done.[10] But some insiders we spoke to were concerned that this work had not gone nearly deep enough to truly prepare frontbenchers for the scale of the task ahead. And, ultimately, there is no substitute for direct experience, and no getting away from the fact that they will face a steep learning curve on taking office.

Attlee's second key advantage was that the machine itself was already changing by the time his government came to power. Keynes' *General Theory of Employment, Interest and Money* had been published nine years earlier, and he had been energetically lobbying for his ideas in government, the media, and academia ever since. Although the Treasury still tried to cling to the old order, the cataclysm of war made this impossible. Keynes himself was brought into the civil service, along with key disciples like James Meade, socialising his new ideas across government. Extensive government planning and control of the economy was introduced, giving Labour a ready-made apparatus with which to operate its own peacetime economic planning. In 1944, the Treasury even committed itself to the goal of maintaining full employment—the heart of the Keynesian agenda.[11]

This is not to say that everything was simple or easy for Attlee's government. The wartime planning apparatus was not perfectly suited to peacetime aims, and the Treasury remained at best a partial convert to Keynesianism. The most senior civil servants—people like Lord Edward Bridges—were likely to be most attached to the old ways of laissez-faire. Some have suggested that this helps to explain some early failures of economic planning.[12] But the fact remains that Attlee was operating in a more favourable environment than the one that would greet Corbyn if he entered Downing Street tomorrow.

Today, alternative economic ideas are far from having taken hold in our most powerful institutions. Pockets of radicalism are emerging, like the "Exploring Economics" network set up in 2016 by civil servants—many of them veterans of student campaigns to change economics education. It aims to encourage questioning of the received wisdom about how economics should be done, through activities ranging from debates on the merits of GDP as a measure of progress, to training modules on feminist economics, to guides demystifying the Treasury rulebook for non-economists.[13] But, just as in the 1940s, there is a generational divide between its members, who tend to be more junior—their worldview shaped by the experience of the crash—and the older generation who still hold most of the power. The permanent secretaries who run Whitehall's 18 departments are the epitome of the British establishment. Over half of them went to private school, two-thirds went to Oxbridge, 13 are male, and all are white.[14] Twelve have backgrounds in economics or business, including a former oil executive at the Cabinet Office and former bankers at the Home Office and Ministry of Defence.[15] It is difficult to imagine these people cheerfully pivoting to serve a radical Corbyn government.

More fundamentally, there is simply no ready-made intellectual framework waiting to replace neoclassical economics in the way that Keynesianism did with laissez-faire. New currents of thought are emerging, from feminist to ecological to post-Keynesian and Marxist economics—but they do not yet add up to a new paradigm ready to usurp the reigning orthodoxy. All of this means that we should be under no illusions: the task facing a Corbyn government would be unlike that faced by any other left government in UK history.

The twin stories of Benn and Hoskyns can also give us some pointers on how we might square up to this challenge. Benn, a largely isolated figure in a less than radical administration, did not have the power to reorient the government machine: he could only try to work around it. This is not a model for a future Corbyn government to emulate. Good relations with officials are essential to getting things done; some have suggested that Benn's own suspicion and mistrust of his officials worsened the breakdown of their relationship and left him still more marginalised within government.

This is not to say that a Labour government will not need to confront the institutional conservatism of the civil service head-on. As Joel Barnett, Treasury minister under the Callaghan Labour government, once said, "When [senior officials] are united they can be devastating, particularly when arguing against a proposition".[16] A changing of the guard at senior level may well be essential, although Britain's tradition of civil service independence means it will not be straightforward. Hiring and firing permanent secretaries is not directly within ministers' gift, although there are precedents for them departing by mutual consent when it is clear that the two simply cannot work together.[17] And ministers have a substantial say in new appointments, which must ultimately be approved by the prime minister.[18] It will also be crucial that new ministers have access to independent sources of advice outside the civil service. Among other things, this means building a strong pipeline of special advisors—people chosen not just for their intellectual abilities, but for their political nous and strategic instincts, their ability to forge coalitions and drive through change.

But really transforming the state demands deeper structural changes. Labour's ultimate aim must not be to sidestep the civil service but to transform it. As John Hoskyns saw, the big prize is to repurpose the machine itself for the needs of new times. And, for all his lamentations in 1982 that Thatcher seemed uninterested in this agenda, Hoskyns got his wish in the end.[19] Thatcher may not have taken on board his most radical proposals, which would have replaced most of the career civil service with private sector appointees. But there is little doubt that she waged war on Whitehall, and that she did so with the explicit aim of neoliberalising the state. If we want to build a post-neoliberal economy, it is vital that we study this history—both to understand the legacy we will need to unpick, and to learn lessons about how such changes might be accomplished.

The neoliberal ghost in the machine

Thatcher was always instinctively hostile to the civil service, not only because of her anti-statism but also because she felt its top echelons were "soaked in the Keynesian approach to economics ... both too powerful and too 'wet'".[20] In this at least, she was probably right. In the early days of the government, many of its supporters blamed the failure to implement monetarist policies on "sabotage" from the Bank of England.[21] The government's first wave of welfare cuts were hampered by a series of mysterious leaks which could only have come from senior officials—and which Labour made hay with in its 1983 election campaign.[22] (The government later came down hard on leakers, with several being charged under the Official Secrets Act.)

In her first term, Thatcher took a slash-and-burn approach to the bureaucracy. Almost immediately on coming to office, she introduced a ruthless approach to cost-cutting and "value for money". She picked an early fight with the civil service unions on pay, culminating in a major strike in 1981 which she was determined to defeat, and did—one of her first big victories over striking workers.[23] The resulting loss of morale caused an exodus of officials. Some suspected that this had been part of the plan all along, accelerating the remaking of the state Thatcher was seeking to bring about. She also took a very close interest in the appointment of top officials, seeking to ensure that new appointees were "one of us". Although an inquiry cleared her of "politicising" senior appointments, in retrospect it is clear that she was consciously pushing through a cultural shift—replacing traditional bureaucrats with go-getting entrepreneurial types, more amenable to her neoliberal vision.

Having razed the building to the ground, in her second term Thatcher began rebuilding it in her image. Norms from the private sector were imported into Whitehall, in what came to be known as "new public management". The most important skills for civil servants were no longer in policy development but the management of people and resources—along lines approved by the new neoliberal consensus. Thatcher began experimenting with spinning out civil service functions into separate public agencies or privatised entities—a conscious effort to break down the power of the state and replace it with new, more marketized forms of delivery.[24] (Ironically, this is a direct cause of the "quangocracy" which so many Tories love to hate.) Meanwhile, the mainstream civil service was increasingly sidelined from policy itself, with the abolition of the Central Policy Review Staff (an independent "think tank" based in the Cabinet Office) and the building up of the Downing Street Policy Unit.[25]

But it was Blair (followed by the coalition and Tory governments) who finished the job Thatcher started, and it is his legacy as much as anyone's that a future Labour government will have to dismantle. A prescient academic paper written in 1992 asked whether Thatcher had achieved a lasting revolution in the state, or whether it could be reversed. It concluded that, bereft of any ideology of its own, Labour might simply not care to undo Thatcher's reforms—indeed, they were already accepting her mantras of privatisation and marketisation as simply "good public management".[26] And so it proved. Although incoming ministers were certainly suspicious of the civil service, Blair made no efforts to clear out Thatcher's people and appoint his own (although Gordon Brown did eventually get rid of Terry Burns, the monetarist permanent secretary to the Treasury).[27] A 1999 White Paper called *Modernising Government* spoke approvingly of Thatcher's reforms, and explicitly positioned the Blair government's own agenda as a continuation of her good work.[20]

Indeed, Blair went even further than Thatcher in two key areas which present serious challenges for an incoming radical government: the grip of mainstream economics on policy making, and the ever-closer entwining of corporate interests with the state. These two things have gone hand in hand. A key strategy of neoliberalism across the world has been to insist that its prescriptions are just good economics. This justifies taking economic policy out of the democratic sphere and handing it over to "experts". But beneath the surface, these supposedly neutral technocratic approaches have systematically given more power to corporations and economic elites.

This means that a left movement must set its sights higher than simply replacing a neoliberal technocracy with a progressive technocracy. A truly radical agenda for government must be about democratising the machine, reclaiming big economic decisions for the democratic sphere, and putting power in the hands of people. This is not only right in principle, it is also right strategically. As a former senior figure in Syriza told us, only this can create a lasting and powerful counterweight to the pressures a governing party will face to conform to the norms of the establishment. In the rest of this chapter, we look at three steps to achieving this: kicking corporate influence out of Whitehall; ending the tyranny of the economist; and building new, more democratic modes of government.

Kicking corporations out of Whitehall

Blair's enthusiasm for private sector expertise is well known. His encouragement of secondments (whereby private sector employees were temporarily parachuted into the civil service) created a revolving door between government and business, with the close relationship between HMRC and the Big Four accountancy firms—essentially the key enablers of tax avoidance—being one notorious example. He was fond of talking about "open-minded" and "inclusive" government, which turned out to mean opening the door wider to corporate lobbyists. A 1999 report from the Cabinet Office approvingly cited the example of a competitiveness review that had effectively allowed "business leaders" to write policy, noting that—unsurprisingly—the policy in question was well received by the business community.[29] David Cameron took this further with the euphemistically named "open policy making".[30]

The problems of corporate lobbying and the "revolving door" are well known. What is less well understood is that lobbying is only the tip of the iceberg. Corporate interests are now not just allowed but actively encouraged to help write their own rules. Policy making and big business have become entangled in a huge and sprawling edifice of corporate influence that will require a serious and sustained effort to unravel. Measures like transparency on lobbying, or tighter restrictions on former officials going to work for the people they used to regulate, will barely scratch the surface of this problem. What is needed is serious reform of Whitehall itself.

Blair's drive to "remove unnecessary regulation" and minimise "unnecessary burdens" on business has been extended to the point where protecting corporate interests has been elevated to the highest objective of government policy.[31] The coalition government introduced a policy called "one-in, one-out regulation", whereby any measure that would cost business money had to be accompanied by scrapping an existing measure that would save them an equal amount. If raising the minimum wage would cost employers more, you needed an "out". If introducing standards to cut air pollution would cost car manufacturers more, you needed an "out". This policy has been steadily ratcheted up to become "one in, three out"—putting almost impossible hurdles in the way of new legislation to curb business interests. The deadly consequences of this agenda, which had long passed under the radar, were brought suddenly and shockingly into the public eye when the Grenfell Tower fire killed 72 people and injured 70 others.[32] As questions were raised as to how this was allowed to happen, it emerged that fire safety inspections were among the "unnecessary red tape" that had been scrapped, that rules on the use of flammable cladding were woefully inadequate, and that "one in, one out" had been used to justify refusing to mandate sprinkler systems in new buildings.[33] Speaking at Labour Conference in 2017, Diane Abbott described the disaster as a "direct consequence" of "deregulation of fire standards and inspection".[34] The general secretary of the Fire Brigades Union demanded that ministers be "held to account for overseeing a deregulatory regime that failed to keep people safe in their homes".[35]

To their shame, previous Labour oppositions never vociferously opposed this agenda. Clearly, an incoming government must immediately scrap the "one in, three out" rule—not doing so would make it nigh on impossible to implement manifesto commitments like boosting employment rights, whose costs to employers would need to be balanced by massive amounts of counterproductive deregulation elsewhere. But once again, behind the headline policy there is a tangled web that also needs to be unravelled. As part of "one-in, three-out regulation", all departments have to submit an impact assessment for any new proposals to something called the Regulatory Policy Committee (RPC). If the RPC deems the assessment of the cost to business inadequate, they can send it back, effectively vetoing the new policy until they are satisfied. They are not mandated to look at any other aspect of the assessment, such as the impacts on society or the environment, or whether the policy is likely to achieve its objectives. All that matters is the cost to business.

You might expect this committee to be staffed with experts, but if so you'd be wrong.[36] The current membership includes a partner at PricewaterhouseCoopers, the chief lobbyist for TATA Steel (formerly chief lobbyist at the Institute of Directors), and a councilman of the City of London Corporation—effectively the finance industry's representatives in government.[37] If a Corbyn government decides to keep a version of the Regulatory Policy Committee, it must be completely repurposed—with a mandate to hold departments accountable to the interests of the many not the few, and a membership to match. It should be tasked to scrutinise the impacts of regulation on climate change and inequality, not just the costs to business. It should be filled with worker and consumer representatives and environmental experts, not just economists and business lobbyists.

Across government, Labour will also need to undo the poisonous legacy of this approach and rebuild its capacity to regulate the private sector effectively. Take the "Public Health Responsibility Deal", which replaced proper regulation of salt, sugar, and alcohol with voluntary measures decided by an industry roundtable that includes the likes of Mars and Diageo.[38] Or "Focus on Enforcement", a programme that invited the farming lobby to propose changes to how farms are inspected.[39] If Labour is serious about rebalancing power in our economy, it will need to make clear that this era is over—and that Whitehall must adapt.

If deregulation means that government has been operating with one hand tied behind its back, austerity has well and truly tied back the other hand. Departments like Health and Social Care, Housing, Communities and Local Government, and Work and Pensions have seen their staff numbers cut by up to 40 per cent.[40] This in turn has accelerated the revolving door, as departments increasingly rely on secondments from the private sector to make up capacity.[41] There is simply no way that Whitehall can be expected to hold its own against corporate lobbying in this context. As long ago as 2012, one of us experienced this first-hand as a charity lobbyist, warning the DWP that if it didn't face down the insurance industry then millions of people could be pushed into rip-off pension schemes. Officials pleaded with a charity that employed six people to get them some legal advice on how to do this, since cuts meant they could no longer access departmental lawyers. And if there is one thing a Corbyn government ushering in a new era of democratic ownership is going to need, it is good lawyers.

Likewise, serious banking reform—an area that is both highly technical and deeply political—will require serious policy capacity if well-resourced bank lobbyists are not to run rings around the civil service. The inequality of arms between the Syriza government and the Troika was one factor in the former's catastrophic defeat: it was said that "the Greeks come with

Word documents and the Europeans come with Excel sheets". In one meeting, German finance minister Wolfgang Schäuble is said to have arrived with reams of briefings covering every aspect of the Greek economy, while Yanis Varoufakis showed up with only his smartphone.[42] It is easy to see a similar problem rearing its head if Labour seriously tries to take on the City of London, which has long mastered the deployment of complexity and technical detail to throw sand in the wheels of effective regulation. After a decade of austerity, the pressure will be in the direction of rescuing crisis ridden schools and hospitals and rebuilding crumbling infrastructure. Hiring more back-office policy staff will never be as politically popular—but we neglect it at our peril.

One way a Corbyn government could send an early signal of a new approach to corporate interests in Whitehall would be by scrapping or radically overhauling departmental boards. Although not the key channel for corporate influence, they illustrate starkly how a neoliberal mindset has permeated the culture of government. Departmental boards were introduced as part of a drive to make departments run more like businesses and beefed up under the coalition government. Guidance now states that their "independent" non-executive directors should be "largely drawn from the commercial private sector".[43] In this topsy-turvy world, having a direct commercial interest in the department's work is not a cause for concern but rather a source of celebrated private sector expertise. (The guidance was revised in 2011 to remove references to directors being "independent", suggesting that conflicts of interest should be "managed" rather than avoided.)[44] Among other things, boards are responsible for departments' overall strategy, "vision and mission"—something one might think was a matter for the democratic process— and, in the extreme, they can pass a vote of no confidence in the permanent secretary and recommend that they should be sacked.[45]

It is debatable how much formal influence departmental boards really have—partly because departments just aren't the same as companies, and so their role and purpose in practice is unclear. But they undoubtedly operate as an informal channel for corporate capture—and one that has managed to pass beneath the public and media gaze. A recent study noted that non-execs "have remained largely invisible ... Yet they have privileged access to the highest level of government, and the potential to influence key decisions on how the country is run".[46] One of the non-execs interviewed said, "I feel that the most valuable role I play is as a sounding board for senior civil servants".[47] Another boasted, "Our commercial background has shifted the department's approach to how it manages the private sector".[48]

So who are these shadowy non-execs? For the most part, they read like a who's who of the British corporate elite. The BEIS board includes the chief executive of easyJet and a director of BP.[49] The lead non-executive at the Department for Transport is also chair of the UK's largest private construction and engineering firm.[50] The government lead non-executive is the chairman of Barclays Bank.[51] How can we hope to take on vested interests in our economy when the officials charged with implementing policy are accountable to those same interests? Departmental boards may only be the tip of the iceberg, but scrapping them would be a symbolic first step towards rooting out corporate influence from top to bottom, right across government.

Ending the tyranny of the economist

Blair was fond of claiming that we lived in a "post-ideological age".[52] The 1997 Labour Manifesto proclaimed, "New Labour is a party of ideas and ideals but not of outdated ideology. What counts is what works".[53] His government would be guided "not by dogma but by an open-minded approach to understanding what works and why".[54] The pitch was that he was socialist in his ends, but pragmatic in his means. Yet without a solid political-economic analysis of the means, his commitment to "what works" effectively meant accepting the existing Thatcherite consensus—namely that in most cases, "what works" is more market, more private sector, and more competition. The ends, too, in practice turned out to be principally economic growth—a perspective steeped in trickle-down economics that allowed soaring inequality to pass unremarked and unchecked.

Beneath the innocuous rhetoric of evidence-based policy, the creeping neoliberalisation of the policy machine was advancing unabated. But what counts as evidence? Whose insights should we be "open-minded" to? The answers turned out to be principally "economics" and "the private sector", and they are answers around which Whitehall has increasingly been remoulded.

The Treasury is notoriously steeped in orthodox economic thinking. In 2014, then Permanent Secretary Sir Nicholas Macpherson gave a speech entitled "The Treasury View" which reads like a list of neoliberal articles of faith.[55] In it, he insists that "markets generally work"—admitting that this "may appear a brave proposition following the worst financial crisis in eighty years". Free trade is good: "Britain has played a critical role in resisting modern forms of protection, in the form of regulation" (otherwise known as workers' rights and environmental standards). The Treasury must "encourag[e] enterprise and entrepreneurialism, for example through changes to the corporate tax system" (read: tax cuts). None of this is ideological, he insists: the Treasury is there to serve the government of the day. This is merely time-honoured wisdom about "what works".

In recent decades, the Treasury has acquired ever more power to spread this view across Whitehall.[56] MPs sometimes joke that there are three main parties of government: Labour, the Tories, and the Treasury. The latter exerts power both directly, by controlling spending, and indirectly, by writing the rules other departments must follow when making new policy. Paradoxically, the Treasury itself is still one of the smallest government departments, and its officials tend to be relatively young and inexperienced. This means that a handful of people with "a business background, a stern haircut, and just enough economics knowledge to be dangerous" have enormous power to overrule the judgements of genuine experts wielding actual evidence—often based on little more than reheated dogma.[57] One former Treasury official told us that state aid rules were often (wrongly) invoked as a reflex response to anyone suggesting a non-market answer to a problem. The whole system, he said, makes market solutions the path of least resistance.

The Corbyn leadership is well aware of these problems, and commissioned former civil servant Bob Kerslake to look into how the Treasury might be reformed.[58] Among other things, he was asked to explore whether the Treasury should be broken up to curb its power—making two separate ministries for government finances and long-term economic strategy, as is common in other countries (and was briefly tried in the UK in the 1960s with the ill-fated Department for Economic Affairs). Kerslake concluded that this wouldn't be worth the disruption involved: conflicts and power struggles would simply be played out between ministries rather than inside them. Certainly, rearranging Whitehall furniture is unlikely to deliver unless we also change what its occupants are doing. (Having said this, in some cases the two may go hand in hand: for instance, one former political advisor we spoke to suggested that the Home Office would never be capable of administering a humane immigration policy—its culture was simply too toxic and too deep-rooted—and the only way to achieve this would be to take it out of their hands and give it a new departmental home.)

In the case of the Treasury, the need for reform goes much deeper than simply creating two new departments staffed by the same people and operating under the same rules. As Kerslake suggests, it starts by shaking things up at the top. What if, instead of reducing the deficit and promoting growth, the Treasury's mandate was to raise people's quality of life, reduce inequality, and promote ecological sustainability? What if as well as a financial secretary to the Treasury, we had an environmental secretary to the Treasury? And what if the Treasury's web of influence across government was transformed by an injection of new people and new thinking?

One place to start might be to reverse the rise and rise of the neoclassical economist (and, perhaps worse, the PPE or business school graduate, carrying all the neoliberal assumptions and none of the expertise). Recruiting more economists was one of Blair's key priorities.[59] A 2000 report called *Adding It Up* set out his government's strategy for rolling out economic analysis across Whitehall.[60] Since it was written, the number of government economists has tripled.[61] Economists and former Treasury officials also increasingly run other departments, including the Department for Transport, the Department for Work and Pensions, the Home Office, and the Department for Culture, Media and Sport.[62]

It is not that economists are inherently bad. It is that the economics they are being asked to do is bad, and that this flawed economic calculus is being applied to decisions on everything from protecting bees to combating loneliness. Economic models now act as a substitute for democratic debate. Since Blair's reforms, all new policy has to be accompanied by a cost-benefit analysis (CBA). CBA works on the principle that the complex and unknowable future effects of policy can be reduced to a single number. All possible impacts can be given a price tag, and from there it is a simple calculation to work out which policy option is most cost-effective. Of course, some impacts are less easy to value than others—like, say, the benefits of cleaner air from banning polluting vehicles. This means they systematically get given less weight than, say, the costs to car manufacturers' bottom line. In this way, CBA acts as a powerful "nudge" towards neoliberal solutions.

Although this may seem like a sideshow of interest only to wonks, in fact its consequences are real and far-reaching. Off-the-record conversations with civil servants reveal how it has rewired Whitehall's thinking. One official complained of having to try to justify the benefits of community cohesion in pounds and pence. Another recounted the experience of the "Growth Review", which forced officials charged with reducing waste or increasing biodiversity to prove their contribution to growth or see their funding cut. Perhaps most disturbing, an official at the Department for Business dismissed the concerns of his environmental counterparts about having to monetise the benefits of protecting ecosystems: deep down, he suggested, they know that the benefits don't justify the costs. It could be argued that these officials would behave differently under new political masters. But the point is that decades of this approach have made neoliberalism the default "common sense" of government. This won't change until officials are given new tools for the job.

The Treasury's Green Book—a manual steeped in the assumptions of orthodox economic thinking—has become the Bible for conducting CBA. Former cabinet secretary Gus O'Donnell has described it as "evaluating something that is not going to happen, using assumptions about motives and behaviour that bear little relationship to reality, and valuations that are plucked out of thin air".[63] As evidence, it's often about as useful as astrology. Yet this is the gold standard for analysis in Whitehall, seen as more "rigorous" and "objective" than, say, the knowledge of frontline doctors and nurses about how best to improve services in the NHS. John McDonnell has said that Labour will bring forward proposals to reform the Green Book; they must be ready to implement those reforms immediately on taking office.[64]

The story is the same when we look at the internal models the Treasury uses to understand the economy and predict the impacts of policy. For instance, HMRC's "Computable General Equilibrium" (CGE) model assumes that if the economy is left alone, there will be full employment. In other words, it is incapable of comprehending that government intervention might actually create jobs. It assumes that the economy is made up of rational individuals who constantly perform complex calculations in their heads. And it is not designed to value non-market factors such as environmental and health benefits—even when they might indirectly benefit the economy.

Such a model is bound to conclude that any social or environmental action—like restricting carbon emissions—will be bad for the economy.[65] It is also programmed to say that limiting the private sector through tax or regulation is a bad idea. In 2013, the Treasury released analysis claiming that the coalition's cuts to corporation tax would boost investment and GDP, raise wages, and increase the tax take overall.[66] Needless to say, the projected benefits have not materialised. (The Treasury does not release any analysis of how its models' forecasts fared when compared with economic reality.)

There are countless other rules and models buried across Whitehall that skew decisions towards neoliberal solutions. There are the public accounting rules which include publicly owned companies in their measure of public debt, something almost no other country does (most countries monitor central and local government borrowing, but treat public corporations separately from this, since they are commercially independent). If Germany applied this measure, its public debt would soar from 71 per cent of GDP to 181 per cent, mainly because of its public banks.[67] The rules also treat public borrowing purely as a liability, ignoring the valuable public assets it creates. This creates an obvious bias against public ownership, making it look fiscally reckless even when it is economically sensible. One of the key reasons the UK Green Investment Bank was first denied borrowing powers and then privatised was to keep its debts off the government's books. Labour's plans to create a new National Investment Bank, as well as a Post Bank under the auspices of the Post Offices, would certainly fall foul of these rules if they remained unchanged. If we want a German-style banking system, we need the German-style internal rules that enable it.

Then there are the models used to assess economic benefits of new transport links, which skew investment towards London and the South East. Most of the projected benefits of the High Speed 2 rail link (HS2) come from time savings made by London workers. Because these workers tend to be paid more, their time is valued more highly than workers in the rest of the country. This actively fuels the cycle of regional inequality: because London is richer, the supposed economic benefits of investing in London's infrastructure are greater. Because the North is poorer, it is deemed economically sensible to continue starving it of investment. In his 2017 Conference speech, McDonnell pledged to "end the Treasury bias against investing in the nations and regions".[68]

It should by now be fairly obvious that these models are fundamentally useless to a Labour government wanting to understand the potential impacts of investing in renewables, improving transport links in the North, or raising corporation tax. Indeed, they are practically hardwired to say that these policies are economically disastrous. Unless these rules are overhauled, civil servants across government will be using a yardstick which is totally at odds with the new government's worldview. At best, this means the government will lack meaningful evidence to inform decisions. At worst, it could become a powerful stick to beat the new government with: it's not hard to imagine disgruntled officials leaking analysis to the media which "proves" that the government's green deal will hurt the economy, or that a new National Investment Bank would be a disaster for the public finances.

Of course, the whole idea that big political decisions can be outsourced to economic models needs to be challenged: modelling needs to be demoted to its rightful place as just one way of thinking about such decisions. But it's still vital that we invest in developing new models which better represent the way the economy really works: which allow for imbalances of power, which understand that human beings aren't the rational automatons of classical economic theory, and which recognise that the environment isn't "out there" somewhere but is the foundation on which the economy rests. Such models are being developed in various academic institutions, but more work is needed before they can be used to inform policy.[69]

A Corbyn government could learn from Blair's playbook in planning for this transformation. Just as Blair embarked on a recruitment drive for economists, so there will be a need both to recruit economists who think differently and to restore the status of other disciplines, like social research and geography. Just as university funding was pumped into microeconomics, so it now needs to be pumped into new economic thinking to create a pipeline for tomorrow's experts. Just as Blair set up a dedicated "Performance and Innovation Unit" to drive through reforms without getting bogged down in existing norms and hierarchies, so Labour could set up a New Economics Unit tasked with developing and promoting new models and new analytical frameworks.[70] This could draw on the existing Exploring Economics network, giving those within the civil service who already understand that change is needed a mandate to make it happen.

Perhaps most importantly, just as Blair drove the push for "evidence based policy" and "joined up government" from the centre, so there will be a need for strong central leadership to make clear that the rules of the game have changed. All of these plans must be ready at the outset of a Corbyn government, and the civil service must be left in no doubt what is expected of it. It will be tempting to start with more high-profile matters—rail renationalisation, saving the NHS, raising the minimum wage. But the fact is that unless the government machine is pointed in a different direction, all of these efforts will risk sinking into the quagmire of the status quo.

But this isn't just about building better models. It is also about overturning the whole idea that we can outsource big decisions to some numbers in a spreadsheet: that there is a magical "right" answer to the question of how to balance growth today with sustainability tomorrow, or the interests of workers with the interests of shareholders—in short, about who should win and who should lose from economic policy—which the economic priesthood is uniquely able to provide. One of the most insidious impacts of neoliberalism is the idea that politics can be reduced to the rational calculations of experts. In an era where algorithms increasingly seem to control every aspect of our lives—from whether we can get a bank loan to what adverts we see on Facebook—it's time to put human values and judgement back at the heart of policymaking. This means finding radically new, more democratic, and participatory ways of doing things.

Building the new democracy

At its heart, the movement that swept Corbyn to victory in the Labour leadership elections is about democracy and empowerment. It is opposed to the overweening power of elites—both economic and political—who have controlled things for too long. Its approach to transforming government can never be just about new technocrats applying better processes: it must also be about pushing power downwards and breaking the grip of a centralised, centrist establishment on our political life.

As Hilary Wainwright has pointed out, and as we saw in earlier chapters, in this respect the Corbyn movement are not the heirs of 1945.[71] Attlee's government espoused a technocratic Keynesianism in which left-wing experts would control the levers of the economy, rather than right-wing experts. Radical democracy was not on the agenda. By contrast, Corbyn's political project is not simply about replacing private elites with public elites, but about transferring power from elites to the people. Hence the Corbyn leadership showing more interest in ideas about worker ownership, or passenger control of publicly owned railways, than Attlee's government ever did. As John McDonnell put it in his speech to the Marx Memorial Library, "Yes you need the expert management, but who else is expert in providing these services but the workers themselves, who else is expert on receiving these services but the customers and the passengers, and who else is expert on protecting the common interest but the elected representatives?"[72]

In an earlier speech at The World Transformed 2017, he put it another way: "In addition to taking over that structure, we're changing the relationship from one of dominance to participation and control".[73] This impulse for participation must be applied to government itself as much as to how we transform the economy. That means new forms of participatory, bottom-up policy making, at both local and national levels. Instead of the false objectivity of economic models and cost-benefit analysis, we need new tools that help people to debate complex and deeply political trade-offs between the economy and the environment, today and tomorrow, or the north and the south. Instead of smoke-filled rooms and revolving doors, we need town halls and people's assemblies.

For the biggest decisions, we can learn from the experience of other countries with citizens' assemblies and constitutional conventions. Iceland called a citizens' assembly in 2009 to propose a new fundamental law in the wake of the financial crisis—a highly successful process right up until the point when the new ruling parties refused to implement their recommendations.[74]

Ireland called its own constitutional convention in 2011, with two-thirds of its members randomly selected from the public and the other third made up of politicians, inspired by grassroots pressure in the form of a self-organised citizens' parliament.[75] Among other things, this led to the 2018 referendum which overturned the ban on abortion. Labour's proposed constitutional convention could draw on these experiences to ensure the widest and most open participation and popular legitimacy. Beyond the usual headline issues such as Lords reform and voting reform, the convention itself could also be a vehicle for debating new ways to deepen participatory democracy.

For day-to-day policy decisions within Whitehall, listening to those affected most by policy should become as much a part of the everyday routine as running numbers through a model—whether it's teachers and nurses who know best how to improve schools and hospitals, disabled people who have to deal with the benefits system day in, day out, or people of colour whose lives are shaped and constrained by institutional racism. Just as Thatcher and Blair made it part of the new "common sense" that the private sector knew best how to run things, so Corbyn must cement a new common sense, which insists that people know best how to improve their own workplaces and communities.

This means replacing the consultative forums, boards, and committees which currently give corporations privileged access to policy with new ones that empower citizens—both over big questions of departmental strategy, and over individual policy decisions. It means reforming the governance of public services so that new school curricula or NHS reorganisations can never again be imposed on teachers, parents, doctors, and patients against their will. These must be durable institutional changes that bind future governments, not just ad hoc consultative methods used by a Corbyn government while in office—baking in a long-term transformation of power relations.

When it comes to assessing individual policy decisions, more use could be made of methods like multi-criteria analysis (MCA), which better capture the complexity of the real world—illuminating trade-offs between different groups or outcomes, and doing justice to things that can't be given a price tag.[76] MCA is routinely used by businesses and non-governmental organisations to make strategic decisions, but is looked down on by the Treasury as second-rate or too "subjective". Crucially, such tools should be used not just as another way for Whitehall experts to decide the "best" option, but as a way for wider publics affected by policy to debate and deliberate over its effects. Their conclusions could then be fed into the policy process in the same way that cost-benefit analyses are today.

For spending decisions, especially at local level, we can make more and better use of participatory budgeting—as John McDonnell hinted in a recent speech.[77] Many have been inspired by the success of Porto Alegre in Brazil, where this method was pioneered, in giving disenfranchised residents a voice and shifting spending towards things that really improved the lives of the poorest. Its application in the UK has so far been marginal, restricted to disbursing small pots of money for community initiatives rather than democratising council budgets themselves. (For instance, one highly praised scheme in Glasgow gave a local community group just £200,000 to spend).[78] Worse, it has sometimes been used as a way of asking citizens to decide how to make spending cuts. Even left-of-centre councils, like Bristol, have used participatory budgeting as an engagement exercise where school children have been "challenged to balance the books".[79] But there is no reason it could not be applied to bigger budgets—giving local people a voice in shaping local services, priorities for upgrading the transport network, new housing developments, or community regeneration.

To do this well, we need to learn the lessons of how participatory budgeting has been used and abused in the past. Crucially, participatory budgeting worked in Porto Alegre in the context of wider reforms to local government to prevent it from being sidestepped by vested interests.[80] Another key lesson from the worldwide spread of participatory budgeting was how easily what began as a radical left experiment mutated into a "good governance" tool that was turned to distinctly neoliberal ends. As Brazilian expert Leonardo Avritzer recently put it, "the point of participatory budgeting is to democratise the state, not to append new participatory mechanisms to a system where the status quo remains unchanged".[81]

Indeed, this is a key lesson of the history of participatory politics more generally. What has been dubbed the "first wave" of enthusiasm for participatory policy was often top-down and elite-driven.[82] This may be an improvement on no participation at all, but it is participation in a very limited and controlled sense. One of the dangers of such top-down participatory practices is that they are easily co-opted. Since the global financial crisis, we've seen a "second wave" of participation—from Ireland to Spain and beyond—which has been much more driven from below by social movements.[83]

Scaling up this politics is not only about finding the right methods—it is also about where the driving energy for the use of those methods comes from. For instance, citizens' juries have often been used as part of top-down participatory strategies, where the sponsoring authority has the power to set the agenda and to shape the evidence citizens are shown. But this does not mean that these tools cannot be adapted and used as part of more bottom-up participatory strategies. Similarly, one reason participatory budgeting in Porto Alegre was a very different beast than it has become in the UK was the presence of powerful and engaged social movements.[84] Successful reform of the state is intimately linked to building power outside the state—as we discuss in Chapter Five.

On this front, we can learn from cities like Barcelona and the "new municipalism" of Barcelona en Comú (BeC), a movement which grew out of the *indignados* social movements and took power at the city level in 2015. It is pioneering more participatory methods, based on ideas of radical democracy, to hardwire citizen involvement into local services and decision-making.[85] This may be easier to achieve at the smaller scale of the city. On the other hand, there are obviously constraints on what can be delivered at this level. BeC has been hampered by the limited power of Spanish local government, and by hostility from local and national officials as well as global capital. Some have raised concerns that it is not possible for the reality to match the rhetoric, leading to "participatory frustration" among citizens. So what does this mean for the UK left? Among other things, that we need to take devolution seriously if we really want to re-energise our democracy.

The Kerslake Review recommended that the best way to break the Treasury's stranglehold on spending and economic decision-making was not to break it up, but to devolve more of its powers and budgets to local councils.[86] Labour's 2017 Manifesto committed to extending devolution, including considering a more federalised UK. It is vital that the model for this devolution makes a decisive break with the Cameron/Osborne era—where the Treasury itself held all the cards in negotiating devolution deals with councils, the only answer to renewing local democracy was to invest power in figurehead mayors, and devolution of budgets was all too often a cynical attempt to offload responsibility for cuts. Instead, devolution must be about allowing local people to set priorities for their area and ensuring local councils have the resources and powers to deliver them. Again, citizens' assemblies can play a role here, as piloted by the Electoral Reform Society's Democracy Matters project—an experiment with developing citizen-led proposals for devolution in Southampton and Sheffield.[87]

Participation requires resources, and so effective devolution must also go hand in hand with reversing the decimation of local government by austerity. Cuts to the central government grant have left councils more reliant on what they can raise through business rates and council tax, a disaster for deprived areas. Many are left desperately competing to attract private investment into the area. For some, even maintaining basic services is now an impossibility, with Tory-run councils in Northamptonshire and East Sussex stripping them back to the bare minimum.[88] Long years of this have taken their toll on the ability of many local politicians to imagine alternatives—an effect that has been dubbed "austerity realism".[89] They have also eroded citizens' trust in local councils as vehicles for democratic change. Just as Thatcher deliberately smashed the power of local government in the 1980s, so Labour must purposely rebuild it as part of a wider strategy for building new sources of popular power.

To make matters worse, cuts have also hollowed out the local voluntary and community sector that could sit at the heart of a new participatory politics—giving the lie to the Cameron-era rhetoric of the "Big Society".[90] The loss of grant funding has left many small grassroots organisations struggling to survive, competing for what money is available and with less and less capacity to give disenfranchised citizens a voice. As one local councillor puts it, "To build up a strong civic society takes a long time. And then you cut it down. It's like planting a tree. It will take years for it to grow again".[91] All the more reason to start now, with a long-term strategy to lay the groundwork for a more participatory culture. Nor does this have to wait for a change of government, vital though that is. Even within their constrained resources, left councils can begin learning lessons from places like Barcelona and experimenting with new, more participatory models for both the economy and politics.

Finally, reform must extend to institutions that take whole domains of economic policy out of the democratic arena—with the Bank of England top of the list. Central bank independence has been a sacred tenet of neoliberal thinking for decades—though evidence of its benefits is slim. Yet central banks are inescapably political: the Bank of England has huge power not just over the City but the entire economy. Most recently, its multi-billion-pound programme of quantitative easing (QE) has contributed to widening inequality, benefitting the wealthiest by pushing up asset prices while failing to stimulate the economy. Clearly, monetary policy and financial regulation need to change to shift power away from technocrats and City lobbyists and towards the public interest.

Beneath the façade of technocratic political neutrality, central banks have a long history of making political interventions to sabotage governments they do not like, particularly governments of the left. In the 1960s, the German Bundesbank "engineered a sharp recession to oust the government" of Chancellor Ludwig Erhard, by restricting banks' ability to offer loans.[92] Its President, Karl Blessing, later admitted: "We had to use brute force to put things in order".[93] In 2015 the governor of the Bank of Greece, a hangover from the previous administration, repeatedly made "flagrant intervention[s]" designed to undermine the Syriza government, including releasing damaging figures on the state of the Greek financial sector on the eve of negotiations with the Troika.[94]

A similar fate could easily befall a radical Labour government. The Bank of England has the power to raise interest rates, and could justify this as economically necessary to offset the impacts of more government borrowing and spending. A sharp rise in interest rates would hurt borrowers, including middle-class homeowners, potentially tipping the balance of public opinion against the government. Under Labour's Fiscal Credibility Rule, the Bank also holds the keys to boosting public investment during a downturn. As we saw in Chapter Three, the Rule can be suspended during difficult times when the economy can no longer be stimulated by lowering interest rates. But this can only be triggered by the Bank's Monetary Policy Committee (MPC), currently made up of five senior Bank of England staff and four external economists. It is unclear whether this would have happened had the Rule been in operation even at the height of the post-2008 recession, even in the absence of any political motivation to undermine the government.

There are a number of ways a future Labour government could address this. It could, as a minimum, replace the governor of the Bank of England (and other senior staff) with someone more sympathetic. It could overhaul the Bank's internal structures, like its Court of Directors—currently overwhelmingly white, male, and skewed towards the City.[95] The Court's chair, Bradley Fried, is co-founder of private equity firm Grovepoint Capital. Other members include Anne Glover, the head of a venture capital firm; Don Robert, chair of credit reporting agency Experian; and Dorothy Thompson, an oil company executive who was previously CEO of Drax (a company whose coal-fired power station in Yorkshire has long been the target of environmental protests).

As with other branches of government, the Bank's internal processes could also be reformed to make this complex area of policy more genuinely open and accountable to the people. Physical relocation of the Bank away from Threadneedle Street—where it has been since 1734—to somewhere outside London (such as Birmingham, as proposed by the Turner Report) might also help with an agenda of democratising its power.[96] Ultimately, Labour must find the courage to say that central bank independence is not untouchable. Its rationale is that politicians cannot be trusted with control of interest rates, since they have dangerous incentives to artificially over-inflate the economy. But even mainstream commentary is now beginning to suggest that this is a hangover from an era where inflation was a much bigger threat to developed economies, and to question whether it can still be justified now that the real danger is not inflation but stagnation or deflation.[97] Monetary policy is a critical lever for controlling our increasingly financialised economy. There is no obvious reason why it should be immune from an agenda of reclaiming democratic control.

A left agenda for reforming the state must be not just about assuming control of the machine, but about reshaping it to make it accountable to the people, not to private interests. The ideas set out in this chapter are necessarily only rough pointers on how we might do this: there is an urgent need for more detailed thinking. The Institute for Government—which describes itself as "the leading think tank working to make government more effective"—is too deeply immersed in the establishment and orthodox thinking to be much help here.[98] It is time the left set up its own alternative.

* * *

It is also important to be clear that this agenda is not at odds with reclaiming a strong role for the state, whether via public ownership of our banks, public investment in our transport networks, or establishing the legal frameworks we need to combat climate change. Rather, this is about transforming the state itself so that this power can be wielded in a more genuinely progressive and democratic way. Nor is it about a crude anti-expert populism. As we explore in Chapter Five, we need to democratise the notion of expertise itself, breaking down barriers between "expert" economists and "non-expert" citizens.[99] This is different from saying there is no role for evidence and experts, especially when it comes to understanding complex systems like the economy and the biosphere. It is vital that we overhaul the way this evidence is produced to overcome the legacy of neoliberalism. But such top-down changes to the government machine may be brittle and vulnerable to being easily undone by succeeding governments of the right. Truly changing the way the bureaucracy functions is a generational task, one which took Thatcher over a decade to achieve.

Meanwhile, democratising and decentralising the machine has the potential to achieve lasting change which will be much harder for a future Conservative government to reverse: change in which millions have a stake and power is dispersed. If it's to be sustainable, this change must be led by powerful and independent social movements. Giving up power almost always seems less attractive once you hold it, and grassroots movements will need to keep even a Corbyn government accountable on its promises about devolution and democracy. The lessons of past experiments tell us that imposing participatory democracy from above is an oxymoron. Ultimately, change will only stick if it is demanded from below.

CHAPTER FIVE: GET READY TO ORGANISE

"Something very interesting has happened in Spain: the people have finally discovered that they are smarter than their own politicians".
—*Sánchez León, historian*

On Friday 3 July 2015, huge crowds gathered in Athens' Syntagma Square. It was two days before they would go to the polls and deliver a massive *Oxi* ("No") vote against the terms of Greece's bailout deal. That evening, Syriza prime minister Alexis Tsipras emerged from his office to make the short walk to address the rally. The crowds, which stretched for miles, carried him in triumph to the square.[1] Tsipras stepped onto the platform to huge cheers, and urged the assembled demonstrators to "say a proud 'no' to ultimatums and those who terrorise you".[2]

On Monday 6 July, just three days later, everything had changed. Tsipras met with European negotiators and agreed a deal almost identical to the one the Greek people had rejected. Overnight, the Syriza leadership went from heroes to pariahs. "In small villages Syriza representatives were leaving their homes at 5am, and returning very late, to avoid meeting anyone. They were ashamed", recalls Stathis Kouvelakis, a former member of the party's central committee. "In Athens, party people didn't turn up to their jobs for days—they couldn't face their colleagues. Well-known figures didn't dare go shopping in their own neighbourhoods".[3] Within the movement itself, the sense of defeat and devastation was overwhelming. In the next elections, turnout plummeted.

Of course, the story of the Greek bailout referendum is extreme and unique. But it does illustrate a broader truth about the relationship between radical political parties and the social movements that sweep them to power. In or out of government, such parties depend on mass mobilisation to bolster their programme. But in cultivating this mobilisation, they unleash forces they cannot control. Conversely, when social movements pour their faith and their energies into individual political leaders, building up sky-high expectations for their ability to deliver radical change, disillusionment and demobilisation can quickly follow. So how can political parties and social movements work together to achieve transformative change? How can we combine efforts to wield power in the state with efforts to build new sources of power outside the state?

The party and the movement

There is a long history of debate on the left about the relationship between radical parties and social movements (and a separate but related debate about the merits of building power within and outside the state). This isn't the place for an extensive dive into these theoretical debates. But it is helpful to explore a little of how they have played out in practice over the past few decades, since it helps us to understand how we got to where we are—and where we might go from here.

A good place to start is the spring of 2011, when a wave of occupations swept the globe. "People's assemblies" were set up in public spaces in an expression of defiance against the ongoing fall-out of the financial crisis and the economic system that had produced it. Inspired by that year's Egyptian revolution, on 15 May a demonstration in Madrid became a spontaneous camp in Puerta del Sol, which in turn became a mass movement known as the *indignados* or 15M. Less than two weeks later, the same thing happened in Athens' Syntagma Square. Occupy Wall Street followed in September, and Occupy St Paul's in October.

It is no accident that this anger found expression in social movements and not through formal politics. The occupations' emphasis on direct democracy traces its ancestry directly to the anarchist-inspired movements of the 1990s.

These were characterised by horizontalism, a rejection of formal power structures, and "prefigurative politics"—building examples of the world we want to see, rather than fighting for it through political institutions. Large swathes of the grassroots Corbyn base came of age politically in these movements: from the anti-globalisation protests of the 1990s, through the anti-war and climate movements of the 2000s, and the anti-cuts and anti-fees movements of the 2010s. They saw little hope for change in political parties who all embraced the same neoliberal consensus.

But the aftermath of the global financial crisis shook these assumptions. In the United States and United Kingdom, the occupations had no immediate political outlet, and eventually fizzled out. This prompted serious soul-searching about the limits of horizontalist organising. Some activists questioned whether the allergy to leadership and institutional power was to blame for Occupy's failure to articulate a positive programme or to build its initial momentum into something bigger and more lasting. It began to dawn on people that the movements into which they had poured their energies were prefixed by "anti-", and that this might be part of the problem.

Looking for answers, some on the left turned to the ideas of Antonio Gramsci about hegemony: the way political movements exercise leadership in wider society, both by shifting the balance of power and by reshaping the dominant "common sense".[4] Neoliberalism came to be understood as a hegemonic project that could only be superseded if the left developed something similar of its own. These ideas have been popularised in the United States by books like Occupy activist Jonathan Smucker's *Hegemony How-To*, which argues that social movements must contest both battles for power and battles for narrative; and, in the UK, by *Inventing the Future*, by Nick Srnicek and Alex Williams, which argues for a left political project based on the idea of a post-work society.[5]

This has been a vital corrective to a left political culture that had become suspicious of power in any form and prone to marginalise itself. The rise of Corbyn's Labour also means that many activists can now see a path to change through formal politics that simply wasn't there before. But this does not mean that the instincts that lay behind horizontalist social movements were misguided or irrelevant. The insight that the state can be oppressive, the ideals of participatory democracy, the value of building alternatives in the here and now—these things are all compatible with Gramsci's ideas. And, while some might be inclined to dismiss any kind of local or community-based action as what Srnicek and Williams dubbed "folk politics", most would agree that this kind of organising is still necessary: the point is that it is not sufficient.

For this new left, there isn't a binary choice between top-down and bottom-up politics, between having a big political vision and making change at the grassroots. The possibilities of the new politics—moulded in social movements but inspired by Corbyn's Labour—lie precisely in the intersection between these two things. The critical task is to build new structures and sources of power that consciously and effectively displace the old ones. The state and the national media are vital levers for doing this. But so are community energy co-ops, local banks, community education projects, and workplace organising. What matters is that they are all part of a wider strategy, one that is serious about what it takes to achieve transformative change.

This emerging grassroots consensus seeks to forge a new politics that uses the power of the state and other institutions to support participatory organisation of the economy. Hilary Wainwright distinguishes between "power over" (coercive power) and "power to" (transformative power). Gaining "power over" the state is not an end in itself, but a means of building "power to", including through new forms of social organisation outside the state.[6]

Before Corbyn came along, many young activists had abandoned a party political system that seemed to have abandoned them. Yet the nature of Labour's ongoing civil war, combined with the demands of a snap election, has meant that much of this movement's energy is now being directed towards distinctly "party-centric" activities—be it fighting successive leadership elections or getting out the vote for the 2017 general election. There is a danger that activists swing from an outright rejection of electoral politics and leadership figures to a wholesale and uncritical investment in them. Forging a path between these two poles is one of the critical tasks facing the UK left today. What is needed is a powerful social base that can be relied upon to support a left government in moments of need, but can also challenge and hold it to account; and that is capable of building power both inside and outside the Labour Party.

The Corbyn leadership appears to understand this. In a 2017 speech at The World Transformed, John McDonnell spoke of the critical role of grassroots movements:

> When we go into government, our biggest resource won't just be the brilliant minds that are advising us ... it will be the mass base that we can build to support us, not just [as] football spectators clapping along the team, but actually being part of ... the very direct implementation of the policies they want to achieve.[7]

Referencing the seminal 1979 pamphlet *In and Against the State*, McDonnell acknowledged the radical left's ambivalent relationship with state power. As the original pamphlet put it, "it is the state's resources we need—its relations we don't".[8] He also hinted that, as we argued in Chapter Three, a strong grassroots base would be vital in confronting the inevitable backlash from vested interests. Labour needed "a base that can survive that potential assault—and more importantly, build up the popular basis of support that will ensure that assault is not even contemplated". Particularly in a context where Labour does not have the full support of the Parliamentary Labour Party, social movements will provide a vital counterweight—creating mass pressure and a popular mandate such that even right-wing Labour MPs feel they cannot afford to sabotage the government's programme. In the event that Labour finds itself in a minority or coalition government, cementing a new political consensus beyond the Labour Party will be even more vital.

This approach may also prove essential to holding the leadership itself to account when being "in" the state threatens its ability to act "against" the state. The role of social movements is not simply to act as uncritical devotees but as "critical friends", unencumbered by the constraints of elected office, which can hold the government to its promises and push the boundaries of the possible. This raises an important question, one which is being debated intensely on parts of the Corbynite left.[9] Are the grassroots to be regarded as the foot soldiers of the party, to be mobilised in defence of its agenda? Or is the party primarily the parliamentary wing of the movement, to be held to account by civil society? And when we talk about "the grassroots", how are we seeing the relationship between the party membership and wider social movements? Should radical left activists be throwing all of their energies into the Labour Party, or building aligned sources of power outside it?

Preliminary answers to such urgent questions can perhaps be found by looking at recent radical political projects elsewhere in Europe. In Greece and Spain, the anti-austerity movements found political expression more quickly than in the UK, in the form of Syriza and Podemos. Podemos in particular is often held up as a shining example of how to reconcile bottom-up movement politics with top-down electoral politics. Both are inspiring in their own ways and have a lot to teach us. But neither offer a blueprint which magically resolves the tension between parties and movements: instead, they allow us to see those tensions play out in real time. As we will see, they are grappling with the same issues that now confront the Corbyn base.

Lessons from abroad: Podemos and Syriza

In different ways, Syriza and Podemos each have strong roots in social movements. And both have (or had) strong internal forces pushing them beyond old-style party politics. However, as they came closer to power, this balancing act was harder to maintain—and the centralising wing of both parties came to predominate.

Of course, all this happened in a very different context from that of today's UK. In both Greece and Spain, the hardship inflicted by austerity meant that people were angry and they were organised—on a massive scale. In Spain, "it felt as if all of Spanish society was on the streets".[10] In Greece, according to one estimate, over a quarter of the population took part in the 2011 occupations of the squares. Similar numbers were part of solidarity networks that sprung up to provide food, medical care, and other essential services.[11] The UK has seen nothing on this scale in living memory. If we don't have to deal with the level of economic crisis seen in Greece and Spain, the flip side of this is that we also don't have the same levels of popular mobilisation with which to work.

The link between these social movements and the emergence of new political forces was also much more immediate than it is for Corbyn's Labour. Podemos grew out of the *Indignados* or 15M movements that erupted after the 2011 occupations, which were defined by opposition to both an unjust economic system and a corrupt political system. It was led by a group of young left-wing academics who wanted to channel this popular energy into an electoral project. Sirio Canós Donnay, Podemos' representative in London, describes it as a product of both the success and the failure of the street movements: "It doesn't matter how loud we shout on the streets if there is no-one willing to listen ... why isn't the majority in the squares translating into the ballot boxes?"[12]

Syriza grew from a coalition of existing left-wing parties—the most prominent of which, Synaspismos, had been more open to the anti-globalisation and anti-war movements than many of its peers. In turn, the Greek social movements of the 2000s, unlike Occupy Wall Street, saw their role as "not to evade politics and its central decision-making in the state, but to confront it".[13] According to author and activist Kevin Ovenden, this meant the relationship between Syriza and its base was different from traditional political parties.[14] It was not a question of passively switching voting loyalties, but was born of collective struggle in movements that had a life of their own, and that realised Syriza's election victory was just the beginning and did not mark the end of the need to mobilise.

And yet, when those who have seen the Syriza government first-hand reflect on its ultimate failure to deliver its radical anti-austerity programme, they often conclude that all this was not enough. Of course, many argue that Syriza's programme simply couldn't be delivered inside the euro, movement or no movement. As Paul Mason puts it: "No mass movement in Greece alone would have been strong enough to defeat what Europe did". But he goes on to say that "Syriza did not consistently mobilise it. And the movement itself distrusted Syriza"—perhaps with good reason.[15]

A former senior figure in Syriza told us that a lack of depth in the popular base was one reason the party's agenda did not survive the sustained battering it received from the domestic and European establishment. People had voted for Syriza because they were angry with the status quo—not because they had a deep understanding of a positive radical economic agenda. Once elected, he said, Greek prime minister Alexis Tsipras was under huge pressure to become a "normal" politician:

> Governments are inside the state and have big pressure from the state—you have to create balance and counter power, pressure from the movements and the left. If you don't have it, you will lose ... if you are something else, you will need a power to keep you something else.[16]

Although the movement did not disappear once Syriza was elected, it did lose momentum. Its most capable people were drawn towards parliament, its energies directed towards electoral politics.[17] As Andreas Karitzis points out, although working within and outside the state are not mutually exclusive, in practice people have limited time and energy. The more of it is poured into political parties, the less is available to sustain the movements they depend on.[18] This is a particular problem when social movements rely on a small handful of committed activists to drive them forward (as was the case with, for example, UK Uncut). This is the dilemma faced by organisations like Momentum today.

But there's another side to this story: did Syriza really want a mass movement behind it? Kouvelakis argues that it did not: "They didn't want a strategy of popular mobilisations", being more focused on traditional parliamentary politics.[19] The leadership did not even try to recruit parliamentarians from the ranks of the social movements, he says. Instead they were more focused on making overtures to the political establishment—including bringing in former Pasok MPs and wooing the military. The aim was to build credibility, to convince the establishment that they could be trusted: "We are in the process of becoming a normal party". And indeed, the media's line shifted from blanket attacks on Syriza to an attempt to isolate their left wing. On this reading, Syriza's radical programme was a casualty not just of European elites, but of Syriza's own political calculation: that the support of *domestic* elites mattered more than the support of its own movement. One person we spoke to emphasised that this was also a choice between two halves of Syriza's electoral base itself: between older voters and public servants who disliked austerity because it was undermining the pre-crisis political and economic system, and younger, more radical voters who wanted to overturn that system. "They chose the part that tried to conserve the system, and they became part of the system really fast".[20]

This went hand in hand with growing centralisation of power within the party itself, turning it into a more conventional top-down electoral machine. The early overtures to the Greek establishment would not have been accepted by the party base had it been asked. The final bailout deal was rejected by the party's central committee and by several of its MPs, but was pushed through by the leadership with the support of other parties. Power had been centralised in a small core around Tsipras: "They had marginalised the party and were not accountable to anyone".[21] As Ovenden puts it: "Despite the democratic culture of the party, in government the pressures of conventional parliamentary management asserted themselves".[22]

We might be tempted to dismiss this as an anomaly—a radical political project bending and breaking under the immense strain of eurozone pressures. It is also worth noting that, unlike Corbyn's Labour, Syriza was never a mass party—its membership peaked at 35 thousand. But it's striking that similar criticisms have been levelled at Podemos, the archetypal movement-led, participatory party. The tensions between top-down and bottom-up politics, it seems, cannot be wished away so easily.

From the outset, Podemos internalised the logic of the squares and assemblies, with participatory democratic processes to shape its manifestos and select its candidates. Power over key decisions is held by the citizens' assembly and subsidiary regional assemblies, all of which operate on the principle of one member, one vote. Membership of the party is open to anyone, without fees or prior participation. It has also sought to maintain organic connections with wider social movements, particularly through its "circles", which are open to anyone—including non-party members—and are specifically tasked with building links outside the party.[23] In a 2015 interview, Eduardo Maura, Podemos' international representative, stressed the importance of social movements not being subsumed into the party: "The pace [of institutional politics] is so different that you oblige movements to adapt to it. If you do this you are going to kill them. Movements need to be autonomous and self-regulating".[24]

But many have been disappointed and disillusioned with how this democratic experiment has played out in practice. From the outset there has been a tension between Podemos' commitment to bottom-up democracy and Pablo Iglesias' strong-minded charismatic leadership: "It pledged to hand control to grassroots activists, despite the fact the party depended on one man's popularity".[25] Iglesias himself has always been on the centralising wing of the party, and has surrounded himself with a group of close advisors who in practice exert a high level of control. At the party's founding assembly, Vistalegre, all of

Iglesias' proposals on party structure and strategy were approved, with some complaining that the way they were voted on was designed to ensure this outcome. Spanish commentator Rafael Narbona was scathing: Podemos had "taken advantage of the legacy of the 15M, made use of the assembly model, but in the end constituted itself as a traditional party".[26] One Podemos activist we spoke to described "an internal structure built with a siege mentality that centralises an excessive amount of power in the leader's office".[27] While Podemos' grassroots do have more power than in other parties (although again, studies have found that the decisions they make often mirror the preferences of the leadership), the intermediate structures that should hold the leader to account—such as the citizens' council—are not strong enough to do so.[28]

At first sight, this might seem to have little relevance to a Corbyn leadership actively committed to extending party democracy. Faced with a relentless onslaught from the political establishment, it has hardly been an option for Corbyn to tread Syriza's path and try to compromise. Instead, the mass base has been his key asset, and strengthening its power key to bolstering his position. But this may not always be the case, particularly if and when the party makes the transition from opposition to government. At the time of writing, there has yet to be a serious test of whether Corbyn's commitment to party democracy will survive when the membership is against him as well as when it is with him.

The dangers of a "siege mentality" are certainly relevant to Corbyn's inner circle, scarred by seemingly endless battles with the party right and the media. And anyway, there are questions over whether the movement is sufficiently independent of the leadership to hold it to account effectively. Senior figures we spoke to expressed concern that most Labour members, while instinctively anti-austerity and anti-Tory, do not have a deep sense of the party's agenda, identifying more with Corbyn as leader than the programme for which he stands. The experiences of Podemos and Syriza tell us that there are real dangers in this.

Notwithstanding their shortcomings, both the Greek and Spanish experiences offer significant cause for optimism. The early days of Syriza were full of possibility, even if this potential was ultimately crushed by a combination of overwhelmingly adverse circumstances and Syriza's own choices in response to those circumstances. This period produced some inspiring moments of popular empowerment—from the workers' takeover of state broadcaster ERT to community-led anti-mining movements in Keratea and Skouries. The successful referendum campaign was both the movement's greatest triumph and the moment its hopes for radical change were finally destroyed. Ovenden argues that the Greek experience, for all its flaws, does point the way towards a path between anti-party "movementism" and party-centric electoralism.

In Spain, many people now see most cause for hope and optimism in the local alliances which Podemos has catalysed and supported, which have taken power in Spanish cities: in people like Ada Colau, an anti-eviction activist politicised by protests against globalisation and the Iraq war, who was elected mayor of Barcelona in 2015 at the head of the left coalition Barcelona en Comú (BeC).[29] Along with Ahora Madrid, a similar platform that has taken power in the capital, BeC is now being held up as a model for how political parties working closely with social movements can achieve radical change at the city level.

Of course, they have still not gone as far or as fast as the movements would like (BeC's leaders acknowledge their first year was a rude awakening to the hard reality that "being in government does not necessarily mean that you are in power").[30] But it is precisely the job of social movements to demand more—maintaining the energy for radical change whilst also appreciating that holders of electoral office will not always be able to fully deliver. Of course, maintaining these connections between top-down and bottom-up politics is easier at the smaller scale of the city than it is at national level— another good reason to make radical devolution a key part of the left's platform.

There are three key lessons, then, that we can draw from these experiences. First, radical governments need a solid power base in wider society in order to implement their agenda—one that is both well informed and well organised. If the base lacks strength or depth, the radical agenda will not survive the inevitable battering from opposing forces. Second, this base needs to be independent, able to hold governments themselves to account. The distinctive pressures of winning power and being inside the state mean that if social movements are simply subsumed into political parties, their energies will dissipate. Third, these pressures can mean that political leaders' commitment to both party democracy and wider social movements weakens over time. The means of holding them accountable must be robust and resilient to withstand this.

As Karitzis concludes: "The fate of any left government depends on our ability to build new social and institutional structures that empower people. And the duty of a left government is not just to exercise diminished power, but also to function as a facilitator for such popular empowerment to take place".[31] Kouvelakis echoes this: "The political practice of radical left parties vitally needs to articulate parliamentary politics with popular mobilizations; when the second is lost, the first becomes weightless".[32] This is not as simple as saying that party leaders must be directly accountable to movements to prevent them "selling out": rather, it demands an appreciation that parties and movements are different beasts which operate according to different logics. Movements are in a position to be utopian, to demand the impossible and in doing so expand the boundaries of the possible. Parties, especially those in government, must make choices within these boundaries.

In the context of Labour, this means we need a party membership that is both powerful enough to hold the leadership to account and strategically aware enough to use this power intelligently. Outside the party, we need a strong social movement base which can both strengthen the party's arm by shifting the balance of forces in its favour, and create space for it to go further by holding its feet to the fire. The left will need to shift from an oppositional mindset to one that engages with the realities and the responsibilities of building power. It will need to modify its default tendency to denounce any compromise as a betrayal and any politician who makes it as a sell-out. We must take responsibility not just for the rightness of our positions but also for the practical effect of our interventions. Just as with the Thatcher project, compromises, tactical retreats, and strategic prioritising are inevitable. The debate must be about whether a given compromise is right for the success of the long-term project, rather than about whether the party should be compromising at all. Of course, there is an important distinction between temporary tactical retreats and the strategic abandonment of the project itself (the ultimate fate of the Syriza government). It is vital that the party's social base is strong enough and independent enough to anticipate and prevent the latter course. In this way, the movement can steer a path between uncritical support of the leadership and hyper-purist abandonment of it when things get tough—embracing its role and responsibility as the leading edge of transformative change.

Senior Labour figures we spoke to recognise the need for this. They want to see members able to critically engage with Labour's policy development. And they want strong social movements outside the party that can continue to push the window of political possibility to the left. As an insurgent opposition leader, Corbyn has done this job very effectively on everything from austerity to rail nationalisation to energy bills. But as the party moves closer to power, and the pressure of pragmatism intensifies, it will need others to play this role and create the space for it to go further—both in civil society and in smaller radical parties such as the Greens. In the rest of this chapter, we look at how this might be achieved in five key areas: building power; building new narratives; building economic alternatives; building ideas; and building leaders.

Building power

In *Hegemony How-To*, Smucker argues that the role of social movements is two-fold: to wage the battle for power (shifting the balance of forces in institutions and wider society) and the battle for narrative (contesting the public discourse and symbolic cultural practices). First, let's look at building power. At its heart, this is about how social movements can grow and scale by reaching out to new constituencies, bringing disparate groups into alignment to forge what Gramsci called a "collective will". Taking on board the participatory instincts of recent social movements, it is also about how they can empower the people worst affected by our economic system—the people whom left politics claims to represent—to build their own leadership.

Gramsci called this "articulation": the process of fragmented individuals coming to identify as a group with common interests. Traditional Marxism assumed that common economic interests were simply an objective fact, and political identities emerged as an expression of that fact. But Laclau and Mouffe, two Gramscian theorists influential on the new left (particularly with Podemos), argue that it is not this simple. It is not only that the working class is fragmented (for example between secure well-paid professionals and the low-paid precariat, distinctions that also fracture along racial and gender lines). It is that we all occupy a series of overlapping identities, not just as workers but as renters, debtors, or citizens. How we perceive these roles and which of them define our politics are the product of struggles for meaning and power.[33] Constructing these alliances is part of the role of social movements, through which people come to see their personal problems as rooted in structures of oppression they can take on collectively, rather than their individual failings.

Smucker gives the examples of Black Lives Matter and of foreclosed homeowners after the crash. In the UK, we could point to the rise of renters' unions, seeking to build new forms of collective power to resist the power of the extractive economy in the form of landlords. We could look to those, like the Independent Workers' Union of Great Britain, who are organising outsourced cleaners and precarious workers in the "gig economy", or to GMB's landmark court victory against Uber. Groups like Migrants Organise and the campaign to shut down Yarl's Wood are building the power of migrants and organising against racist structures. The Just Treatment campaign is organising patients against the exploitative practices of big pharma and the high drug prices they produce. Groups like Reclaim the Power successfully held off fracking for years by organising with the communities directly affected. All of these movements in different ways are building counterweights to the power of extractive capital.

They are pivotal to building and sustaining the new democratic economy, and to creating the strong social base that could underpin a radical government.

Activists forged in such movements who now find themselves Labour members are grappling with the question of how to do this kind of organising within a political party itself. New activists' assumptions about how change happens are bumping up against the assumptions of the party machine. Nowhere was this more apparent than in the 2017 election "ground war". Armies of young activists who turned up to go door knocking for the first time were sometimes confused and dismayed to find that they were not expected to have proper conversations about the things they cared about: "canvassing" just meant identifying Labour voters, making sure they were planning to get out and vote, then moving on to the next address as quickly as possible.

Momentum activists who wanted to do things differently often faced— and still face—resistance from local parties. As in America with Bernie Sanders' "Big Organising", fresh approaches to political organising—or rather, the rediscovery of old approaches—are shaking up the assumptions of top-down electoralist machine politics. The challenge is to ensure that this new blood reshapes the party's own common sense about how to organise, rather than the other way around.

Some argue that Momentum cannot play a broader role for precisely this reason: it is an electoral machine, pure and simple, and we will need to build other spaces for campaigning and community organising. But this seems a shortsighted approach to the promising potential of an organisation of over 40 thousand members, many of whom are experienced grassroots organisers. It is also a fatalistic attitude to the potential for party politics to be reinvented in a way that rebuilds organic connections with the communities it claims to represent. Nonetheless, we need to recognise the strong pressures pushing Momentum groups away from new kinds of organising, and take active steps to counteract them.

New Socialist co-editor Tom Blackburn has coined the phrase "Corbynism from Below" to convey the need to build a stronger culture of bottom-up movement organising and to rebuild roots in working class communities.[34] This means creating spaces that bring people together to address their immediate problems, whilst also giving them an analysis of how these problems are political rather than personal, and a powerful experience of acting collectively to do things differently. These can range from setting up community pubs and social clubs to food banks, clothing banks, and community land trusts. The party's recently formed Community Organising Unit positions it well to invest in this kind of activity. Of course, we also need a strong ecosystem of civil society efforts that are independent of the Labour Party.

Many point to the solidarity economy that emerged in Greece after the crisis as an example of how this can be done—albeit arising from a place of extreme necessity. As one volunteer put it, "We are at the end, but from this end we try to help each other".[35] Initiatives ranged from the "potato movement", which cut out supermarket middlemen to connect rural producers directly with urban consumers, to collectives offering free legal advice to those being evicted from their homes. Volunteers set up free social clinics, food kitchens, and evening classes, all run by assemblies on the participatory model of the squares. National networks were formed connecting these new initiatives, now under the umbrella of Solidarity4All. Syriza set up a fund to support the network financially, but it remains independent.

Crucially, this solidarity movement is not just about crisis relief: it is about sowing the seeds for political and economic transformation. Solidarity4All is clear on this:

> For us, this ... is not only about relief, but about the way to build another world ... The solidarity movement acknowledges that its potential for social transformation goes hand in hand with the fight for political change.[36]

The solidarity movement seeks to create new political identities by bringing people together across boundaries, connecting the dots between their problems to expose their systemic causes, and giving a powerful experience of working together to build co-operative solutions. A food collection network might also organise campaigns against housing evictions. The active participation of migrants in solidarity networks acts as a way to break down barriers and undermine the far right:

> In every case, the target is the participation and activation of those very people who have the problem, the break of social isolation and individualisation of the problem, against despair, personal interest, social fragmentation that feeds fascist tendencies, for the strengthening of social cohesion and of the community spirit in every neighbourhood.[37]

In the same way, for UK community organising to be genuinely transformative, it must be more than an attempt to patch up holes in the welfare state: it must be part of an effort to build new political identities and communities, to tell a new story about where problems like hunger and homelessness actually come from and how we can fight them together. Crucially, grassroots organisers need a strong sense of this political compass to guide their work. Conversely, the lived experiences of people most oppressed by the system must inform the political programme. This is where popular education, community organising, and the development of new ideas go hand in hand.

This process must build political blocs which transcend the racialised identities promoted by the far right. It is not new to suggest that the way to displace a far-right politics that divides people based on race is with a politics that unites people based on shared economic interests. The point here is that it is not enough to do this at the level of discourse, with rhetorical strategies that deflect blame for economic problems away from immigrants and onto elites. Nor can we assume that if we address people's underlying economic grievances, racism will magically disappear without the need to tackle it head-on. Apart from anything else, as Novara journalist Ash Sarkar points out, we can't afford to wait for a Labour government to do this before draining the poison out of a resurgent far right: "It's essential we start to transform the political landscape that a Labour government would inherit".[38]

Our task is to chart a path between the anodyne liberalism that says all that is needed to tackle racism is to promote cultural inclusion, and the reductionist socialism that says all we need to do is to address the "real" economic issues. Tackling racism absolutely means tackling economic marginalisation: but it means doing so in a way that deliberately and consciously brings people together across racial divides, whilst mobilising vigorously against the far right. Just as Solidarity4All resisted Golden Dawn by bringing immigrants and Greek-born citizens together in spaces built on solidarity, so Sarkar argues that we should use the weight of Momentum to do the same in the UK.

This cuts against the grain for a lot of left organising. Smucker points out that the culture of many left movements—from the language we use to the kinds of tactics we employ—is more concerned with maintaining community and identity within the group than with building new communities and identities outside it. There are a range of reasons for this, from decades spent cultivating the habit of losing to the simple human need to huddle in a friendly group when surrounded by a society from which we often feel alienated.

Smucker argues that the psychological effects of constantly waging oppositional battles can exacerbate these tendencies. It is not hard to see how this plays out in the Labour Party today: the endless attacks on the party encourage a "bunker mentality" and an intense loyalism, amongst both the Corbyn leadership and its supporters. One insider we spoke to noted the perplexing paradox that local party battles between Momentum slates and the party right were almost entirely content-free, defined not by the ideas the candidates stood for but by their identity: their membership of internal factions, their age and experience (or alleged lack of it). The more organisations like Momentum are sucked into wars of position, not in wider society but within the Labour Party itself, the less able—both organisationally and psychologically—they are to do the vital work of reaching out and building broad social bases of support for a new politics.

This is not to say that battles for party democracy aren't important—on the contrary, they are critical. And unfortunately, it seems clear that the fight for the soul of the Labour Party will not be concluded any time soon—even, perhaps especially, with the advent of a Labour government. But it cannot be allowed to suck all of the movement's time and energy, nor can it be allowed to create a poisonous defensive mentality which shuts down our ability to organise outside. There would be no faster way to exhaust the radical potential of this new grassroots base, so eager to do things differently.

Building new narratives

The battle for power and the battle for narrative are intimately linked. Thatcher's Conservatives certainly understood this. The 1977 *Stepping Stones* report on strategic communications put it this way:

> A Tory landslide is not enough, if it only reflects the electorate's material dissatisfaction since 1974. A landslide is needed, but it must represent an explicit rejection of socialism and the Labour-trades union axis; and the demand for something morally and economically better.[39]

Echoing this, Tom Blackburn writes of Corbynism today:

> it would be wrong to interpret [the 2017 election result] straightforwardly as 12.8 million votes for socialism. The party's new left must

remember that it has to actively cultivate popular support for a radical political alternative.[40]

The *Stepping Stones* report argued that the Conservatives needed to tell a compelling story about what was going wrong with the UK economy and why their free-market policies were the way to put it right. By making this the dominant story in the public debate, they not only won the coming election, but set up the new government with a clear popular mandate to drive through transformative change.

Crucially, this narrative strategy was intimately linked to their strategic assessment of the balance of power (discussed in Chapter Two). In particular, the report argued that the Conservatives' communications needed to comprehensively discredit the trade unions in order to remove one of the major "political obstacles" to their agenda—laying the groundwork for the smashing of union power once in government. "Skilfully handled", it said, "the rising tide of public feeling could turn the unions from Labour's secret weapon into its major electoral liability".[41]

In the same way, the Corbyn movement needs to develop a clear story about the economy that can shift what is regarded as "common sense" and lend weight to its strategy for rebalancing power. This clear mandate for change, broadly accepted across wider society and not just within the Labour Party itself, could be particularly critical should Labour find itself heading a minority government or coalition. Building bridges with the more radical voices in other parties, such as the Greens and Scottish National Party, may also prove invaluable in this context.

Cameron's Conservatives absorbed these lessons too. The left was blindsided by the Conservatives' success in turning a crisis of neoliberalism into a crisis of government spending through rhetorical sleight of hand that saw the airwaves full of Tory politicians repeating the mantra that we'd maxed out the nation's credit card, that they were dealing with the mess the Labour government left, that Labour had spent too much and crashed the economy. Making the state rather than the banks the culprit justified their true political project—a wider stripping back of the state—whilst cementing the idea that there was "no alternative" to austerity politics. The left's attempts to explain that austerity didn't make economic sense failed to cut through this powerful story. One campaigner likened it to "bringing a spreadsheet to a knife fight".[42]

This prompted a flurry of interest in American cognitive linguist George Lakoff's book *Don't Think of an Elephant*, which argues that the way we frame issues—the categories we use—influences how people perceive and understand the world.[43] The left needed to use new frames of its own: trying to argue against austerity within our opponents' existing frames only served to strengthen their grip. At the same time, there was a revival of interest in Gramsci's idea of "common sense": the unconscious way in which people see the world, influenced by dominant ideologies and cultural stories as well as their own experiences. Successful political projects need to tell a coherent story about how the world works, where its problems come from and how to fix them, and to establish this as the new "common sense".[44] It is clear that this thinking has influenced Labour's approach: Corbyn even used the phrase in his 2017 conference speech when he said, "It is Labour that is now setting the agenda and winning the arguments for a new common sense about the direction our country should take"—and, later, "There is a new common sense emerging about how the country should be run".[45]

It has also deeply influenced Podemos. From the outset, Pablo Iglesias' media presence has been a key weapon in the party's arsenal, and communications have been a core part of their strategy. Inspired by Ernesto Laclau's interpretation of Gramsci, Iglesias and those around him sought to build a new political consensus using what Laclau calls "floating signifiers"—neutral ideas that can be filled with meaning, like democracy or *la casta* ("the elite")—to reshape the debate. Instead of left and right, the new political divide would be between those at the top and everyone else. Corbyn's Labour has adopted a similar strategy, with the slogan "for the many not the few" (mischievously borrowed from New Labour, but imbued with new meaning) and talk of a "rigged economy".[46]

Recent research suggests that this kind of anti-elite populist rhetoric could be effective at tapping into people's existing instincts about inequality (what Gramsci called "good sense") and shifting their perspective on the economy.[47] But it must be used in a way that points to systemic problems and solutions, rather than corrupt individuals: the latter risks exacerbating both people's fatalism and the tendency to scapegoat. It must also be used in a way that adopts a clear and expansive definition of who counts as "the people". The recent rise of right-wing populists, from Nigel Farage and Marine Le Pen to Donald Trump, makes abundantly clear that the rhetorical clothes of anti-elitism can easily be worn by racist nationalists for whom "the people" does not include migrants or people of colour. In his first speech to the European Parliament after Brexit, Farage declared:

> What the little people did, what the ordinary people did—what the people who'd been oppressed over the last few years who'd seen their living standards go down did—was they rejected the multinationals, they rejected the merchant banks, they rejected big politics and they said actually, we want our country back, we want our fishing waters back, we want our borders back.[48]

This dynamic has played out perhaps most starkly in the rise of Ciudadanos, Podemos' right-wing evil twin—a populist party which plays on anti-elite sentiment but takes a hard line on immigration. It has even been suggested that Podemos' rise paved the way for this twisted tribute act. (When Podemos first rose to the top of the polls, the CEO of a major Spanish bank said that they needed a "Podemos of the right". Soon after, Ciudadanos' funding duly soared.)[49] Nor is this anything new: in using anger at an unjust economic order to fuel hatred of outsiders and minorities, the new right-wing populists are repeating a very old historical pattern. A 1930s Nazi propaganda poster bore the slogan "Smash the enemy, international high finance".[50] If we don't nail down these "floating signifiers", they can easily float off to the right. Hate is not a zero-sum commodity, and we cannot afford to assume that stoking people's justified anger with elites will make them less likely to hate foreigners. Instead, our narratives need to use this anger as a jumping-off point to tell a positive story about how we can build an economy that serves the common good. This was the real success of Labour's 2017 election campaign: as Corbyn said in his conference speech, and as even his opponents grudgingly agreed, the manifesto was—together with the membership—one of the two "stars" of the campaign.[51]

So what does this mean for the grassroots movement? It might seem like the battle for narrative is one to be waged by politicians in speeches and media interviews.

But Gramsci's idea of common sense is much more sophisticated than this. It arises from people's everyday experiences, the cultural messages they encounter, their interactions with others, as well as the messages they absorb through the national media. For Gramsci, common sense starts to shift when a disconnect emerges between people's lived experience and the dominant narrative: it no longer makes intuitive sense.[52]

Luis Gimenez, a long-time member of Podemos' press team and author of one of the first supportive books about the party, identifies the press and broadcasters as critical in this process, writing: "People think that politics happens in parties or collectives, but that's not true ... Politics happens in the media".[53]

This emphasis is certainly debatable. There is considerable evidence that the mass media is in fact becoming less powerful in defining the common sense. The Brexit vote is a good example. High-profile warnings on the economy not only failed to persuade people to vote Remain; they actually reinforced their determination to stick two fingers up to a political establishment backed up by economic experts they no longer trusted. The story they were hearing did not seem to mesh with the reality of life in post-industrial communities. Likewise, the relentless media onslaught against Corbyn did not dent his popularity at the polls in the way many expected. There is a growing gulf between the stories told by the mainstream media and the everyday political conversations taking place in people's homes and communities.

The left needs to intervene at both these levels. Of course we must contest the domain of traditional mass media—creating an echo chamber as the Conservatives managed to do with austerity, with the same story being told by a diverse range of voices. This will be helped by projects like the New Economy Organisers' Network (NEON) Spokesperson Network, which trains progressive spokespeople and books them into the media, and their Communications Hub, which provides campaigners with up-to-the-minute framing research and helps co-ordinate rapid responses to unfolding events. We need to build on our success at using social media to reach new audiences and sidestep the traditional media, as Momentum did so successfully by producing viral video content during the 2017 election campaign, and as Labour has since begun doing with videos like "Our Town".[54]

And the dominance of right-wing media, whose hysterical attacks on the Corbyn leadership are only likely to escalate if the party takes power, must certainly be addressed. As in other spheres, this demands structural changes to tackle unaccountable concentrations of media power—not by imposing greater state control, but by breaking them up and replacing them with more decentralised, democratic alternatives. For instance, left-wing media watchers Dan Hind and Tom Mills propose legislation limiting media ownership alongside the creation of a network of regional media co-operatives and a "British Digital Corporation" to support new democratic media.[55]

But we also need doorstep conversations, popular education programmes, co-operative spaces where people can hear the new story and experience it directly. Indeed, with our mass membership and organising capability, we are arguably stronger on this territory. And our stories are stronger if they grow from this on-the-ground experience. Shifting the narrative is not synonymous with media strategy: it is about much more than this.

Building economic alternatives

One way to cement the new narrative is to show in practice that new economic solutions can work, refuting Thatcher's famous mantra that "There Is No Alternative". As the experience of Greece's solidarity economy shows, creating a different economy from the ground up can not only help those suffering but be powerful in helping achieve change at the top. This is one of the key ways that we can begin to displace the economic power of big institutions even before a Labour government comes to power.

Social movements can play a part in this through initiatives like community energy co-ops and community land trusts. Just as Greek solidarity networks saw bankrupt small businessmen rub shoulders with hard-left activists, so community energy projects in the UK have built alliances far beyond the usual suspects. In places like Balcombe, threatened with fracking under people's homes, local residents have come together with environmental activists to build their own renewable energy solutions. The Hebridean islanders of Eigg came together to buy back their land from private landowners and place it in a community trust. Democratic housing solutions are being pioneered across the country, from LILAC, a sustainable co-housing development in Leeds, to community land trusts like Granby Four Streets in Liverpool and London CLT in Mile End—taking land permanently out of the market and using it to provide affordable homes.[56] Such actions are the seeds of a new democratic economy. They will need state support to survive and thrive, but until we have a government able and willing to give that support, it falls to social movements to keep the seeds alive.

Where progressives are in power at city and regional level, they can also play their part. Many have been inspired by Barcelona en Comú's efforts to build new local economic alternatives while strengthening social movements—for instance, by taking energy and water into local public ownership. Closer to home, Nottingham City Council have set up Robin Hood Energy, a publicly owned energy supply company. This gives local people lower energy bills, directly displaces the economic power of the Big Six energy companies, and proves that publicly owned energy can work. Replicating this across the country would provide a solid foundation for a Labour government's energy policy.

The "Preston Model" has become a byword for how local councils can use their power to build a more resilient, democratic local economy. As we saw in Chapter One, Preston councillors have worked to "repatriate" their procurement spending to keep money circulating in the local economy, by choosing to support local small businesses rather than outsourcing to big business. The council are paying and promoting the real Living Wage. They are also working to incubate new co-operative businesses in areas where local firms do not already exist. This model is widely credited with Preston's impressive regeneration over recent years.

We need a serious effort to replicate and extend these experiments. What is being called the new "municipal socialism" is vital for many reasons. It improves people's lives in the here and now, demonstrating what radical politicians can achieve when in power. It shows that another way of doing things is possible. And, perhaps most importantly, it strengthens the connective tissue of the democratic economy while weakening the pull of the extractive economy. The more local people can draw on the community for essential services, and the less they depend on firms like Carillion and G4S, the harder it will be for vested economic interests to hold a Labour government to ransom. Of course, the pressures of austerity and the erosion of local government powers mean that delivering radical initiatives is not easy for local councils (as even Preston itself has found). They need to be supported both from above (with resources and expertise from the party centre) and from below (by organic social movements such as a strong co-operative movement, or campaigns like Switched On London, which demanded a public energy company for the capital).

Building ideas

Compelling stories and economic alternatives crucially need to be under-pinned by new ideas. We need an intellectual framework that helps us understand the economy, how it works and how to change it, just as Keynes' theories informed the politics of the 1940s, and Hayek's the 1970s. This frame-work is beginning to emerge on the left, and we have tried to sketch out some of its key elements in Chapter One. But it is still much less unified and well theorised than those that underpinned previous transformative shifts.[57] As we saw in Chapter Four, it is not yet ready to displace orthodox economics.

We also need plenty of "shovel-ready" policy solutions that exemplify and extend the new politics. Here the left is trying to bridge a generational deficit in new thinking, on a shoestring, and without the luxury of time. A broad-brush vision for change is taking shape—itself a remarkable achievement when we remember that just a few years ago the left was bemoaning our ina-bility to offer alternatives. But there is a serious lack of resources for translat-ing this into detailed policy development, let alone the kind of battle plans set out in the Ridley Plan. This task cannot be met by the Labour Party alone. Like the neoliberals, we must build new institutions outside of the political party.

As we have seen, the neoliberal project was driven forward in the decades before the 1970s by an elaborate web of organisations stretching across the globe, with the Mont Pelerin Society—and later, the Atlas Foundation—at its centre. Philip Mirowski has christened this the "Neoliberal Thought Collective", and likens its structure to that of a Russian doll: layers of interlocking institu-tions, from the highly public to the highly secretive, all committed to the same goal—to normalise neoliberal thinking in powerful institutions and in the public mind.[58]

There were academic strongholds, such as the University of Chicago Economics Department and the London School of Economics; think tanks, which themselves spawned a range of specialist offshoots to make media and political interventions; and philanthropic foundations, which both bankrolled the operation and provided it with services (for instance, the Volcker Fund maintained a "directory" of neoliberal intellectuals which by 1956 already had 1,841 names).[59] When pitching to funders, its members would acknowledge that these were part of a single pipeline for the generation and dissemination of ideas. But publicly, they carefully maintained the illusion that they were a spontaneous ecosystem of independent entities. Slowly but surely, the neoliberals created their own echo chamber.

This story has become a familiar one to many on the left. It is now commonplace to say that we need to emulate the right's network of think tanks. But surprisingly little serious effort has been devoted to the question of how we might actually do this. It is clear that a left project of this sort can't simply replicate the tactics of the right, though we can of course learn from them. Most obviously, the right's strategy for hegemony was essentially an elitist one. They certainly did contest the arena of public discourse: in his first speech to the Mont Pelerin Society, Hayek proclaimed:

What to the politicians are fixed limits of practicability imposed by public opinion must not be similar limits to us. Public opinion on these matters is the work of men like ourselves ... who have created the political climate in which the politicians of our time must move.[60]

But this was a tactic in what remained at heart an elitist strategy. The main goal was to mould a new generation of top decision makers: to "capture the minds of the crucial elites ... by innovating new economic and political doctrines that those elites would recognise as being in their interest".[61] This was the shortcut to power. Mass popular consent would come later, if at all. As Mirowski puts it, "These elite saboteurs would bring about the neoliberal market society far more completely and efficaciously than waiting for the fickle public to come round to their beliefs".[62]

By contrast, a "Democratic Thought Collective" would have a different strategy. It would aim to build mass popular engagement and support for radical ideas, *as well as* developing policy and contesting the battle for ideas in powerful institutions. As we saw in Chapter Four, a radical democratic strategy does not mean we can afford to neglect the job of reshaping the establishment. If we fail to do so, we will be constantly working against the grain of institutions that we need to work for us. But it does mean that we cannot rely solely on these tactics.

So what would building a left-wing "Russian doll" look like? There are three key layers to this: academia (whose role is to provide new fundamental research based on new frameworks for understanding the economy); think tanks (whose role is both to translate these ideas into implementable policy, and to intervene in the media to shift public debate to the left); and popular education (whose role is both to involve the grassroots in developing new progressive ideas, and to deepen their understanding of those ideas).

Academia

In looking for the root causes of the supposed spread of dangerous left-wing ideas in the United States, the Powell Memorandum pointed the finger squarely at academia. American universities, especially social science departments, were, it claimed, full of subversives. This mattered not just because their research output shaped the intellectual consensus: in fact, this was a secondary problem. Much more concerning was the fact that they pumped out graduates with a left-wing worldview who went on to populate the media, politics, and other well-placed positions in society: "Yale, like every other major college, is graduating scores of bright young men ... who despise the American political and economic system".[63] Today, partly thanks to the determined efforts of the Mont Pelerin Society, it is economics departments that produce the decision-makers of the future, and these departments are dominated by orthodox thinking.

Powell argued that corporations should build counter-power by insisting on "balance": demanding that textbooks be revised to give more prominence to pro-enterprise theories; securing speaking slots on panels (they must "exert whatever degree of pressure—publicly and privately—may be necessary to assure opportunities to speak"); influencing faculty appointments by arguing they should be more diverse. Today, campaigns like the student-led Rethinking Economics and academic-led Reteaching Economics—which sprang up after the 2008 crash, led by young people frustrated that they were still being taught discredited theories with little real-world application—are vital for tipping the scales in the other direction. They advocate for pluralism in the classroom— the teaching of feminist, ecological and Marxist schools of thought—which, as Powell saw, can be an effective way of shifting highly conservative institutions away from orthodoxy. This will take time: the universities remained hostile to Thatcher well into the 1980s, when 364 economists signed a letter opposing her policies and Oxford University refused her an honorary degree.[64]

These campaigns have the potential to gradually transform the academy, as well as building a pipeline of future leaders. Already, alumni of the student movement are represented in the Bank of England, the Treasury, and various other government departments, where they helped set up the civil service network Exploring Economics (discussed in Chapter Four). But we also need more support for progressive academics themselves: strengthening networks for intellectual exchange, and expanding the resources available for alternative economics (something a Labour government could do once in power, just as Blair boosted funding for microeconomics).

Think tanks

The ecosystem of left think tanks is nothing like as strong as the one that laid the foundations for neoliberalism. But the combined resources of the main players—the New Economics Foundation (NEF), Institute for Public Policy

Research (IPPR), and the union-funded Centre for Labour and Social Studies (CLASS)—actually compare rather well to the firepower of the neoliberal think tanks in the 1970s and 1980s. It is too easy on the left to fall back on the trope that the right succeeds by virtue of its almost unlimited resources, that we are the underdogs who can't compete on this terrain. But this isn't always true.

Of course, the neoliberals did have vast amounts of money, not to mention high-level access and influence. But when we look specifically at the experience of the UK's Thatcherite think tanks, the contrast does not hold water. The IEA started out with a "part-time staff of one" and a "cramped office scarcely able to accommodate a visitor". At its peak in the 1980s, it employed 15 people. The Centre for Policy Studies made do with seven. At this time it had a budget of around £150,000.[65] NEF and IPPR currently outgun this considerably in terms of people and resources: both currently have annual expenditures in excess of £3 million (although this funding comes with strings attached, and only a fraction is available for truly radical policy innovation, for which it is true that funding is harder to come by).[66]

Professor Radhika Desai has argued that it was precisely their narrow elite focus, and the high level of centralisation of British political life, that allowed the neoliberal think tanks to embed themselves so successfully into the establishment's thinking even on a shoestring budget. A few dinners with journalists or meetings in Whitehall could go an awfully long way. Left think tanks committed to mass participation face a potentially more resource intensive challenge. Participatory assemblies allowing people to debate the policies that matter to them, economics training events up and down the country— these things cost money. To meet this challenge, we will likely need to leverage our corresponding advantage—hundreds of thousands of grassroots activists who may be willing to chip in small amounts of money to fund new projects.

So what might those new projects look like? The UK's leading neoliberal think tanks had a clear division of labour—not based on subject specialism, but on their strategic role in the political project. The IEA was the respectable, sober-suited academic research outfit. The Centre for Policy Studies (CPS) was essentially the policy wing of Thatcher's Conservative party faction: unlike the IEA, it was not set up as a charity, because it was too close to the Tory party to claim its activities were non-political.

The Adam Smith Institute was the attack dog—the media outrider who would make quick and dirty interventions in the public debate, proposing extreme policy ideas to help shift the centre of gravity to the right. (It still plays this role today, concocting gimmicky media stories like "Tax Freedom Day"—the day each year when the average person stops "working for the state".)[67] These three think tanks were supported by a range of other influential outfits, such as Chatham House on foreign policy and the Royal United Services Institute (RUSI) on defence.

It is not clear that any of the left think tanks currently in existence have a similarly defined sense of their role in the ecosystem. Once upon a time, NEF was the extreme outrider and IPPR was more associated with Labour's soft left—but in today's changed political landscape their respective niches are increasingly unclear. CLASS, being funded by the trade unions, is more overtly close to Labour and could perhaps play a role similar to the CPS. But it seems inevitable that we will also need new organisations—smaller, nimbler, with less institutional baggage and a clearer sense of their purpose. Journals and magazines can play an important role as centres for debate and discussion— as outlets like *New Socialist, Renewal, Red Pepper, Soundings,* and *openDemocracy* already do. The recent takeover of *Tribune* magazine by *Jacobin* is an interesting development on this front. Finally, The World Transformed could come to play a much bigger role in grassroots-led policy development. Already recognised as the most vibrant and energetic forum for the discussion of new progressive ideas, it is now branching out to make this a forum that operates all year round, not just at an annual festival.[68]

Popular education

The World Transformed could also be a key player in the third layer of the Russian doll: popular education programmes. (The 2017 festival included a

strand of events on this theme, which is now a central part of the organisation's strategy.) Workers' education was critical to the socialist movements
of the nineteenth and early twentieth centuries, but has largely died out as
a tradition. Early working-class movement leaders often felt held back by
their lack of formal education, or frustrated by the limitations of the education offered to them. In response, a growing movement arose for workers'
self-education through evening classes and study groups. We need to redis-
cover this tradition if we are to build a powerful and informed mass base for
Corbynism.

One historical precedent is the Plebs League, set up in 1909 by a group
of working-class students at Ruskin College, led by Noah Ablett, a miner
from the Rhondda. Ruskin College was founded as a training ground for
future working-class political and union leaders—but tensions quickly
arose between its academics and philanthropic backers, who thought workers should get an establishment-approved "good" education, and the likes of
Ablett, who insisted that education was always political, and stood for "the
education of the workers in the interests of the workers".[69] Attempts to erad-
icate Marxism from the curriculum became the flashpoint for this dispute,
which the students ultimately lost.

Unable to realise their vision for radical education from below within
Ruskin College, they set about building it elsewhere. The Plebs League set up
socialist evening classes across South Wales, Lancashire, the North East, and
the west of Scotland. By 1927, over a thousand classes were running with more
than 30 thousand students. Several would go on to become leading figures in
the labour movement, including William Mainwaring, who became a Labour
MP, and Arthur Cook, who went on to lead the miners' union. It also helped set
up the Central Labour College in London, intended to rival Ruskin College and
funded by the miners' and railway workers' unions.

Importantly, the League insisted that radical education should be "owned
and controlled by the workers themselves".[70] The leaders of Ruskin College had
made concerted efforts to recruit wealthy philanthropic donors to counteract

the influence of union funding. The Plebs League insisted that workers' education must be funded solely by workers' organisations—but they wanted it to be controlled by the rank and file, not the union bureaucracy. How to fund popular education programmes is a similarly knotty issue today. Now as then, genuinely radical projects can be very difficult to fund sustainably. (The Central Labour College folded in 1929 after the impacts of the Great Depression hit the finances of its sponsoring unions hard.) This in turn gives rise to the danger of educational initiatives becoming "some wealthy backer's plaything"—whether an eccentric individual or a large foundation.[71]

It is also worthwhile to look at how and what the Plebs League taught. They felt it was important for workers to be able to draw on Marxist theoretical frameworks for making sense of the economy, but also that these must be related to their own lived experience, not simply handed down as abstract laws. They placed a high premium on developing their skills as critical thinkers. Drawing on the methods of the Socialist Labour Party (SLP)'s evening classes, this was about more than simply imparting knowledge. Rather, it was about enabling people to think for themselves, to hold their own in debates with confidence, and to spread these capacities to others in their communities. Tom Bell, an organiser with the SLP, had said of their classes: "Every worker who went through the entire session came out a potential tutor for other classes".[72]

Of course, these historical examples were very much rooted in their time and place, with an audience of (largely male) industrial workers. We can also learn a lot from the experience of feminist and black liberation movements. Consciousness-raising groups, pioneered by New York Radical Women, are a good example. While early twentieth century workers' education was predicated on the "science" of Marxism, consciousness-raising draws on the wisdom inherent in people's day-to-day experiences. By sharing these experiences, groups could come to see their personal problems as part of a wider system of oppression, and begin to build an understanding of how to tackle them collectively. These movements have also been influential on the efforts of today's left to build safe and inclusive spaces where everyone's voice can be heard.

In turn, consciousness-raising was partly inspired by the civil rights movement. Groups like the Black Panther Party were pioneers of using education to empower oppressed minorities. Point five of the Party's ten-point platform stated:

> We believe in an educational system that will give to our people a knowledge of the self. If you do not have knowledge of yourself and your position in the society and in the world, then you will have little chance to know anything else.[73]

In 1973 the party set up Oakland Community School, a day school providing community-led education for Black youth, which is still going 50 years later. Echoing the Plebs League's emphasis on building independent thinkers, one former student said, "they taught us how to think, not what to think".[74]

As Hilary Wainwright has argued, this reflects a deep question for the left about the kind of knowledge needed to run society. Is this knowledge to be gained through a scientific understanding of the whole system, or do we also value the "tacit knowledge" people gain through their experience of participating in that system?[75] The emerging consensus in today's left is "both". We can give people useful frameworks to think about the economy—indeed, we have tried to do so in Chapter One—but we reject the neoliberal insistence that economics is a science that can be understood only by experts. Ultimately, what we seek to promote is debate and dissent. This does not mean there is no role for expertise, but it does mean that popular education is about more than imparting that expertise from on high.[76]

The most interesting approaches to popular education today, influenced by the ideas of Brazilian radical educator Paolo Freire, focus on giving people the confidence to engage in economic debates; encouraging them to see that their lived experience gives them just as much right to an opinion as a sharp-suited economist; and equipping them to pass on their knowledge to others. Gramsci would have approved: he saw the generation of a new common sense as a two-way exchange between political or intellectual leaders and the people, in which "every teacher is always a pupil and every pupil is a teacher".[77] NEON's Summer School for activists and campaigners, Global Justice Now's "Demand the Impossible" programme for young people, and Economy's (albeit less political) work with tenants' associations and community groups, are all good examples of this.[78] But they are few and far between. Although interest in popular education is growing across the movement, from the leader's office to organisations like London Young Labour and The World Transformed, this has yet to translate into programmes on anything like the scale needed.

To change this, we need action both within and beyond the Labour Party. Historically, political parties have been key vehicles for popular education—but today, the role of the political education officer in local constituency Labour Parties has often atrophied. It must urgently be rebuilt, putting these officers at the heart of a new, well-resourced network. We need evening classes, weekend retreats, and summer schools for local activists. We need more mass participatory gatherings where people can discuss and debate policy—and better channels for this to inform policy development.

We also need civil society initiatives that reach out far beyond the party membership, and that link theoretical knowledge with practical organising. For instance, we can imagine programmes that bring together renters in a local area to share their experiences, learn about the root causes of the housing crisis, develop practical organising skills, and plan action together—whether it's joining a renters' union, putting pressure on a problem landlord, campaigning for rent control, or establishing a community land trust. The experiences and priorities of these newly organised groups should then be fed directly back into policy development and debates within the Labour Party.

Building leadership

In all of this work, we need to be developing and supporting a strong cohort of movement leaders from diverse backgrounds, with a particular focus on those with under-represented identities. Whether it be media spokespeople, parliamentary candidates, policy staff, or community organisers—there simply hasn't been a strong pipeline of radical leaders for a generation or more. For one thing, with the left so far from power, radicals have simply not been learning how to run things. For another, as we've seen, for decades much of the radical left was suspicious of the whole idea of leadership. This means the pool of talent available for the party and the movement to draw on is worryingly shallow. It also means that those who do act as leaders and spokespeople are under immense strain—especially women and people of colour in the public eye, who often have to deal with sustained backlash on social media.

Building a leadership isn't just about acquiring hard skills, like economics knowledge or media training, although some of that will be needed. (For example, after decades of the Blairite consensus, many MPs openly admit that they are just as much in need of economics training as party members.) It is also about building communities that support and nurture the whole person—groups of people with a shared analysis but a diversity of life experiences, capable of working together from street level to the House of Commons. Crucially, it's about a new style of leadership—one based not on big egos, hierarchies, and strict discipline, but on the ability to collaborate, to listen, and to empower others to lead. Several people we spoke to emphasised the need for better social and emotional support for developing leaders, and for greater emphasis on the soft skills of co-operation, communication, and emotional resilience this kind of leadership demands.

Too little attention has been paid to the role the Mont Pelerin Society played in supporting its own community of leaders. Its story is usually told as one of powerful and sinister figures pulling strings—but in fact, in the early days its members were just as isolated from the political mainstream as many on the radical left felt in the 1990s and 2000s. "The importance of that meeting", as Milton Friedman said of the inaugural 1947 Swiss gathering, which occasioned his first visit to Europe, "was that it showed us that we were not alone".[79] On the left, key figures in the Plebs League saw the role of institutions like the Central Labour College in part as providing for a "little community" where the "interchange of ideas" could take place, before participants went back to their own communities to lead, organise, and educate.[80]

Projects like NEON's Campaign Lab (and more recently, Movement Builders and OrgBuilders) and Campaign Bootcamp have done important work that recognises the importance both of networks and a new style of leadership. We need an equally strong set of leadership programmes for the political and policy space: ones that support social movement leaders to become parliamentary candidates, and parliamentary candidates to become ministers or shadow ministers; or that support the thinkers and special advisors of the future. These are critical to building the umbilical links between movement and party, and the strong bench of what Gramsci called "organic Intellectuals" that we will need in order to succeed. Although the party itself provides some such programmes, they are limited in scope and, according to insiders, not as useful as they could be.

Smucker's insight that left-wing groups are often too focused on their members' sense of belonging doesn't mean that this sense of belonging is not important. Paradoxically, it also doesn't mean that we are necessarily good at looking after our people. The point of leadership pipelines and community networks should not be to provide a comforting space for us to hibernate from reality, but to energise and refresh us to go out into less comforting spaces— be that organising against racism in working-class communities, or weathering right-wing attacks in the media and parliament.

* * *

Transformative shifts in the economy require much more than just a political party ready to take state power. Both the neoliberal experience and the history of early twentieth century socialism point to the importance of a robust exchange of ideas and a strong community of current and future leaders. And the recent history of radical movements in Greece and Spain tells us that independent social movements with deep roots in communities are essential to counteract not just the power of the establishment, but the pressure on any sitting government to abandon its radicalism. Not only that, they are central to the project itself. The democratic economy we are trying to build requires the active participation and empowerment of citizens and the building of local economic alternatives.

The job of the grassroots is not simply to get Labour elected and to defend it in government. Rather, it's the other way around: the job of the Labour Party must be to serve the movements that will help transform the economy, society, and politics. If the Corbyn project is to survive and fulfil its potential, it will need both an informed, empowered, and strategically aware party membership, and a strong ecosystem of social movements outside the party. Our task now is to build both.

CONCLUSION

Today in the United Kingdom, perhaps uniquely among the major industrial economies, a mass left-wing party committed to overturning the status quo stands on the threshold of power. For all the dangers and challenges the current situation presents, it's important to recall how absurdly unlikely this would have seemed just five years ago. As recently as 2015, it looked as though neoliberalism had reasserted itself after the crisis, more unassailably dominant than ever, and there was little prospect of the Labour Party seriously trying to change this. Even the social movements committed to challenging neoliberalism were stuck in opposition mode, struggling to articulate a positive alternative.

Reminding ourselves just how far we have come in a few short years should both encourage us, and strengthen our resolve when we consider how far we still have to go. In this context, the biggest risk is not that Corbyn's Labour cannot win an election. Politics today is nothing if not volatile: if we do not win today, we may yet win tomorrow, especially if we learn and strengthen as we go. The biggest risk is that Labour wins power but loses the prize: that it is unable, for whatever reason, to survive in government and to implement a radical agenda. This scenario truly would spell the end of the UK left's hopes for a generation, as well as paving the way for the far right to step into the breach. We all have a responsibility to ensure that does not come to pass.

At its best, the Corbyn project amounts to nothing less than a democratic transformation of the economy and of politics—informed as much by the participatory ideals and solutions emerging from twenty-first century social movements as by the inheritance of an older socialist tradition. It is about transferring power and ownership from the few to the many—from economic elites to ordinary citizens—through an exciting array of new and old democratic forms, from worker ownership and public banks to land trusts and municipal energy companies.

History tells us that transformative shifts of power and ownership on this scale require much more than simply a government with a vision. They require a movement, inside and outside government, with a strong sense of where it is going and how to get there. They require clarity about the relative strengths of those from whom we are seeking to take power and those to whom we are seeking to give it. They cannot be achieved overnight, or even in a single term in government. Some sense of long-term strategy is therefore essential. Also crucial is action to make sure that the institutions and levers of government are reformed so as to be capable of enacting this strategy.

This does not mean having a strategic blueprint perfected in advance and carved into stone, which must then be adhered to rigidly at all times. Rather, it is about having a clear sense of what we are trying to change, and what it will take to achieve it.

Hindsight is a wonderful thing, and the rearview mirror can make shifts like the neoliberal revolution seem straightforward and clean-cut: either a historical inevitability or an intentional coup, ruthlessly planned and executed with military precision. And it's a peculiar disease of the UK left to exaggerate the strategic brilliance and power of our opponents while underestimating our own assets. In fact, the process of shifting a dominant paradigm is always emergent, uneven, and replete with setbacks. To those in the thick of the neoliberal project, things often seemed chaotic and success certainly did not seem inevitable.

We must not forget how messy and contingent large-order systemic change can be. Desai describes Thatcher's leadership victory as "something of a chance affair"—not so far removed from the strange set of circumstances that produced Corbyn's leadership, against the expectations of almost everybody, not least of Corbyn himself. Like Corbyn, Thatcher's faction were for a long time insurgents within their own party, having to fight their opponents within as well as without, and not enjoying the party's full support even once in government. At the end of Thatcher's first term, the jury was still out on what she had achieved. In 1983, Arthur Seldon, a key figure at the IEA, did not even vote for her, so frustrated was he by her lack of radicalism. In 1984, Sir John Hoskyns could still bemoan the absence of precisely the kind of hard-nosed battle planning we admire the neoliberals for today:

> The much used word "strategy" is not understood as the step-by-step removal of constraints (administrative, political, economic) so as to make an insoluble problem soluble. There is a confusion between winning today's battles, which is one thing, and making tomorrow's battles winnable, which is quite another.[1]

The difficult and unpredictable nature of transformative change is even more starkly illustrated by the case of Chile, the original laboratory for neoliberal policies. Between 1975 and 1989, under the Pinochet right-wing military takeover and at the urging of Chicago School economists, Chile implemented two waves of privatisation. The first wave was a near-total failure. Not only companies nationalised by Allende but a host of older public concerns—including 16 banks and thousands of mines, real estate holdings, and agro-industrial enterprises—were auctioned off to elites at bargain-basement prices. Despite the accolades afforded the "Chilean miracle" by Milton Friedman and others, the actual results of this policy were a major embarrassment. All but five of the banks and many of the other enterprises failed and had to be taken back into public hands. By 1983 the government-controlled portion of the economy once again equalled that under Allende, with critics mockingly referring to a "Chicago Road to Socialism". Only with the second wave of privatisation, beginning in 1985, did the transfer of these firms to the private sector stick.[2]

These lessons from history should reassure us. Our situation, shambolic and under-prepared as it can often seem, is perhaps not as different from that of previous transformative projects as we might imagine. We will never feel perfectly ready, and it is not always possible to get everything right first time. We must be prepared to experiment, fail, and try again. We must be comfortable with debate and dissent within the movement during this process: as there was under both Attlee and Thatcher, there will always be both those urging caution and pragmatism to stabilise the project and prevent it from collapsing, and those urging it on faster to achieve its radical potential.

In particular, we must be ready to adapt to changing circumstances—including resistance, reaction, and the threat of economic dislocation. Those who have power do not give it up lightly. Labour may hope that its economic agenda contains enough for some of the forces of capital to welcome or at least accept it, perhaps encouraged by the alternative of a disastrous Tory Brexit. But we need to be prepared that this gamble may not pay off. In this context, a strategy for neutralising the power of vested interests—and especially that of global financial markets—becomes critical.

Ultimately, the success of such a strategy will depend on some form of democratic counter-power. Democracy is both the means and the end of this political project. And extending democracy is not only its *raison d'être*: it is also its most powerful weapon against both institutional inertia and overt reaction. We transform the state not simply by replacing neoliberal technocrats with progressive technocrats (though we will certainly need to do this), but by radically democratising and decentralising it. We transform society not simply by taking control of the state, but by building new sources of people power outside it, capable of building, deepening, and defending the project in communities, in workplaces, in the policy debate, and in the media.

CONCLUSION

In doing this, we must constantly keep in mind that "we the people" is a rhetorical sword that can be wielded by right-wing nationalists just as much as by democratic socialists. Our democratic "we" needs to be explicitly inclusive of migrants, people of colour, and all those excluded or demonised by fascism. Defending and acting in solidarity with these communities must go hand in hand with building a new, democratic economy and society.

The mass base of Corbynism thus has a pivotal role to play—and not simply as foot soldiers whose task is to propel a left-wing government into power and keep it there. Rather, we should see things the other way around: the point of securing a left-wing government is to use the levers of state power to transform both the state itself and the economy in ways that empower us all.

Jeremy Corbyn is not the movement's saviour, nor can any leader be passively relied upon to bring about the change we need. For the project to succeed we must all have a clear sense of the world we are trying to build and the role we can each play in creating it. The words of the poet Percy Bysshe Shelley, often repeated and shared during the 2017 general election campaign, are as appropriate as ever in reminding us of the true agents of transformative change:

> *Rise like Lions after slumber*
> *In unvanquishable number—*
> *Shake your chains to earth like dew*
> *Which in sleep had fallen on you—*
> *Ye are many—they are few.*[3]

MOVEMENT DISCUSSION GUIDE

The purpose of this book is to promote discussion and debate in the movement about the strategic challenges facing the UK left on the road to systemic change. This guide is designed to help you continue the conversation. We encourage you to get together with a group of friends, with your local party, or with whatever grassroots groups you organise with to discuss the questions below, or others that may occur to you. The guide is there to be used however you like, but can be followed as a self-guided five-session reading group, discussing one chapter per session. This can also be adapted for those who haven't read the book using the questions that relate to the shorter articles and videos we've signposted. You can find all this content and more online at http://www.peoplegetready.org.uk.

Chapter One: People Get Ready!

Questions

1. Go around the group and each say a few words about what drew you to left politics and the change you want to see in the world. How optimistic do you feel about the prospects for change today? What do you see as the greatest challenges?

2. What does the "democratic economy" mean to you? Do you agree that this is an important part of the change we need? What other ideas do you think are important?

3. Thatcher said: "Economics are the method; the object is to change the heart and soul". What did she mean? Do you think this is true for the left today?

4. Choose an area that matters to you, or that your group has been working on (eg housing, work, healthcare). How has neoliberalism affected this area? How might the left undo this legacy and build a more democratic economy in this area?

Resources

Joe Guinan & Martin O'Neill, "The institutional turn: Labour's new political economy": http://renewal.org.uk/articles/the-institutional-turn-labours-new-political-economy.

Chapter Two: Get Ready for Change

Questions

1. Go around the group and each say one thing that struck you when reading this chapter—a story or quote you liked, something that made you think differently or that you disagreed with.

2. What do you think the experiences of the Attlee and Thatcher governments have to teach us about how governments can achieve transformative change? How do these lessons apply to Labour today?

3. Choose one of either the Ridley Report or the Powell Memorandum. Read it and discuss what you think today's left could learn from its approach. What would a modern left version of this strategy look like?

4. Choose an area that matters to you, or that your group has been working on (eg housing, work, healthcare). What vested interests would need to be overcome in order to transform this area? What sources of power can the left draw on?

Resources

The Ridley Plan: https://www.margaretthatcher.org/document/110795
The Powell Memorandum: https://scholarlycommons.law.wlu.edu/powellmemo/

Chapter Three: Get Ready for Reaction

Questions

1. This chapter deals with some quite technical economic issues. Go around the group and each say one thing you found confusing or would like to understand better. Make a list and discuss how you might find answers to your questions.

2. In the video, Grace Blakeley argues that Labour needs to take on the banks today just as Thatcher took on the unions in the 1980s. Do you agree? If so, what does this mean in terms of both policy and organising?

3. Do you think a Labour government would be likely to face serious backlash from vested interests, including the City of London, or do you think there are ways this could be avoided? If so, what might the government and the movement need to do to prepare and respond?

4. Read the article "John McDonnell is right: We need a new left internationalism". This develops the chapter's argument that international co-operation will be needed to seriously tame the forces of global capital. Do you agree? If so, what should we be doing to help build a new political consensus internationally as well as at home? And how does this relate to surviving in a hostile international environment in the meantime?

Resources

Video: Grace Blakeley at The World Transformed: https://twitter.com/i/status/1044153784325345281

Recording: The World Transformed session, "A Movement in Government": https://soundcloud.com/theworldtransformed/a-movement-in-government-bad-audio-quality

Christine Berry: "John McDonnell is right—we need a new left internationalism": https://www.versobooks.com/blogs/4086-john-mcdonnell-is-right-we-need-a-new-left-internationalism

Chapter Four: Get Ready to Govern

Questions

1. Choose one of the three suggested readings below (or use your reading of Chapter Four). Discuss how you think the Treasury might act as a barrier to radical change and what can be done to overcome this.
2. This chapter argues that in order to transform the economy, we need to radically democratise the state, and that this will only succeed if it is demanded from below. Do you agree?
3. If so, what should the movement be doing to build pressure for change—in the public debate, within the Labour Party or at local level? What does this mean for your group or organisation right now?

Resources

The Kerslake Review of the Treasury: http://www.industry-forum.org/wp-content/uploads/2017/03/9076_17-Kerslake-Review-of-the-Treasury-_-final_v2.pdf

Dave Powell, "Transforming the Treasury—the biggest and best idea of all": https://www.opendemocracy.net/ourkingdom/david-powell/transforming-treasury-biggest-and-best-idea-of-all

Sir Nicholas Macpherson, "The Treasury View: A testament of experience": https://www.gov.uk/government/speeches/speech-by-the-permanent-secretary-to-the-treasury-the-treasury-view-a-testament-of-experience.

Chapter Five: Get Ready to Organise

Questions

1. In the chapter, a former Syriza member says: "Governments are inside the state and have big pressure from the state—you have to create balance and counter power, pressure from the movements and the left". Do you agree?

2. What do you think are the different roles of political parties and social movements in achieving social change? What do the experiences of Podemos and Syriza teach us about this?

3. Read Ash Sarkar's article and discuss what struck you about it. What could organisers in your area do to help build the kind of grassroots movements she talks about? What initiatives are already happening that you think help to do this and how could you support them?

4. In the video, John McDonnell talks about the ways in which radical people came together in the past to build their understanding of the world and how to change it, and how we can do the same today. What is currently happening in your local area that plays this role? If there isn't enough happening, how could you make it happen?

Resources

Video: John McDonnell on political education: https://twitter.com/TWT_NOW/status/1040671839100563457

Recording: The World Transformed session, "Making the case for political education": https://www.youtube.com/watch?v=ZaiN5vtWFjA&feature=youtu.be

Ash Sarkar: "This isn't just a culture war—we need a radical anti-fascist movement right now": https://www.theguardian.com/commentisfree/2018/aug/21/anti-fascist-movement-far-right

Rosie Baines: "Framing the economy – how to win the case for a better system": https://www.opendemocracy.net/neweconomics/framing-economy-win-case-better-system/

ENDNOTES

Foreword: Owen Jones

1   Sarah Butler, "Nearly 10 million Britons are in insecure work, says union", *The Guardian*, 5 June 2017.
2   Patrick Collinson, "Four in 10 right-to-buy homes are now owned by private landlords", *The Guardian*, 8 December 2017.
3   Jonathan Ford, "Water privatisation looks little more than an organised rip-off", *Financial Times*, 10 September 2017.
4   Ofwat, "The economic regulation of the water sector", National Audit Office, 14 October 2015, https://www.nao.org.uk/wp-content/uploads/2014/07/The-economic-regulation-of-the-water-sector.pdf; Gill Plimmer, "Privatised water costs consumers £2.3bn more a year, study says", *Financial Times*, 6 June 2017.
5   Hansard, https://publications.parliament.uk/pa/cm199293/cmhansrd/1993-02-09/Orals-2.html.
6   Andrew Cumbers, *Renewing Public Ownership: Constructing a Democratic Economy in the Twenty-First Century*, CLASS: Centre for Labour and Social Studies, 10 October 2017, 9, http://classonline.org.uk/pubs/item/renewing-public-ownership1.
7   Matthew Elliott and James Kanagasooriam, *Public opinion in the post-Brexit era: Economic attitudes in modern Britain*, London, Legatum Institute, October 2017, https://www.li.com/activities/publications/public-opinion-in-the-post-brexit-era-economic-attitudes-in-modern-britain.

Introduction

1   Antonio Gramsci, *Selections from the Prison Notebooks*, trans. Quintin Hoare and Geoffrey Nowell Smith (London: Lawrence & Wishart 1971), 276.
2   Jeremy Corbyn, "Speech to Labour Party Conference", 27 September 2017, https://labour.org.uk/press/jeremy-corbyn-speech-to-labour-party-conference/.
3   Geoff Eley, *Forging Democracy: The History of the Left in Europe, 1850–2000*, (Oxford: Oxford University Press 2002), ix.
4   Gary Younge, "Journalists' lack of curiosity about Corbyn was professional malpractice", *Prospect Magazine*, 16 June 2017, https://www.prospectmagazine.co.uk/magazine/journalists-brazen-dismissal-of-corbyn-was-professional-malpractice.

5   Tom Mills, "It Was a Fantasy: Centrist Political Commentators in the Age of Corbynism", *New Socialist*, 12 June 2017, https://newsocialist.org.uk/it-was-a-fantasy/.

6   Pankaj Mishra, *Age of Anger: A History of the Present* (New York: Farrar, Straus and Giroux 2017).

7   The Luddites were the original "machine-breakers", reacting against changes in the capitalist mode of production that posed an existential threat to their way of life. E. P. Thompson's magisterial study helped rescue them from "the enormous condescension of posterity": see E. P. Thompson, *The Making of the English Working Class* (London: Victor Gollancz 1965), 12, 547–602.

8   Naomi Klein, *The Shock Doctrine: The Rise of Disaster Capitalism* (New York: Picador 2007).

9   Barry Eichengreen and Peter Temin, "The Gold Standard and the Great Depression", *Contemporary European History*, Vol. 9, No. 2 (2000), 183–207.

10 Alex Nunns, *The Candidate: Jeremy Corbyn's Improbable Path to Power* (London: O/R Books 2018), second edition, 287–90.

11 Monique Charles, "Grime Labour", *Soundings*, No. 68, Spring 2018, 40–52.

12 Enzo Traverso, *Left-Wing Melancholia: Marxism, History, and Memory* (New York: Columbia University Press 2016).

13 John McDonnell, *The Economic Policy of the Labour Party: Speech to the Marx Memorial Library*, 2 October 2018.

14 R. H. Tawney quoted in Ross Terrill, *R. H. Tawney and His Times: Socialism as Fellowship* (Cambridge, MA: Harvard University Press 1973), 173.

15 Dieter Plehwe, "Introduction", in Philip Mirowski and Dieter Plehwe, *The Road from Mont Pèlerin: The Making of the Neoliberal Thought Collective* (Cambridge, MA: Harvard University Press 2009), 15.

16 Daniel Stedman Jones, *Masters of the Universe: Hayek, Friedman, and the Birth of Neoliberal Politics* (Princeton: Princeton University Press 2012), 134–35; Kim Phillips-Fein, *Invisible Hands: The Businessmen's Crusade Against the New Deal* (New York: W. W. Norton 2009), 43–44.

17 Milton Friedman, *Capitalism and Freedom* (Chicago: University of Chicago Press 2002), 40th anniversary edition, xiv.

Chapter One

1   Ben Sellers, "#JezWeDid", in Tom Unterrainer (ed.), *Corbyn's Campaign* (Nottingham: Spokesman 2016), 28.

2   Ibid., 37.

3   Andrew Lilico, "All that matters now is stopping Corbyn", *CapX*, 12 June 2017, https://capx.co/all-that-matters-now-is-stopping-corbyn/.

4   Harriet Agerholm, "Jeremy Corbyn was just 2,227 votes away from chance to be Prime Minister", *The Independent*, 9 June 2017, https://www.independent.co.uk/

ENDNOTES

news/uk/politics/corbyn-election-results-votes-away-prime-minister-theresa-may-hung-parliament-a7782581.html.

5   For UK inequality data, see *World Inequality Database,* http://wid.world/country/united-kingdom/.

6   Marjorie Kelly and Ted Howard, *The Making of a Democratic Economy: Building Prosperity for the Many, Not Just the Few* (San Francisco: Berrett-Koehler 2019), forthcoming.

7   See Philip Mirowski and Dieter Plehwe, *The Road from Mont Pèlerin: The Making of the Neoliberal Thought Collective* (Cambridge, MA: Harvard University Press 2009).

8   Quinn Slobodian, *Globalists: The End of Empire and the Birth of Neoliberalism* (London: Harvard University Press 2018).

9   Francis Fukuyama, *The End of History and the Last Man* (New York: The Free Press 1992).

10   Saskia Sassen, "A savage sorting of winners and losers, and beyond", in Craig Calhoun and Georgi Derluguian (eds.), *Aftermath: A New Global Economic Order* (New York: Social Science Research Council and New York University Press 2011), 21.

11   Karl Polanyi, *The Great Transformation: The Political and Economic Origins of Our Time* (Boston: Beacon Press 2001), 3.

12   Benjamin Kentish, "Forty percent of homes sold under Right to Buy now in the hands of private landlords, new analysis reveals", *The Independent*, 8 December 2017, https://www.independent.co.uk/news/uk/politics/right-to-buy-homes-sold-private-landlords-latest-figures-rent-a8098126.html.

13   For example, only 5 per cent of British Gas shares are still held by individuals. See https://www.centrica.com/investors/investor-information/ownership-profile.

14   Mariana Mazzucato, *The Value of Everything: Making and Taking in the Global Economy* (London: Allen Lane 2018).

15   Stephen A. Marglin and Juliet B. Schor (eds.), *The Golden Age of Capitalism: Reinterpreting the Postwar Experience* (Oxford: Oxford University Press 1990).

16   Thomas Piketty, *The Economics of Inequality* (Cambridge, MA: Harvard University Press 2015), 66.

17   Kelly and Howard, *The Making of a Democratic Economy*, forthcoming.

18   The *Elements of the Democratic Economy* series from the Next System Project distils this landscape of theoretical exploration and real-world practice into concise summaries describing each of the institutions involved, assessing their transformative characteristics and potential, and providing on-the-ground examples and a sense of the challenges yet to be overcome. See https://thenextsystem.org/elements. For the origins of some of this thinking, see Gar Alperovitz, *America Beyond Capitalism: Reclaiming Our Wealth, Our Liberty & Our Democracy* (Takoma Park, MD: Democracy Collaborative Press 2011); and Gar Alperovitz, *What Then Must We Do? Straight Talk About the Next American Revolution* (White River Junction, VT: Chelsea Green 2013).

19   Joe Guinan, "Bring back the Institute for Workers' Control", *Renewal*, Vol. 23, No. 4, 2015, 11–36.

20   Joe Guinan, "Social democracy in the age of austerity and resistance: the radical potential of democratising capital", *Renewal*, Vol. 20, No. 4, 2012, 9–19.

21   Joe Guinan and Thomas M. Hanna, "Democratic Ownership in the New Economy", in John McDonnell (ed.), *Economics for The Many* (London: Verso 2018), 108–25.

22   "Corbynomics: The Great Transformation", *The Economist*, 19 May 2018, 19–20. *The Economist* is among the few mainstream publications to pay "Corbynomics" the serious attention it deserves, thanks to the reporting of Duncan Robinson and Callum Williams. See also "Jeremy Corbyn's Model Town", *The Economist*, 21 October 2017, 56–57.

23   André Gorz, *Strategy for Labor: A Radical Proposal* (Boston: Beacon Press 1967), 6.

24   Joe Guinan and Thomas M. Hanna, "Polanyi against the whirlwind", *Renewal*, Vol. 25, No. 1, 2017, 5–12.

25   Labour Party, *For the Many Not the Few*, May 2017, https://labour.org.uk/wp-content/uploads/2017/10/labour-manifesto-2017.pdf; Labour Party, *Alternative Models of Ownership: Report to the Shadow Chancellor and the Shadow Secretary of State for Business, Energy and Industrial Strategy*, June 2017, https://labour.org.uk/wp-content/uploads/2017/10/Alternative-Models-of-Ownership.pdf.

26   See Joe Guinan and Martin O'Neill, "The institutional turn: Labour's new political economy", *Renewal*, Vol. 26, No. 2, 2018, 5–16.

27   Labour Party, *For the Many Not the Few*, 19.

28   Andrew Cumbers, *Reclaiming Public Ownership: Making Space for Economic Democracy* (London: Zed Books 2012), 60.

29   Matthew Elliott and James Kanagasooriam, *Public opinion in the post-Brexit era: Economic attitudes in modern Britain*, London, Legatum Institute, October 2017, https://www.li.com/activities/publications/public-opinion-in-the-post-brexit-era-economic-attitudes-in-modern-britain.

30   Thomas M. Hanna and Joe Guinan, "Democracy and decentralisation are their watchwords: for Corbyn and McDonnell, it's municipal socialism reinvented", *openDemocracy*, 25 March 2016, https://www.opendemocracy.net/uk/thomas-hanna-joe-guinan/democracy-and-decentralisation-are-their-watchwords-for-corbyn-and-mcdonn.

31   Cumbers, *Reclaiming Public Ownership*, 21.

32   Kenneth O. Morgan, *Labour in Power 1945–1951* (Oxford: Oxford University Press 1985), 96–97.

33   Herbert Morrison, *Socialisation and Transport* (London: Constable 1933), 224–25.

34   Jim Tomlinson, *Democratic Socialism and Economic Policy: The Attlee Years, 1945–1951* (Cambridge: Cambridge University Press 1997), 112.

35   Reuben Kelf-Cohen, *British Nationalisation 1945–1973* (London: Macmillan 1973), 59.

36   Clive Jenkins, *Power at the Top: A Critical Survey of the Nationalised Industries* (Westport, CT: Greenwood Press 1976), 16–21.

37   Cumbers, *Reclaiming Public Ownership*, 21. See also Joe Guinan, "Who's afraid of public ownership?" *Renewal*, Vol. 21, No. 4, 2013, 77–84.

38   David Coates, *The Labour Party and the Struggle for Socialism* (Cambridge: Cambridge University Press 1975), 50. See also Guinan, "Bring Back the Institute for Workers' Control".

39   Raymond Williams, *The Long Revolution* (Harmondsworth: Penguin 1965), 330. "In being dragged back to the processes of the old system, yet at the same time offered as witnesses of the new", the nationalised industries, in Williams' bleak verdict, "so deeply damaged any alternative principle in the economy as to have emptied British socialism of any effective meaning".

40   Michael Foot, *Aneurin Bevan: A Biography, Volume Two: 1945–1960* (New York: Atheneum 1974), 106.

41   Hilary Wainwright, *A New Politics from the Left* (Cambridge: Polity 2018), 133, *n. 14*.

42   Nigel Morris, "Labour leadership race: Rivals turn on Jeremy Corbyn in row over Clause IV", *The Independent*, 9 August 2015, https://www.independent.co.uk/news/uk/politics/labour-leadership-rivals-turn-on-jeremy-corbyn-in-row-over-clause-iv-10447690.html; Joe Guinan and Thomas M. Hanna, "Don't believe the Corbyn bashers—the economic case against public ownership is mostly fantasy", *openDemocracy*, 9 September 2015, https://www.opendemocracy.net/ourkingdom/joe-guinan-thomas-m-hanna/dont-believe-corbyn-bashers-economic-case-against-public-owners.

43   Hanna and Guinan, "Democracy and decentralisation are their watchwords".

44   Labour Party Consultation Paper: Democratic Public Ownership, https://labour.org.uk/wp-content/uploads/2018/09/Democratic-public-ownership-consulation.pdf.

45   For a good introduction to the ideas of "energy democracy", see Platform's *Energy Beyond Neoliberalism*: https://www.lwbooks.co.uk/sites/default/files/09_energy-beyondneoliberalism.pdf.

46   Labour Party, *Alternative Models of Ownership*.

47   Ted Howard and Martin O'Neill, "Beyond extraction: The political power of community wealth building", *Renewal,* Vol. 26, No. 2, 2018, 46–53.

48   Aditya Chakrabortty, "In 2011 Preston hit rock bottom. Then it took back control", *The Guardian*, 31 January 2018, https://www.theguardian.com/commentisfree/2018/jan/31/preston-hit-rock-bottom-took-back-control.

49   "Jeremy Corbyn's Model Town", *The Economist*, 21 October 2017, 56–57; Matthew Brown and Martin O'Neill, "The Road to Socialism is the A59: on the Preston Model", *Renewal*, Vol. 24, No. 2, 2016, 69–78.

50   Marjorie Kelly, Sarah McKinley, and Violeta Duncan, "Community wealth building: America's emerging asset-based approach to city economic development", *Renewal*, Vol. 24, No. 2, 2016, 51–68.

51   George Eaton, "How Preston—the UK's "most improved city"—became a success story for Corbynomics", *New Statesman*, 1 November 2018, https://www

.newstatesman.com/politics/uk/2018/11/how-preston-uk-s-most-improved-city-became-success-story-corbynomics.

52   Toby Helm, "McDonnell: Labour will give power to workers through 'ownership funds'", *The Observer*, 8 September 2018, https://www.theguardian.com/politics/2018/sep/08/john-mcdonnell-labour-proposal-workers-ownership-funds.

53   Rudolf Meidner, *Employee Investment Funds: An Approach to Collective Capital Formation* (London: George Allen & Unwin 1978).

54   Adrian Zimmerman, "Economic democracy instead of more capitalism: core historical concepts reconsidered", in John Callaghan et al. (eds.), *In Search of Social Democracy: Responses to Crisis and Modernisation*, (Manchester: Manchester University Press 2009), 279.

55   Mathew Lawrence, Andrew Pendleton, and Sara Mahmoud, *Co-operatives Unleashed: Doubling the Size of the UK's Co-operative Sector*, New Economics Foundation report to the Co-operative Party, 3 July 2018, p. 42, https://neweconomics.org/uploads/files/co-ops-unleashed.pdf.

56   See Joe Guinan, "Socialising Capital: Looking Back on the Meidner Plan", *International Journal of Public Policy*, forthcoming 2019. See also Jonas Pontusson, *The Limits to Social Democracy: Investment Politics in Sweden* (Ithaca: Cornell University Press 1992); Rudolf Meidner, "Why Did the Swedish Model Fail?" *Socialist Register*, Vol. 29, 1993, 211–28.

57   Peter Gowan, "Labour has a Plan", *Jacobin*, 2 November 2018, https://www.jacobinmag.com/2018/11/labour-party-inclusive-ownership-funds-corbyn-mcdonnell.

Chapter Two

1   Charlie Cooper, "Future Labour government should be more radical than Attlee, says Shadow Chancellor", *The Independent*, 21 May 2016, https://www.independent.co.uk/news/uk/politics/labour-government-jeremy-corbyn-most-radical-ever-shadow-chancellor-john-mcdonnell-clement-attlee-a7041311.html.

2   Richard Saville, "Commanding Heights: The Nationalisation Programme", in Jim Fyrth (ed.), *Labour's High Noon: The Government and the Economy 1945–51* (London: Lawrence & Wishart 1993), 37–38; Robert Millward, "The 1940s Nationalizations in Britain: Means to an End or Means of Production?" *Economic History Review*, 1997, Vol. 50, No. 2, 210–12.

3   For a particularly dim view of the Attlee government's record, see Syndicalist Workers' Federation, *How Labour Governed 1945–1951*, Direct Action Pamphlets No. 5, *no date*, reproduced at: https://libcom.org/files/How%20Labour%20governed%201945-51.pdf.

4   Saville, "Commanding Heights: The Nationalisation Programme", 37.

5   Doug McEachern, *A Class Against Itself: Power and the Nationalisation of the British Steel Industry* (Cambridge: Cambridge University Press 1980), 65.

ENDNOTES

6   Willie Thompson, *The Long Death of British Labourism: Interpreting a Political Culture* (London: Pluto Press 1993), 51–52.
7   Brian J. McCormick, *Industrial Relations in the Coal Industry* (London, Macmillan 1979), 32–42.
8   David Greasley, "The coal industry: images and realities on the road to nationalisation", in Robert Millward and John Singleton (eds.), *The Political Economy of Nationalisation in Britain 1920–50* (Cambridge: Cambridge University Press 1995), 39.
9   Kelf-Cohen, *British Nationalisation 1945–1973*, 20. See also Ben Fine, *The Coal Question: Political Economy and Industrial Change for the Nineteenth Century to the Present Day* (London: Routledge 1990).
10 Greasley, "The coal industry: images and realities on the road to nationalisation", 59.
11 John Singleton, "Labour, the Conservatives and nationalisation", in Robert Millward and John Singleton (eds.), *The Political Economy of Nationalisation in Britain 1920–50* (Cambridge: Cambridge University Press 1995), 28.
12 Arnold A. Rogow, *The Labour Government and British Industry 1945–1951* (Oxford: Basil Blackwell 1955), 155.
13 Richard Saville, "Commanding Heights: The Nationalisation Programme", in Jim Fyrth (ed.), *Labour's High Noon: The Government and the Economy 1945–51* (London: Lawrence & Wishart 1993), 43.
14 Kenneth O. Morgan, *Labour in Power 1945–1951* (Oxford: Oxford University Press 1985), 105.
15 Emanuel Shinwell, *Conflict Without Malice: An Autobiography* (London: Odhams Press 1955), 172–73.
16 Morgan, *Labour in Power 1945–1951*, 105.
17 Martyn Sloman, *Socialising Public Ownership* (London: Macmillan 1978), 20.
18 Cumbers, *Reclaiming Public Ownership*, 20.
19 Robert Millward, "The Nature of State Enterprise in Britain", in Franco Amatori, Robert Millward, and Pier Angelo Toninelli (eds.), *Reappraising State-Owned Enterprise: A Comparison of the UK and Italy* (Routledge: London 2011), 24–27. A comprehensive 1903 survey of the evidence by Millward and his colleagues offered as its first conclusion that "there is no systematic evidence that public enterprises are less cost effective than private firms". Robert Millward, David Parker, Leslie Rosenthal, Michael T. Sumner and Neville Topham, *Public Sector Economics* (London: Longman 1983), 258. Nor are they alone: for a full examination of the efficiency debate regarding public ownership, see Thomas M. Hanna, *Our Common Wealth: The Return of Public Ownership in the United States* (Manchester: Manchester University Press 2018), 36–50. For a summary of the measure of total factor productivity, see Diego Comin, "Total Factor Productivity", in Steven Derlauf and Larry Blume (eds.), *The New Palgrave Dictionary of Economics* (Hampshire: Palgrave Macmillan 2008), second edition, 260.
20 Robin Blackburn, *Banking on Death, or, Investing in Life: The History and Future of Pensions* (London, Verso 2002), 506.

21   Guinan, "Social democracy in the age of austerity and resistance".
22   David Parker, *The Official History of Privatisation, Volume I: The Formative Years 1970–1987* (Abingdon: Routledge 2009), 1.
23   Christopher Johnson, *The Economy Under Mrs Thatcher 1979–1990* (London: Penguin 1991), 144.
24   Ernst & Young, *Privatization: Investing in State-Owned Enterprises Around the World* (New York: John Wiley & Sons 1994), 4.
25   HM Treasury, *Implementing Privatisation: The UK Experience* (London: HM Treasury 2002), p. 4.
26   Parker, *The Official History of Privatisation, Volume I*, 1.
27   Andrew Gamble, *The Free Economy and the Strong State: The Politics of Thatcherism* (Durham, NC: Duke University Press 1988), v.
28   Margaret Thatcher, *The Downing Street Years* (New York: HarperCollins 1993), 677.
29   Richard Heffernan, "UK Privatisation Revisited: Ideas and Policy Change, 1979–92", *The Political Quarterly*, 2005, Vol. 76, No. 2, 267.
30   Alexander Gallas, *The Thatcherite Offensive: A Neo-Poulantzasian Analysis* (Chicago: Haymarket 2016), 201.
31   Stephen Wilks, *The Political Power of the Business Corporation* (Cheltenham: Edward Elgar 2013), 115.
32   Parker, *The Official History of Privatisation, Volume I*, 448.
33   Ibid., 290–91.
34   Ibid., 290–91, 317, 541 *n. 5*.
35   Wilks, *The Political Power of the Business Corporation*, 124.
36   John Boughton, *Municipal Dreams: The Rise and Fall of Council Housing* (London: Verso 2018), 169.
37   David Parker, *The Official History of Privatisation, Volume II: Popular Capitalism, 1987–1997* (Abingdon: Routledge 2012), 505, *table 18.3*.
38   Wilks, *The Political Power of the Business Corporation*, 124.
39   Margaret Thatcher, "Interview for *Sunday Times*", 3 May 1981, Margaret Thatcher Foundation, https://www.margaretthatcher.org/document/104475.
40   In this, it may have been modelled at least in part on the Fabian Society, given Friedrich Hayek's central role in its creation and the esteem in which he held Beatrice Webb's ability to shape public opinion. See Nick Bosanquet, *After the New Right* (London: Heinemann 1983), 26, 41 *n. 3*. See also Quinn Slobodian, *Globalists: The End of Empire and the Birth of Neoliberalism* (London: Harvard University Press 2018), 124.
41   Stedman Jones, *Masters of the Universe*, 134–35.
42   Phillips-Fein, *Invisible Hands*, 157–58.
43   Lewis F. Powell, Jr, *Attack on the American Free Enterprise System*, U.S. Chamber of Commerce, 23 August 1971, available from the Powell archives at Washington and Lee School of Law, http://law2.wlu.edu/powellarchives/page.asp?pageid=1251.
44   Ibid.

45   Ibid.
46   Phillips-Fein, *Invisible Hands*, 160–162. Nancy MacLean, *Democracy in Chains: The Deep History of the Radical Right's Stealth Plan for America* (New York: Viking 2017), 125–26.
47   Jane Mayer, *Dark Money: The Hidden History of the Billionaires Behind the Rise of the Radical Right* (New York: Anchor Books 2017).
48   Nicholas Ridley, *'My Style of Government': The Thatcher Years* (London: Fontana 1992), 2–3.
49   Conservative Research Department, Economic Reconstruction Group, *Final Report of the Nationalised Industries Policy Group*, 30 June 1977, available at Margaret Thatcher Foundation, https://www.margaretthatcher.org/document/110795.
50   Henk Overbeek, *Global Capitalism and National Decline: The Thatcher Decade in Perspective* (London: Unwin Hyman 1990), 154.
51   Conservative Research Department, Economic Reconstruction Group, *Final Report of the Nationalised Industries Policy Group*, 22–23.
52   Ibid., 20.
53   Ibid., 15.
54   Overbeek, *Global Capitalism and National Decline*, 188.
55   "Appomattox or civil war", *The Economist*, May 27, 1978.
56   Conservative Research Department, *Final Report of the Nationalised Industries Policy Group*, 24.
57   Ibid., 11, 25.
58   Ibid., 25.
59   Ridley, *'My Style of Government'*, 4; Gallas, *The Thatcherite Offensive*, 81.
60   John Hoskyns et al., *Stepping Stones*, 1977 (private memo, available online at https://c59574e9047e61130f13-3f71d0fe2b653c4f00f32175760e96e7.ssl.cf1.rackcdn.com/5B6518B5823043FE9D7C54846CC7FE31.pdf.
61   Gallas, *The Thatcherite Offensive*, 113.
62   Ibid., 114.
63   Overbeek, *Global Capitalism and National Decline*, 188.
64   Antonio Gramsci, "War of Position and War of Manoeuvre", in David Forgacs (ed.), *The Antonio Gramsci Reader: Selected Writings 1916–1935* (New York: New York University Press 2000), 225–28.
65   Thatcher, *The Downing Street Years*, 141.
66   Gallas, *The Thatcherite Offensive*, 143.
67   Ibid., 144, 168.
68   Ibid., 180–81.
69   Ibid., 165.
70   Aditya Chakrabortty, "End these offshore games or our democracy will die", *The Guardian*, 7 November 2017, https://www.theguardian.com/commentisfree/2017/nov/07/end-offshore-games-democracy-die-paradise-papers.

71   Beth Stratford, "Falling house prices could be the reboot our economy desperately needs. But only if we prepare a soft landing", *openDemocracy,* 13 February 2018, https://www.opendemocracy.net/neweconomics/falling-house-prices-reboot-economy-desperately-needs-prepare-soft-landing/.

72   Rana Foroohar, *Makers and Takers: The Rise of Finance and the Fall of American Business* (New York: Crown Business 2016).

73   Mathew Lawrence, personal communication to the authors, 8 November 2018.

74   Adam Cohen, *Nothing to Fear: FDR's Inner Circle and the Hundred Days that Created Modern America* (New York: Penguin 2009).

75   Nick Taylor, *American Made—The Enduring Legacy of the WPA: When FDR Put the Nation to Work* (New York: Bantam 2009), 7.

Chapter Three

1   John McDonnell, "Governing from the Radical Left", speech at The World Transformed, 25 September 2017.

2   Jim Pickard, "Labour plans for capital flight or run on pound if elected", *Financial Times,* 26 September 2017, https://www.ft.com/content/e06aa3a6-a2c5-11e7-b797-b61809486fe2; "Jeremy Corbyn: It's right to plan for run on pound", *BBC News,* 26 September 2017, https://www.bbc.com/news/uk-politics-41393021.

3   Ben Pimlott, "Introduction: Neil Kinnock's New Deal", in Ben Pimlott (ed.), *Labour's First Hundred Days,* Fabian Society tract No. 519, April 1987, 3.

4   Christopher Clifford, "The rise and fall of the Department of Economic Affairs 1964–69: British government and indicative planning", *Contemporary British History,* Vol. 11, No. 2, 1997, 94–116; Paul Ormerod, "Economics and finance: forward planning and holding tight", in Ben Pimlott (ed.), *Labour's First Hundred Days,* Fabian Society tract No. 519, April 1987, 12.

5   Richard Pryke, "Labour and the City: The Predictable Crisis", *New Left Review,* Vol. I, No. 39, September-October 1966, 3.

6   Samuel Brittan, *Steering the Economy: The Role of the Treasury* (Harmondsworth: Penguin 1971), 292.

7   Pryke, "Labour and the City: The Predictable Crisis", 15.

8   Harold Wilson, *The Labour Government 1964–70* (Penguin: Harmondsworth 1971), 64–65. Wilson claimed to have retorted that "if I went to the country on the issue of dictation by overseas financiers, I would have a landslide"—to which the Governor of the Bank of England "ruefully" said that he believed he would. See also Andrew Glyn, "Capital Flight and Exchange Controls", *New Left Review,* Vol. 1, No. 155, January-February 1986, 37–49.

9   Brittan, *Steering the Economy,* 292–93.

10   Harold Wilson quoted in Coates, *The Labour Party and the Struggle for Socialism,* 99.

11   Noel Thompson, *Political Economy and the Labour Party* (London: Routledge 2006), second edition, 184.

ENDNOTES

12 The Alternative Economic Strategy would have flanked traditional reflationary measures with innovative policies including "public ownership, planning, price controls, industrial democracy and import restrictions". Mark Wickham-Jones, *Economic Strategy and the Labour Party: Politics and Policy Making, 1970–83* (London: Palgrave Macmillan 1996), 5.

13 John Medhurst, *That Option No Longer Exists: Britain 1974–76* (London: Zero Books 2014), 96.

14 Tony Benn, "The Real Choices Facing the Cabinet", Memorandum by the Secretary of State for Energy, 2 November 1976, CP(76) 117, CAB/129/193/7, http://discovery.nationalarchives.gov.uk/details/r/C9614765.

15 William P. Rodgers quoted in Eric Helleiner, *States and the Reemergence of Global Finance: From Bretton Woods to the 1990s* (New York: Cornell University Press 1994), 124.

16 See Ken Coates (ed.), *What Went Wrong: Explaining the Fall of the Labour Government* (Nottingham: Spokesman 2008), second edition.

17 David Smith, *The Rise and Fall of Monetarism: The Theory and Politics of an Economic Experiment* (London: Penguin 1991); Kathleen Burk and Alec Cairncross, *'Goodbye, Great Britain': The 1976 IMF Crisis* (New Haven: Yale University Press 1992).

18 Thompson, *Political Economy and the Labour Party*, 226.

19 Nicholas Ridley quoted in David Keys et al., *Thatcher's Britain: A Guide to the Ruins* (London: Pluto Press and New Socialist 1983), 2.

20 Alan Budd quoted in David Harvey, *Spaces of Hope* (Berkeley: University of California Press 2000), 7.

21 Jonah Birch, "The Many Lives of François Mitterrand", *Jacobin*, 19 August 2015, https://www.jacobinmag.com/2015/08/francois-mitterrand-socialist-party-common-program-communist-pcf-1981-elections-austerity/.

22 Daniel Singer, *Is Socialism Doomed? The Meaning of Mitterrand* (New York: Oxford University Press 1988), 3–7.

23 Philip Short, *Mitterrand: A Study in Ambiguity* (London: Bodley Head 2013), 311.

24 Singer, *Is Socialism Doomed?*, 101–02.

25 Ibid., 106.

26 Ibid., 107.

27 Birch, "The Many Lives of François Mitterrand".

28 Christopher Hitchens, "Staking a Life", *Lapham's Quarterly*, 2011, https://www.laphamsquarterly.org/crimes-punishments/staking-life.

29 Christian Stoffaës, "The nationalizations: an initial assessment, 1981–1984", in Howard Machin and Vincent Wright (eds.), *Economic Policy and Policy Making Under the Mitterrand Presidency 1981–1984* (New York: St. Martin's 1985), 144.

30 Birch, "The Many Lives of François Mitterrand"; Singer, *Is Socialism Doomed?*, 114.

31 Singer, *Is Socialism Doomed?*, 116.

32 Donald Sassoon, *One Hundred Years of Socialism: The West European Left in the Twentieth Century* (New York: The New Press 1996), 546.

33   William Mitchell and Thomas Fazi, *Reclaiming the State: A Progressive Vision of Sovereignty for a Post-Neoliberal World* (London: Pluto Press 2017), 76–86.
34   Helleiner, *States and the Reemergence of Global Finance*, 140.
35   Ibid., 7.
36   Ibid., 104.
37   Short, *Mitterrand*, 312.
38   Peter A. Hall, "The Evolution of Economic Policy under Mitterrand", in George Ross, Stanley Hoffmann, and Sylvia Malzacher (eds.), *The Mitterrand Experiment: Continuity and Change in Modern France* (Cambridge: Polity Press 1987), 55–56.
39   Singer, *Is Socialism Doomed?*, 106.
40   Wayne Northcutt, *Mitterrand: A Political Biography* (New York: Holmes & Meier 1992), 96.
41   Hall, "The Evolution of Economic Policy under Mitterrand", 56–57.
42   Singer, *Is Socialism Doomed?*, 132.
43   Ibid., 127–28, 9.
44   Michael McLeay, Amar Radia and Ryland Thomas, "Money creation in the modern economy", *Bank of England Quarterly Bulletin* 2014 Q1, http://www.bankofengland .co.uk/publications/documents/quarterlybulletin/2014/qb14q1prereleasemoney-creation.pdf.
45   Richard Roberts and David Kynaston, *City State: A Contemporary History of the City of London and How Money Triumphed* (London: Profile Books 2002), ix.
46   John Kay, *Other People's Money: Masters of the Universe or Servants of the People?* (London: Profile Books 2015); Adair Turner, *Between Debt and the Devil: Money, Credit and Fixing Global Finance* (Princeton: Princeton University Press 2016), 62–63.
47   Sir John Cunliffe, *Speech: Are firms underinvesting—and if so why?* Greater Birmingham Chamber of Commerce, 8 February 2017.
48   Adair Turner, *Between Debt and the Devil*, 63.
49   Jan Toporowski, "Brexit and the discreet charm of haute finance", in David Bailey and Leslie Budd, *The Political Economy of Brexit* (Newcastle: Agenda Publishing 2017), 40.
50   Nicholas Shaxson, *The Finance Curse: How Global Finance is Making Us All Poorer* (London: Bodley Head 2018), 4. See also Michael Hudson, *Killing the Host: How Financial Parasites and Debt Destroy the Global Economy* (New York: ISLET 2015).
51   *Bank of England Quarterly Bulletin*, Vol. 29, No. 4, November 1989.
52   Jean-Louis Arcand, Enrico Berkes, and Ugo Panizza. *Too much finance?* IMF Working Paper No 12/161, (2012). https://www.imf.org/external/pubs/ft/wp/2012/wp12161. pdf.
53   Bank of England, *Why is the UK financial system so big, and is that a problem?* (London: Bank of England 2014); Lucia Alessi and Carsten Detken, "*Identifying excessive credit growth and leverage*", European Central Bank Working paper series, No. 1723, (2014).
54   Bank of England, *Why is the UK financial system so big?*

55 Thatcher, *The Downing Street Years*, 141.

56 Graham Turner, *Financing Investment: Final Report* (London: GFC Economist Ltd and Clearpoint Advisors Ltd 2018).

57 George Parker, "McDonnell strikes emollient tone with City leaders", *Financial Times*, 17 June 2018, https://www.ft.com/content/f852ca7e-70c0-11e8-852d-d8b-934ff5ffa.

58 Labour Party, Labour's Fiscal Credibility Rule, http://labour.org.uk/wp-content/uploads/2017/10/Fiscal-Credibility-Rule.pdf. See also Simon Wren-Lewis, "Labour's Fiscal Credibility Rule in Context", in John McDonnell (ed.), *Economics for the Many* (London: Verso 2018), 12–22.

59 Bank of England, *Quantitative Easing*, https://www.bankofengland.co.uk/monetary-policy/quantitative-easing.

60 Robert Peston, "Would Corbyn's 'QE for people' float or sink Britain?", BBC, 12 August 2015, https://www.bbc.co.uk/news/business-33884836.

61 Turner, *Between Debt and the Devil*, Ch. 14; Steve Keen, "Manifesto", *Steve Keen's Debtwatch*, http://www.debtdeflation.com/blogs/manifesto/.

62 Simon Wren-Lewis, "A Labour run on Sterling?" *Mainly Macro*, 27 September 2017, https://mainlymacro.blogspot.com/2017/09/a-labour-run-on-sterling.html; Ann Pettifor, "Why business could prosper under a Corbyn government", *The Guardian*, 17 December 2017, https://www.theguardian.com/business/commentisfree/2017/dec/17/why-industry-leader-have-no-need-to-panic-over-jeremy-corbyn-john-mcdonnell.

63 Graham Secker, Matthew Garman, Krupa Patel, Lillian Huang, and Alix G. Guerrini, *Into Thin Air: 2018 European Equity Outlook*, Morgan Stanley & Co., 26 November 2017, 23–24.

64 Robert Miller, "Corbyn is keeping us awake at night, say business chiefs", *The Times*, 23 August 2018, https://www.thetimes.co.uk/article/corbyn-is-keeping-us-awake-at-night-say-business-chiefs-gz6hb09td.

65 Madison Marriage, "Why the UK's uber-wealthy voters fear a Corbyn-led government", *Financial Times*, 6 October 2018, https://www.ft.com/content/85e0e610-a07c-11e0-b19c-da9d6c239ca8.

66 Thomas M. Hanna, *The Crisis Next Time: Planning for Public Ownership as an Alternative to Corporate Bank Bailouts*, The Democracy Collaborative, 2 July 2018, https://thenextsystem.org/sites/default/files/2018-06/TheCrisisNextTime.pdf.

67 Sidney Webb quoted in A. J. P. Taylor, *English History 1914–1945* (Oxford: Oxford University Press 1965), 297; Gregory Elliott, *Labourism and the English Genius: The Strange Death of Labour England?* (London: Verso 1993), 46.

68 Stathis Kouvelakis, "Syriza's Rise and Fall", *New Left Review*, Vol. 2, No. 97 (2016), 46.

69 Kouvelakis, "Syriza's Rise and Fall", 53.

70 Yanis Varoufakis, *And the Weak Suffer What They Must? Europe, Austerity and the Threat to Global Stability* (London: Vintage 2016); Kevin Ovenden, *Syriza: Inside the Labyrinth* (London: Pluto Press 2015).

71 Ovenden, *Syriza;* Interviews with Greek political observers, July and August 2018.

72 Mike Makin-Waite, *Communism and Democracy* (London: Lawrence & Wishart 2017), 262–66.

73 Costas Lapavitsas, *Crisis in the Eurozone* (London: Verso 2012).

74 Kouvelakis, "Syriza's Rise and Fall", 53.

75 We would like to thank Joe Bilsborough, whose research on capital mobility for another project was invaluable here.

76 Jim O'Neill, "I'm an ex-Tory Minister: Only Labour Grasps Britain's Desire for Change", *The Guardian*, 5 October 2018, https://www.theguardian.com/commentisfree/2018/oct/05/ex-tory-minister-labour-grasps-britain-desire-change-corbyn-mcdonnell.

77 "A confident Labour is swaggering left in its economic policy", *The Economist*, 27 September 2018, https://www.economist.com/britain/2018/09/27/a-confident-labour-is-swaggering-left-in-its-economic-policy.

78 Gerald Epstein, "Should Financial Flows Be Regulated? Yes", United Nations, Department of Economics and Social Affairs Working Papers, July 2009, Issue 77, 5.

79 Atish R. Ghosh and Mahvash S. Qureshi, "What's In a Name? That Which We Call Capital Controls", IMF Working Paper WP/16/25, February 2016, https://www.imf.org/external/pubs/ft/wp/2016/wp1625.pdf.

80 Helleiner, *States and the Reemergence of Global Finance*, 150.

81 Glyn, "Capital Flight and Exchange Controls", 38.

82 Ibid.

83 Jomo K. S., "Crisis and Crisis Management in Malaysia, 1997–98", in Wong Sook Ching, Jomo K.S., and Chin Kok Fay, (eds.) *Malaysian "Bail Outs"? Capital Controls, Restructuring and Recovery* (Singapore: Singapore University Press 2005), 23–46.

84 Ethan Kaplan and Dani Rodrik, "Did the Malaysian Capital Controls Work?" in Sebastian Edwards and Jeffrey A. Frankel (eds.), *Preventing Currency Crises in Emerging Markets* (Chicago: University of Chicago Press 2002), 397.

85 Ásgeir Jónsson and Hersir Sigurgeirsson, *The Icelandic Financial Crisis: A Study into the World's Smallest Currency Area and its Recovery from Total Banking Collapse* (London: Palgrave Macmillan 2016), 235, 247.

86 Atish R. Ghosh, Jonathan D. Ostry, and Mahvash S. Qureshi, *Taming the Tide of Capital Flows: A Policy Guide* (Cambridge: The MIT Press 2017), 77.

87 Epstein, "Should Financial Flows Be Regulated? Yes", 10–12.

88 We would like to thank Tom Barker for his archival research on these civil service plans as part of another project.

89 John McDonnell, *The Economic Policy of the Labour Party: Speech to the Marx Memorial Library*, 2 October 2018.

90 Christine Berry, "John McDonnell is right: we need a new left internationalism", *Verso Blog,* 17 October 2018, https://www.versobooks.com/blogs/4086-john-mcdonnell-is-right-we-need-a-new-left-internationalism.

91 Corporate Europe Observatory, *TTIP: "Regulatory co-operation" a threat to democracy*, 21 March 2016, https://corporateeurope.org/international-trade/2016/03/ttip-regulatory-cooperation-threat-democracy; Karen Howlett, "WTO rules against Ontario in green energy dispute", *Canada Globe and Mail*, 20 November 2012, https://www.theglobeandmail.com/report-on-business/industry-news/energy-and-resources/wto-rules-against-ontario-in-green-energy-dispute/article5461941/.

92 Varoufakis, *And the Weak Suffer What They Must?*

93 Benn Steil, *The Battle of Bretton Woods: John Maynard Keynes, Harry Dexter White, and the Making of a New World Order* (Princeton: Princeton University Press 2014).

94 Singer, *Is Socialism Doomed?*, 75–77.

95 Ibid., 117.

96 Ibid., 76.

97 Ibid., 125.

98 John Bew, *Citizen Clem: A Biography of Attlee* (London: riverrun 2016), 460.

99 Sellers, "#JezWeDid", in Unterrainer, *Corbyn's Campaign*, 38–39.

100 Kouvelakis, "Syriza's Rise and Fall".

101 George Eaton, "Corbynism 2.0: the radical ideas shaping Labour's future", *New Statesman*, 19 September 2018, https://www.newstatesman.com/politics/uk/2018/09/corbynism-20-radical-ideas-shaping-labour-s-future.

Chapter Four

1 Dave Richards and Martin Smith, "The lessons of Tony Benn as a Cabinet Minister: Breaking the rules and paying the price", *LSE British Politics and Policy blog*, 19 March 2014, http://blogs.lse.ac.uk/politicsandpolicy/the-lessons-of-tony-benn-as-a-cabinet-minister-breaking-the-rules-and-paying-the-price/.

2 Leo Panitch and Colin Leys, *The End of Parliamentary Socialism: From New Left to New Labour* (London: Verso 2001), 90.

3 Richards and Smith, "The lessons of Tony Benn as a Cabinet Minister".

4 John Hoskyns, "Conservatism Is Not Enough", *Political Quarterly* 55 (1984), 6. Based on a speech given at the Institute of Directors' Annual Lecture in September 1983.

5 Bew, *Citizen Clem*, 356–60; J. C. R. Dow, *The Management of the British Economy 1945–1960* (Cambridge: Cambridge University Press 1964).

6 Ovenden, *Syriza*, xii.

7 David Walker, "Babes in the Whitehall Wood", *The Independent*, 14 January 1997. https://www.independent.co.uk/voices/babes-in-the-whitehall-wood-1283140.html.

8 John McDonnell, *The Economic Policy of the Labour Party: Speech to the Marx Memorial Library* (2 October 2018).

9 Christine Berry, "The making of a movement: Who's shaping Corbynism?", *open Democracy*, 5 December 2017, https://civilsocietyfutures.org/making-movement-who-shaping-corbynism/.

10   Henry Zeffmann, "Corbyn groomed for No. 10 by ex-head of Civil Service Lord Kerslake", *The Times,* 23 October 2017.

11   Ministry of Reconstruction, *Employment Policy: Cmd. 6527* (London: The Stationery Office 1944).

12   R. S. Barker, "Civil Service Attitudes and the Economic Planning of the Attlee Government", *Journal of Contemporary History*, Vol. 21, No. 3 (July 1986), 473–86.

13   Thomas Bearpark, Andrew Heron and Ben Glover, "Economics in government: more open, more diverse, more influential", *Civil Service Quarterly,* 8 August 2017, https://quarterly.blog.gov.uk/2017/08/08/economics-in-govern-ment-more-open-more-diverse-more-influential/.

14   George Arnett, "Elitism in Britain: Breakdown by profession", *The Guardian,* 28 August 2014, https://www.theguardian.com/news/datablog/2014/aug/28/elitism-in-brit-ain-breakdown-by-profession.

15   Author's own research based on departmental websites (correct at time of writing); details available on request.

16   Panitch and Leys, *The End of Parliamentary Socialism*, 90.

17   For example, Terry Burns' departure as permanent secretary to the Treasury under Gordon Brown.

18   Civil Service Commission, *Recruiting Permanent Secretaries: Ministerial Involvement* (London: The Stationery Office 2012), http://civilservicecommission.independent.gov.uk/wp-content/uploads/2012/12/EXPLANATORY-NOTE-PERM-SEC-COMPETITIONS-MINISTERIAL-INVOLVEMENT.pdf

19   John Hoskyns, "Whitehall and Westminster: An outsider's view", *Parliamentary Affairs* 36 (1983). Based on a speech given at the Annual Dinner of the Institute of Fiscal Studies in October 1982.

20   James B. Christoph, "The Remaking of British Administrative Culture", *Administration & Society* 24, No. 2 (26 August 1992), 165.

21   David Laidler, "Review: Dow and Savile's Critique of Monetary Policy—A Review Essay", *Journal of Economic Literature,* Vol. 27, No. 3 (Sep. 1989), 1147–59.

22   Geoffrey K. Fry, "The Development of the Thatcher Government's 'Grand Strategy' for the Civil Service: A Public Policy Perspective", *Public Administration*, Vol. 62, No. 3 (1984), 322–35, https://doi.org/10.1111/j.1467-9299.1984.tb00566.x.

23   Fry, "The Development of the Thatcher Government's 'Grand Strategy' for the Civil Service", 326.

24   Christoph, "The Remaking of British Administrative Culture", 168.

25   Peter Hennessy, "Mrs Thatcher's Poodle?", *Contemporary Record* 2, No. 2 (June 25 1988), 2–4, https://doi.org/10.1080/13619468808580958.

26   Christoph, "The Remaking of British Administrative Culture", 175–76.

27   R. A. W. Rhodes, "New Labour's Civil Service: Summing-up Joining-up", *The Political Quarterly* 71 (2000), 151–66.

28   Cabinet Office, *White Paper: Modernising Government* (London: The Stationery Office 1999).

ENDNOTES

29   Cabinet Office *Professional Policy Making in the 21st Century* (London: The Stationery Office 1999).

30   Cabinet Office, "Open Policy Making Toolkit", UK Government website, 3 January 2017, https://www.gov.uk/guidance/open-policy-making-toolkit.

31   Cabinet Office, *Modernising Government*.

32   Christine Berry, "After Grenfell: Ending the murderous war on our protections", *openDemocracy*, 16 June 2017, https://www.opendemocracy.net/neweconomics/grenfell-ending-murderous-war-protections/.

33   George Monbiot, "With Grenfell, we've seen what 'ripping up red tape' really looks like", *The Guardian*, 15 June 2017, https://www.theguardian.com/commentisfree/2017/jun/15/grenfell-tower-red-tape-safety-deregulation.

34   Samuel Osborne, "Diane Abbott: Grenfell Tower fire 'direct consequence of deregulation, privatisation and outsourcing'", *The Independent*, 24 September 2017, https://www.independent.co.uk/news/uk/politics/grenfell-tower-fire-diane-abbott-direct-consequence-labour-conference-brighton-deregulation-a7964256.html,

35   Matt Wrack, "Deregulation and the Grenfell Tower fire", Fire Brigades Union blog, 20 June 2018, https://www.fbu.org.uk/blog/deregulation-and-grenfell-tower-fire.

36   Christine Berry and Stephen Devlin, *Threat to Democracy: The impact of 'better regulation' in the UK* (London: New Economics Foundation 2015), 29.

37   UK Government, Regulatory Policy Committee: *Our management,* https://www.gov.uk/government/organisations/regulatory-policy-committee.

38   Department of Health, Public Health Responsibility Deal, https://responsibilitydeal.dh.gov.uk/; Graham A. MacGregor et al., "Food and the responsibility deal: how the salt reduction strategy was derailed", *British Medical Journal* 350 (2015); Jonathan Gornall, "Sugar's web of influence 3: Why the responsibility deal is a 'dead duck' for sugar reduction", *British Medical Journal* 350 (2015); Cecile Knai et al. "Are the Public Health Responsibility Deal alcohol pledges likely to improve public health? An evidence synthesis", *Addiction*, Vol. 110, No. 8 (Aug 2015), 1232–46; Department of Health, *Public Health Responsibility Deal—Plenary Group Members*, https://responsibilitydeal.dh.gov.uk/plenary-group-members/.

39   Department for Business, Innovation and Skills, Focus on Enforcement, http://discuss.bis.gov.uk/focusonenforcement/business-focus-on-enforcement-2/; Department for Business, Innovation and Skills. *National Farmers' Union's BFoE Review*, http://discuss.bis.gov.uk/focusonenforcement/business-focus-on-enforcement-2/business-focus-onenforcement-national-farmers-unions-review/.

40   Institute for Government, "Civil service staff numbers", *Institute for Government*, 12 September 2018, https://www.instituteforgovernment.org.uk/explainers/civil-service-staff-numbers.

41   Lord Kerslake, *Rethinking the Treasury: The Kerslake Review of the Treasury* (London: Industry Forum, February 2017), 31.

42   Interview with Greek political observer, 23 October 2018.

43 Cabinet Office, "Enhanced Departmental Boards Protocol", *UK Government website*, 19 February 2013, https://www.gov.uk/government/publications/enhanced-departmental-boards-protocol.

44 Robert Hazell et al., *Critical Friends? The role of non-executives on departmental boards* (London: UCL Constitution Unit 2018), 17.

45 Cabinet Office, "Enhanced Departmental Boards Protocol".

46 Hazell et al., *Critical Friends?*, 17.

47 Ibid., 54.

48 Ibid., 71.

49 Department for Business, Energy and Industrial Strategy, *Our governance*, https://www.gov.uk/government/organisations/department-for-business-energy-and-industrial-strategy/about/our-governance.

50 Department for Transport, "New non-executives appointed to the Department for Transport board", *UK Government website*, 11 June 2013, https://www.gov.uk/government/news/new-non-executives-appointed-to-the-department-for-transport-board.

51 UK Government, *Government Lead Non-Executive and Non-Executive Board Member: Sir Ian Cheshire*, https://www.gov.uk/government/people/ian-cheshire.

52 Institute for Government, *Previous Event: Tony Blair at the IfG*, https://www.instituteforgovernment.org.uk/events/tony-blair-ifg.

53 Labour Party, *General Election Manifesto—New Labour: Because Britain Deserves Better* (London: Labour Party 1997), 1.

54 David Blunkett, Speech to the ESRC (2 February 2002), cited in Peter Wells, "New Labour and Evidence-Based Policy Making: 1997–2007", *People, Place & Policy Online*, Vol. 1, No. 1 (2007), 22.

55 Sir Nicholas Macpherson, "Speech to the Mile End Group by the Permanent Secretary to the Treasury: The Treasury View—a testament of experience", *HM Treasury*, 17 January 2014, https://www.gov.uk/government/speeches/speech-by-the-permanent-secretary-to-the-treasury-the-treasury-view-a-testament-of-experience.

56 Michael Hallsworth, *Policy Making in the Real World: Evidence and Analysis* (London: Institute for Government, April 2011), 64.

57 David Powell, "Transforming the Treasury: The biggest and best idea of all", *openDemocracy*, 12 May 2014, https://www.opendemocracy.net/ourkingdom/david-powell/transforming-treasury-biggest-and-best-idea-of-all; Stian Westlake, "Is it time to break up the Treasury?", *Civil Service World*, 19 November 2015, https://www.civilserviceworld.com/articles/opinion/stian-westlake-it-time-break-treasury.

58 Lord Kerslake, *Rethinking the Treasury.*

59 Cabinet Office, *Professional Policy Making in the 21ˢᵗ Century.*

60 Performance and Innovation Unit, *Adding It Up: Improving Analysis and Modelling in Central Government*, (London: The Stationery Office 2000).

61 According to a recent article in *Civil Service Quarterly* (Bearpark, Heron and Glover, "Economics in government: more open, more diverse, more influential") there are

currently around 1,500 government economists. According to figures in *Adding It Up*, in 2000 there were 518.

62 Author's own research (correct at time of writing), details available on request.

63 Gus O'Donnell et al., *Report: Wellbeing and Policy* (London: Legatum Institute 2014), 20.

64 John McDonnell, *Speech to Labour Party Conference*, 24 September 2018, https://labour.org.uk/press/john-mcdonnells-full-speech-labour-conference-2018/.

65 Frank Ackerman and Joseph Daniel, *(Mis)Understanding Climate Policy: The Role of Economic Modelling* (Cambridge, MA: Synapse Energy Economics, April 2014).

66 HM Treasury, *Analysis of the Dynamic Effects of Corporation Tax Reductions* (London: The Stationery Office, December 2013).

67 Laurie Macfarlane, "From PFI to privatisation, our national accounting rules encourage daft decisions. It's time to change them", *openDemocracy*, 18 January 2018, https://www.opendemocracy.net/neweconomics/pfi-privatisation-national-accounting-rules-encourage-destructive-decisions-time-change/.

68 McDonnell, *Speech to Labour Party Conference*.

69 Yannis Dafermos, Giorgos Galanis and Maria Nikolaidi, *A New Ecological Macroeconomic Model* (London: New Economics Foundation), https://neweconomics.org/uploads/files/08ec800b159197d7a3_qlm6i2e5v.pdf; Tim Jackson, *System Dynamics: FALSTAFF,* https://timjackson.org.uk/ecological-economics/falstaff/.

70 Craig Berry et al., *Reforming the Treasury, Reorienting British Capitalism* (Sheffield: SPERI British Political Economy Brief No. 21, March 2016), 5.

71 Wainwright, *A New Politics from the Left*.

72 McDonnell, *The Economic Policy of the Labour Party*.

73 McDonnell, *Speech: Governing from the Radical Left*.

74 Yves Sintomer, "From Deliberative to Radical Democracy? Sortition and Politics in the 21st Century", *Politics and Society*, Vol. 46, No. 3 (2018), 345.

75 Sintomer, "From Deliberative to Radical Democracy?", 345.

76 Department for Communities and Local Government, *Multi-Criteria Analysis: A Manual* (London: The Stationery Office 2009).

77 McDonnell, *The Economic Policy of the Labour Party*.

78 Case study: Govanhill, Glasgow, *Local Government Association*, 12 December 2016, *https://www.local.gov.uk/govanhill-glasgow*.

79 Bristol City Council, "Pupils try their hand at setting the council's budget", 21 November 2017, http://news.bristol.gov.uk/pupils_try_their_hand_at_setting_the_council_s_budget.

80 Adrian Bua, "Book Review: Popular Democracy: The Paradox of Participation by Gianpaolo Baiocchi and Ernesto Ganuza", *LSE Review of Books*, 15 August 2017, http://blogs.lse.ac.uk/lsereviewofbooks/2017/08/15/book-review-popular-democracy-the-paradox-of-participation-by-gianpaolo-baiocchi-and-ernesto-ganuza/.

81 Leonardo Avritzer, "Conference presentation: Institutionalising Participatory and Deliberative Democracy", *University of Westminster*, 11 November 2017, https://

www.westminster.ac.uk/events/institutionalizing-participatory-and-delibera-tive-democracy

82   Sintomer, "From Deliberative to Radical Democracy?"

83   Sintomer, "From Deliberative to Radical Democracy?", 344–50.

84   Bua, "Book Review: Popular Democracy: The Paradox of Participation by Gianpaolo Baiocchi and Ernesto Ganuza".

85   Wainwright, *A New Politics from the Left;* Ajuntament de Barcelona, *Citizen Participation,* http://ajuntament.barcelona.cat/participaciociutadana/en.

86   Kerslake, *Rethinking the Treasury,* 20.

87   Democracy Matters Project, *Citizens Assembly Pilots,* https://citizensassembly .co.uk/democracy-matters/.

88   "Northamptonshire County Council: 'Radical' service cuts planned", BBC, 2 August 2018; "East Sussex County Council cuts services to 'legal minimum'", BBC, 3 August 2018.

89   Jonathan S. Davies, *Governing In And Against Austerity: International Lessons from Eight Cities* (Leicester: De Montfort University 2017), 23.

90   UNISON, *Community and Voluntary Services in the Age of Austerity: UNISON Voices from the Frontline* (London: Unison 2013).

91   Davies, *Governing In and Against Austerity,* 26.

92   Varoufakis, *And the Weak Suffer What They Must?*

93   Bernard Connolly, *The Rotten Heart of Europe* (London and Boston: Faber and Faber 1995).

94   Ovenden, *Syriza: Inside the Labyrinth,* 131.

95   Bank of England, *Court of Directors,* https://www.bankofengland.co.uk/about/peo-ple/court-of-directors.

96   Turner, *Financing Investment,* 102.

97   "Upsetting the punchbowl: A debate about central bank independence is overdue", *Economist,* 20 October 2018, https://www.economist.com/finance-and-economics/ 2018/10/20/a-debate-about-central-bank-independence-is-overdue.

98   Institute for Government, *About Us,* https://www.instituteforgovernment.org.uk/ about-us.

99   See also Frank Fischer, *Democracy and Expertise: Reorienting Policy Inquiry* (Oxford: Oxford University Press 2009).

Chapter Five

1   Kouvelakis, "Syriza's Rise and Fall", 63.

2   Doug Bolton, "Greek debt crisis: Alexis Tsipras speaks to 25,000 at 'No' rally in Syntagma Square, urging voters to deny 'those who terrorise you'", *The Independent,* 5 July 2015.

3   Kouvelakis, "Syriza's Rise and Fall", 65.

ENDNOTES

4   Antonio Gramsci, *Selections from the Prison Notebooks*, trans. Quintin Hoare and Geoffrey Nowell Smith (London: Lawrence & Wishart 1971).

5   Jonathan Smucker, *Hegemony How-To: A Roadmap for Radicals* (AK Press 2017); Nick Srnicek and Alex Williams, *Inventing the Future: Post-Capitalism and a World Without Work* (London: Verso 2015).

6   Wainwright, *A New Politics from the Left.*

7   John McDonnell, *Speech: Governing from the Radical Left,* available at https://www.youtube.com/watch?v=daIR_8jGqjo.

8   Jeanette Mitchell et al., *In and Against the State* (London: London Edinburgh Weekend Return Group 1979), available online at: https://libcom.org/library/against-state-1979.

9   Bert Russell, "Corbynism from (The Great) Below", *We Are Plan C,* 18 October 2017, https://www.weareplanc.org/blog/corbynism-from-the-great-below/.

10   Owen Jones and Ellie Mae O'Hagan, *Agitpod*: "Episode 24—Sirio Canós Donnay" (Podcast).

11   Solidarity4All, *Building Hope Against Fear and Devastation: Annual Report 2015,* https://issuu.com/solidarityforall/docs/report_2014.

12   Owen Jones and Ellie Mae O'Hagan, *Agitpod*: "Episode 24—Sirio Canós Donnay" (Podcast).

13   Kevin Ovenden, *Syriza: Inside the Labyrinth* (London: Pluto Press 2015), xiii.

14   Ibid.

15   Ibid., 24.

16   Interview with former senior Syriza figure, 26 July 2018.

17   Tom Blackburn, "Corbynism from Below", *New Socialist,* 12 June 2017, https://new-socialist.org.uk/corbynism-from-below/.

18   Andreas Karitzis, "The Dilemmas and Potentials of the Left: Learning from Syriza", *Socialist Register* (2016), 374–81.

19   Kouvelakis, "Syriza's Rise and Fall", 50.

20   Interview with Greek political observer, 23 October 2018.

21   Kouvelakis, "Syriza's Rise and Fall".

22   Ovenden, *Syriza: Inside the Labyrinth.*

23   Podemos, *Organisational Principles*, 2016, https://podemos.info/wp-content/uploads/2016/11/Organisational_Principles.pdf.

24   Eduardo Maura, "Podemos: Politics by the people", interviewed by Andrew Dolan, *Red Pepper,* 22 February 2015, https://www.redpepper.org.uk/podemos-politics-by-the-people/.

25   Giles Tremlett, "The Podemos revolution: How a small group of radical academics changed European politics", *The Guardian,* 31 March 2015, https://www.theguardian.com/world/2015/mar/31/podemos-revolution-radical-academics-changed-european-politics.

26   Bécquer Seguín and Sebastiaan Faber, "Can Podemos Win in Spain?", *The Nation,* 14 January 2015, https://www.thenation.com/article/can-podemos-win-spain/.

27 Private correspondence, September 2018.
28 Santiago Pérez-Nievas et al., "New Wine in Old Bottles? The Selection of Electoral Candidates in General Elections in Podemos", in Cordero and Coller (eds.), *Democratizing Candidate Selection* (London: Palgrave Macmillan 2018).
29 Dan Hancox, "Is this the world's most radical mayor?", *The Guardian*, 26 May 2016, https://www.theguardian.com/world/2016/may/26/ada-colau-barcelona-most-radical-mayor-in-the-world.
30 Sebastiaan Faber and Bécquer Seguín, "Welcome to Sunny Barcelona, Where the Government is Embracing Co-ops, Citizen Activism, and Solar Energy", *The Nation*, 11 August 2016, https://www.thenation.com/article/welcome-to-sunny-barcelona-where-the-government-is-embracing-coops-citizen-activism-and-solar-energy/.
31 Karitzis, "Learning from Syriza", 376.
32 Kouvelakis, "Syriza's Rise and Fall", 69.
33 Ernesto Laclau and Chantal Mouffe, *Hegemony and Socialist Strategy: Towards a Radical Democratic Politics* (London: Verso 1985).
34 Blackburn, "Corbynism from Below?".
35 Solidarity4All, *Solidarity is people's power: Towards an international campaign of solidarity to the Greek people* (Athens: Solidarity4All 2013), 14, available at https://www.solidarity4all.gr/sites/www.solidarity4all.gr/files/aggliko.pdf.
36 Solidarity4All, *Solidarity is people's power*, 20; Solidarity4All, *Annual Report 2015*.
37 Solidarity4All, *Solidarity is people's power*, 16.
38 Ash Sarkar, "This isn't just a culture war: We need a radical anti-fascist movement right now", *The Guardian*, 21 August 2018, https://www.theguardian.com/commentisfree/2018/aug/21/anti-fascist-movement-far-right.
39 Hoskyns et al., *Stepping Stones.*
40 Blackburn, "Corbynism from Below".
41 Hoskyns et al., *Stepping Stones.*
42 Christine Berry, "Flipping the script on our economic stories", *Red Pepper*, 15 March 2018, https://www.redpepper.org.uk/flipping-the-script-on-our-economic-stories/.
43 George Lakoff, *Don't Think Of An Elephant: Know Your Values And Frame the Debate* (Hartford: Chelsea Green 1990).
44 Gramsci, *Selections from the Prison Notebooks.*
45 Jeremy Corbyn, *Speech to Labour Party Conference*, 27 September 2017, https://labour.org.uk/press/jeremy-corbyn-speech-to-labour-party-conference/.
46 Financial Times, "Corbyn sets out stall: 'We won't play by their rules' in 'rigged economy'", *Financial Times*, 20 April 2017, https://www.ft.com/content/685ca457-d190-3976-ba1b-13e7d8058522.
47 *Framing the Economy: How to Win the Case for a Better System* (London: NEF, NEON, PIRC & the Frameworks Institute 2018).
48 Nigel Farage, *Speech to the European Parliament*, 28 June 2016. Available at https://www.independent.co.uk/news/uk/politics/nigel-farage-brexit-speech-european-parliament-full-transcript-text-a7107036.html.

ENDNOTES

49   Miguel Lorenzo, "Josep Oliu propone crear 'una especie de Podemos de derechas'", *El Periodico,* 25 June 2014, https://www.elperiodico.com/es/politica/20140625/josep-oliu-propone-crear-una-especie-de-podemos-de-derechas-3329695.

50   Christine Berry, "What would it look like to build a politics that's open to people but closed to big money?", *openDemocracy,* 9 May 2017, https://www.opendemocracy.net/neweconomics/what-would-it-look-like-to-build-a-politics-thats-open-to-people-but-closed-to-big-money/.

51   Jeremy Corbyn, *Speech to Labour Party Conference,* 27 September 2017.

52   Gramsci, *Selections from the Prison Notebooks.*

53   Seguín and Faber, "Can Podemos Win in Spain?"

54   Labour Party, *Our Town,* https://www.facebook.com/labourparty/videos/our-town/1737038089726749/.

55   Dan Hind and Tom Mills, "Media Democracy: A Reform Agenda for Democratic Communications", in Laurie Macfarlane (ed.), *New Thinking for the British Economy* (*openDemocracy* 2018).

56   New Economics Foundation, *Agenda for Change: Building a New Economy Where People Really Take Control* (London: NEF 2016).

57   Larry Elliott, "Ten years after the financial crash, the timid left should be full of regrets", *The Guardian,* 30 August 2018, https://www.theguardian.com/commentisfree/2018/aug/30/financial-crash-capitalism-banking-crisis.

58   Philip Mirowski, *Never Let a Serious Crisis Go to Waste: How Neoliberalism Survived the Financial Meltdown* (London: Verso 2014).

59   Mirowski, *Never Let a Serious Crisis Go to Waste.*

60   Hayek's Opening Address to the first meeting of the Mont Pelerin Society, quoted in Mirowski, *Never Let a Serious Crisis Go to Waste,* 49.

61   Mirowski, *Never Let a Serious Crisis Go to Waste,* 77.

62   Ibid.

63   Powell, *Attack on the American Free Enterprise System.*

64   Radhika Desai, "Second Hand Dealers in Ideas: Think Tanks and Thatcherite Hegemony", *New Left Review,* Vol. I, No. 203 (1994), 62.

65   Ibid., 29–30.

66   NEF, *Annual Report and Accounts,* 2017, available at https://neweconomics.org/uploads/images/2018/02/nef-accounts-2017.pdf; IPPR, *Annual Report and Accounts,* 2017, available at https://www.ippr.org/files/ippr-2017-year-end-accounts.pdf.

67   Adam Smith Institute, *Tax Freedom Day,* https://www.adamsmith.org/taxfreedomday.

68   Dan Sabbagh, "Labour hopes new initiative will revive political education", *The Guardian,* 8 October 2018, https://www.theguardian.com/politics/2018/oct/08/labour-hopes-new-initiative-will-revive-political-education.

69   *The Plebs Magazine,* Issue 1, cited in Colin Waugh, *Plebs: The lost legacy of independent working-class political education* (Sheffield: Post-16 Educator 2009), available online at: http://www.ifyoucan.org.uk/PSE/Home_files/PSE%20Plebs%20pamphlet.pdf.

70   Editorial, *The Plebs Magazine*, Issue 3, cited in Waugh, *Plebs*.

71   Waugh, *Plebs*, 6.

72   Ibid., 15.

73   Black Panther Party, *Ten Point Program*, available online at: https://www.marxists .org/history/usa/workers/black-panthers/1966/10/15.htm.

74   Shani Ealey, "Black Panthers Oakland Community School: A model for liberation", *Black Organising Project*, 3 November 2016, http://blackorganizingproject.org/ black-panthers-oakland-community-school-a-model-for-liberation/.

75   Wainwright, *A New Politics from the Left*.

76   Tom Blackburn, "Waking Up the Giant: Political Education and the Labour Movement", *New Socialist*, 17 June 2018, https://newsocialist.org.uk/waking-up-the-giant/.

77   Roger Simon, *Gramsci's Political Thought: An Introduction* (London: Lawrence & Wishart 1990), x.

78   Aditya Chakrabortty, "What happens when ordinary people learn economics?", *The Guardian*, 20 June 2018, https://www.theguardian.com/commentisfree/2018/jun/20/ ordinary-people-learn-economics-manchester-classes.

79   Phillips-Fein, *Invisible Hands*, 44–46.

80   Waugh, *Plebs*, 21.

Conclusion

1   Hoskyns, "Conservatism Is Not Enough".

2   Joseph Collins and John Lear, *Chile's Free-Market Miracle: A Second Look* (Oakland: Institute for Food and Development Policy 1995).

3   Percy Shelley, "The Mask of Anarchy: Written on the Occasion of the Massacre at Manchester", *Poetical Works*, ed. Thomas Hutchinson (London: Oxford University Press 1970), 344.

BIBLIOGRAPHY

Ackerman, Frank and Joseph Daniel. *(Mis)Understanding Climate Policy: The Role of Economic Modelling.* Cambridge, MA: Synapse Energy Economics, April 2014.

Agerholm, Harriet. "Jeremy Corbyn was just 2,227 votes away from chance to be Prime Minister". *The Independent*, 9 June 2017.

Ajuntament de Barcelona. *Citizen Participation.* http://ajuntament.barcelona.cat/participaciociutadana/en.

Alessi, Lucia and Carsten Detken. "*Identifying excessive credit growth and leverage*". European Central Bank Working paper series, no. 1723, (2014).

Alperovitz, Gar. *America Beyond Capitalism: Reclaiming Our Wealth, Our Liberty & Our Democracy.* Takoma Park, MD: Democracy Collaborative Press, 2011.

Alperovitz, Gar. *What Then Must We Do? Straight Talk About the Next American Revolution.* White River Junction, VT: Chelsea Green, 2013.

Amatori, Franco, Robert Millward, and Pier Angelo Toninelli, eds. *Reappraising State-Owned Enterprise: A Comparison of the UK and Italy.* Routledge: London, 2011.

Arcand, Jean-Louis, Enrico Berkes, and Ugo Panizza. *Too much finance?* IMF Working Paper no 12/161, (2012), https://www.imf.org/external/pubs/ft/wp/2012/wp12161.pdf.

Arnett, George. "Elitism in Britain: Breakdown by profession". *The Guardian*, 28 August 2014.

Avritzer, Leonardo. "Conference presentation: Institutionalising Participatory and Deliberative Democracy". *University of Westminster*, 11 November 2017.

Bailey, David and Leslie Budd. *The Political Economy of Brexit.* Newcastle: Agenda Publishing, 2017.

Bank of England. *Court of Directors,* https://www.bankofengland.co.uk/about/people/court-of-directors.

Bank of England. *Quantitative Easing,* https://www.bankofengland.co.uk/monetary-policy/quantitative-easing.

Bank of England. *Why is the UK financial system so big, and is that a problem?* London: Bank of England, 2014.

Barker, R. S. "Civil Service Attitudes and the Economic Planning of the Attlee Government". *Journal of Contemporary History* 21, no. 3 (July 1986): 473–86

BBC News. "Jeremy Corbyn: It's right to plan for run on pound". 26 September 2017.

BBC News. "Northamptonshire County Council: 'Radical' service cuts planned". 2 August 2018.

BBC News. "East Sussex County Council cuts services to 'legal minimum'". 3 August 2018.

Bearpark, Thomas, Andrew Heron and Ben Glover. "Economics in government: more open, more diverse, more influential" *Civil Service Quarterly,* 8 August 2017.

Benn, Tony. "The Real Choices Facing the Cabinet". Memorandum by the Secretary of State for Energy, 2 November 1976, CP(76) 117, CAB/129/193/7, http://discovery.nationalarchives. gov.uk/details/r/C9614765.

Berry, Craig et al. *Reforming the Treasury, Reorienting British Capitalism.* Sheffield: SPERI British Political Economy Brief No. 21, March 2016.

Berry, Christine. "What would it look like to build a politics that's open to people but closed to big money?" *openDemocracy,* 9 May 2017.

Berry, Christine. "After Grenfell: Ending the murderous war on our protections". *openDemocracy,* 16 June 2017.

Berry, Christine. "The making of a movement: Who's shaping Corbynism?" *openDemocracy,* 5 December 2017.

Berry, Christine. "Flipping the script on our economic stories". *Red Pepper,* 15 March 2018.

Berry, Christine. "John McDonnell is right: we need a new left internationalism". *Verso Blog,* 17 October 2018, https://www.versobooks.com/blogs/4086-john-mcdonnell-is-right-we-need-a-new-left-internationalism.

Berry, Christine and Stephen Devlin. *Threat to Democracy: The impact of 'better regulation' in the UK.* London: New Economics Foundation, 2015.

Bew, John. *Citizen Clem: A Biography of Attlee.* London: riverrun, 2016.

Birch, Jonah. "The Many Lives of François Mitterrand". *Jacobin,* 19 August 2015.

Blackburn, Tom. "Corbynism from Below". *New Socialist,* 12 June 2017.

Blackburn, Tom. "Waking Up the Giant: Political Education and the Labour Movement". *New Socialist,* 17 June 2018.

Blackburn, Robin. *Banking on Death, or, Investing in Life: The History and Future of Pensions.* London, Verso, 2002.

Black Panther Party. *Ten Point Program,* https://www.marxists.org/history/usa/workers/ black-panthers/1966/10/15.htm.

Bolton, Doug. "Greek debt crisis: Alexis Tsipras speaks to 25,000 at 'No' rally in Syntagma Square, urging voters to deny 'those who terrorise you'". *The Independent,* 5 July 2015.

Bosanquet, Nick. *After the New Right.* London: Heinemann, 1983.

Boughton, John. *Municipal Dreams: The Rise and Fall of Council Housing.* London: Verso, 2018.

Bristol City Council. "Pupils try their hand at setting the council's budget. 21 November 2017, http://news.bristol.gov.uk/pupils_try_their_hand_at_setting_the_council_s_budget.

Brittan, Samuel. *Steering the Economy: The Role of the Treasury.* Harmondsworth: Penguin, 1971.

Brown, Matthew and Martin O'Neill "The Road to Socialism is the A59: on the Preston Model". *Renewal* 24, no. 2, (2016): 69–78.

Bua, Adrian. "Book Review: Popular Democracy: The Paradox of Participation by Gianpaolo Baiocchi and Ernesto Ganuza". *LSE Review of Books,* 15 August 2017.

Burk, Kathleen and Alec Cairncross. *'Goodbye, Great Britain': The 1976 IMF Crisis.* New Haven: Yale University Press, 1992.

Cabinet Office. *White Paper: Modernising Government.* London: The Stationery Office, 1999.

Cabinet Office. *Professional Policy Making in the 21st Century.* London: The Stationery Office, 1999.

Cabinet Office. "Enhanced Departmental Boards Protocol". *UK Government website,* 19 February 2013, https://www.gov.uk/government/publications/enhanced-departmental-boards-protocol.

BIBLIOGRAPHY

Cabinet Office. "Open Policy Making Toolkit". UK Government website, 3 January 2017, https://www.gov.uk/guidance/open-policy-making-toolkit.

Calhoun, Craig and Georgi Derluguian, eds. *Aftermath: A New Global Economic Order.* New York: Social Science Research Council and New York University Press, 2011.

Callaghan, John, Nina Fishman, Ben Jackson, and Martin McIvor, eds. *In Search of Social Democracy: Responses to Crisis and Modernisation.* Manchester: Manchester University Press, 2009.

Chakrabortty, Aditya. "End these offshore games or our democracy will die". *The Guardian,* 7 November 2017.

Chakrabortty, Aditya. "In 2011 Preston hit rock bottom. Then it took back control" *The Guardian,* 31 January 2018.

Chakrabortty, Aditya. "What happens when ordinary people learn economics?" *The Guardian,* 20 June 2018.

Charles, Monique. "Grime Labour". *Soundings,* no. 68, (Spring 2018): 40–52.

Ching, Wong Sook, Jomo K. S., and Chin Kok Fay, eds. *Malaysian "Bail Outs"? Capital Controls, Restructuring and Recovery.* Singapore: Singapore University Press, 2005.

Christoph, James B. "The Remaking of British Administrative Culture". *Administration & Society* 24, no. 2 (26 August 1992).

Civil Service Commission. *Recruiting Permanent Secretaries: Ministerial Involvement.* London: The Stationery Office, 2012.

Clifford, Christopher. "The rise and fall of the Department of Economic Affairs 1964–69: British government and indicative planning". *Contemporary British History* 11, no. 2, (1997): 94–116.

Coates, David. *The Labour Party and the Struggle for Socialism.* Cambridge: Cambridge University Press, 1975.

Coates, Ken, ed. *What Went Wrong: Explaining the Fall of the Labour Government.* Nottingham: Spokesman, 2008.

Cohen, Adam. *Nothing to Fear: FDR's Inner Circle and the Hundred Days that Created Modern America.* New York: Penguin, 2009.

Collins, Joseph and John Lear. *Chile's Free-Market Miracle: A Second Look.* Oakland: Institute for Food and Development Policy, 1995.

Connolly, Bernard. *The Rotten Heart of Europe.* London and Boston: Faber and Faber, 1995.

Conservative Research Department. *Final Report of the Nationalised Industries Policy Group.* Economic Reconstruction Group, 30 June 1977, https://www.margaretthatcher.org/document/110795.

Cooper, Charlie. "Future Labour government should be more radical than Attlee, says Shadow Chancellor". *The Independent,* 21 May 2016.

Corbyn, Jeremy. "Speech to Labour Party Conference". 27 September 2017, https://labour.org.uk/press/jeremy-corbyn-speech-to-labour-party-conference/.

Corporate Europe Observatory. *TTIP: "Regulatory co-operation" a threat to democracy.* 21 March 2016.

Cumbers, Andrew. *Reclaiming Public Ownership: Making Space for Economic Democracy.* London: Zed Books, 2012.

Cunliffe, Sir John. *Speech: Are firms underinvesting—and if so why?* Greater Birmingham Chamber of Commerce, 8 February 2017.

Dafermos, Yannis, Giorgos Galanis and Maria Nikolaidi. *A New Ecological Macroeconomic Model.* London: New Economics Foundation, https://neweconomics.org/uploads/files/08ec800b159197d7a3_qlm6i2e5v.pdf.

Davies, Jonathan S. *Governing In And Against Austerity: International Lessons from Eight Cities.* Leicester: De Montfort University, 2017.

Democracy Matters Project. *Citizens Assembly Pilots.* https://citizensassembly.co.uk/democracy-matters/.

Department for Business, Energy and Industrial Strategy. *Our governance,* https://www.gov.uk/government/organisations/department-for-business-energy-and-industrial-strategy/about/our-governance.

Department for Communities and Local Government. *Multi-Criteria Analysis: A Manual.* London: The Stationery Office, 2009.

Department for Transport. "New non-executives appointed to the Department for Transport board". *UK Government website,* 11 June 2013, https://www.gov.uk/government/news/new-non-executives-appointed-to-the-department-for-transport-board.

Derlauf, Steven and Larry Blume, eds. *The New Palgrave Dictionary of Economics.* Hampshire: Palgrave Macmillan, 2008.

Desai, Radhika. "Second Hand Dealers in Ideas: Think Tanks and Thatcherite Hegemony". *New Left Review* I, no. 203, (1994): 27–64.

Dow, J. C. R. *The Management of the British Economy 1945–1960.* Cambridge: Cambridge University Press, 1964.

Ealey, Shani. "Black Panthers Oakland Community School: A model for liberation". *Black Organising Project,* 3 November 2016.

Eaton, George. "Corbynism 2.0: the radical ideas shaping Labour's future". *New Statesman,* 19 September 2018.

Eaton, George. "How Preston—the UK's "most improved city"—became a success story for Corbynomics". *New Statesman,* 1 November 2018.

The Economist. "Appomattox or civil war". May 27, 1978.

The Economist. "Jeremy Corbyn's Model Town". 21 October 2017.

The Economist. "Corbynomics: The Great Transformation". 19 May 2018.

The Economist. "A confident Labour is swaggering left in its economic policy". 27 September 2018.

The Economist. "Upsetting the punchbowl: A debate about central bank independence is overdue". 20 October 2018.

Edwards, Sebastian and Jeffrey A. Frankel, eds. *Preventing Currency Crises in Emerging Markets.* Chicago: University of Chicago Press, 2002.

Eichengreen, Barry and Peter Temin. "The Gold Standard and the Great Depression". *Contemporary European History* 9, no. 2 (2000): 183–207.

Eley, Geoff. *Forging Democracy: The History of the Left in Europe, 1850–2000.* Oxford: Oxford University Press, 2002.

Elliott, Gregory. *Labourism and the English Genius: The Strange Death of Labour England?* London: Verso, 1993.

Elliott, Larry. "Ten years after the financial crash, the timid left should be full of regrets". *The Guardian,* 30 August 2018.

Elliott, Matthew, and James Kanagasooriam. *Public opinion in the post-Brexit era: Economic attitudes in modern Britain.* London, Legatum Institute, October 2017.

Epstein, Gerald. "Should Financial Flows Be Regulated? Yes". United Nations, Department of Economics and Social Affairs Working Papers, July 2009, Issue 77.

Ernst & Young. *Privatization: Investing in State-Owned Enterprises Around the World.* New York: John Wiley & Sons, 1994.

BIBLIOGRAPHY

Faber, Sebastiaan and Bécquer Seguín. "Welcome to Sunny Barcelona, Where the Government is Embracing Co-ops, Citizen Activism, and Solar Energy". *The Nation*, 11 August 2016.

Farage, Nigel. *Speech to the European Parliament*, 28 June 2016.

Financial Times. "Corbyn sets out stall: 'We won't play by their rules' in 'rigged economy'". 20 April 2017.

Fine, Ben. *The Coal Question: Political Economy and Industrial Change for the Nineteenth Century to the Present Day*. London: Routledge, 1990.

Fischer, Frank. *Democracy and Expertise: Reorienting Policy Inquiry*. Oxford: Oxford University Press, 2009.

Foot, Michael. *Aneurin Bevan: A Biography, Volume Two: 1945-1960*. New York: Atheneum, 1974.

Forgacs, David, ed. *The Antonio Gramsci Reader: Selected Writings 1916-1935*. New York: New York University Press, 2000.

Foroohar, Rana. *Makers and Takers: The Rise of Finance and the Fall of American Business*. New York: Crown Business, 2016.

Framing the Economy: How to Win the Case for a Better System. London: NEF, NEON, PIRC & the Frameworks Institute, 2018.

Friedman, Milton. *Capitalism and Freedom*. Chicago: University of Chicago Press, 2002.

Fry, Geoffrey K. "The Development of the Thatcher Government's 'Grand Strategy' for the Civil Service: A Public Policy Perspective". *Public Administration* 62, no. 3, (1984): 322-35.

Fukuyama, Francis. *The End of History and the Last Man*. New York: The Free Press, 1992.

Fyrth, Jim, ed. *Labour's High Noon: The Government and the Economy 1945-51*. London: Lawrence & Wishart, 1993.

Gallas, Alexander. *The Thatcherite Offensive: A Neo-Poulantzasian Analysis*. Chicago: Haymarket, 2016.

Gamble, Andrew. *The Free Economy and the Strong State: The Politics of Thatcherism*. Durham, NC: Duke University Press, 1988.

Ghosh, Atish R. and Mahvash S. Qureshi. "What's In a Name? That Which We Call Capital Controls". IMF Working Paper WP/16/25, February 2016.

Ghosh, Atish R., Jonathan D. Ostry, and Mahvash S. Qureshi. *Taming the Tide of Capital Flows: A Policy Guide*. Cambridge: The MIT Press, 2017.

Glyn, Andrew. "Capital Flight and Exchange Controls". *New Left Review* I, no. 155, (January-February 19860): 37-49.

Gornall, Jonathan. "Sugar's web of influence 3: Why the responsibility deal is a 'dead duck' for sugar reduction" *British Medical Journal* 350, (2015).

Gorz, André. *Strategy for Labor: A Radical Proposal*. Boston: Beacon Press, 1967.

Gowan, Peter. "Labour has a Plan". *Jacobin*, 2 November 2018.

Gramsci, Antonio. *Selections from the Prison Notebooks*, trans. Quintin Hoare and Geoffrey Nowell Smith. London: Lawrence & Wishart, 1971.

Guinan, Joe. "Social democracy in the age of austerity and resistance: the radical potential of democratising capital". *Renewal* 20, no. 4, (2012): 9-19.

Guinan, Joe. "Who's afraid of public ownership?" *Renewal* 21, no. 4, (2013): 77-84.

Guinan, Joe. "Bring back the Institute for Workers' Control". *Renewal* 23, no. 4, (2015): 11-36.

Guinan, Joe. "Socialising Capital: Looking Back on the Meidner Plan". *International Journal of Public Policy*, forthcoming 2019.

Guinan, Joe and Thomas M. Hanna. "Don't believe the Corbyn bashers—the economic case against public ownership is mostly fantasy". *openDemocracy*, 9 September 2015.

Guinan, Joe and Thomas M. Hanna. "Polanyi against the whirlwind". *Renewal* 25, no. 1, (2017): 5–12.

Guinan, Joe and Martin O'Neill. "The institutional turn: Labour's new political economy". *Renewal* 26, no. 2, (2018): 5–16.

Hallsworth, Michael. *Policy Making in the Real World: Evidence and Analysis*. London: Institute for Government, April 2011.

Hancox, Dan. "Is this the world's most radical mayor?" *The Guardian*, 26 May 2016.

Hanna, Thomas M. *Our Common Wealth: The Return of Public Ownership in the United States*. Manchester: Manchester University Press, 2018.

Hanna, Thomas M. *The Crisis Next Time: Planning for Public Ownership as an Alternative to Corporate Bank Bailouts*. The Democracy Collaborative, 2 July 2018.

Hanna, Thomas M. and Joe Guinan. "Democracy and decentralisation are their watchwords: for Corbyn and McDonnell, it's municipal socialism reinvented". *openDemocracy*, 25 March 2016.

Harvey, David. *Spaces of Hope*. Berkeley: University of California Press, 2000.

Hazell, Robert et al. *Critical Friends? The role of non-executives on departmental boards*. London: UCL Constitution Unit, 2018.

Heffernan, Richard. "UK Privatisation Revisited: Ideas and Policy Change, 1979–92". *The Political Quarterly* 76, no. 2, (2005): 267.

Helleiner, Eric. *States and the Reemergence of Global Finance: From Bretton Woods to the 1990s*. New York: Cornell University Press, 1994.

Helm, Toby. "McDonnell: Labour will give power to workers through 'ownership funds'". *The Observer*, 8 September 2018.

Hennessy, Peter. "Mrs Thatcher's Poodle?" *Contemporary Record* 2, no. 2, (June 25 1988): 2–4.

Hitchens, Christopher. "Staking a Life". *Lapham's Quarterly*, 2011.

HM Treasury. *Implementing Privatisation: The UK Experience*. London: HM Treasury, 2002.

HM Treasury. *Analysis of the Dynamic Effects of Corporation Tax Reductions*. London: The Stationery Office, December 2013.

Hoskyns, John, et al. *Stepping Stones*. 1977, https://c59574e9047e61130f13-3f71d0fe2b653c4f-00f32175760e96e7.ssl.cf1.rackcdn.com/5B6518B5823043FE9D7C54846CC7FE31.pdf.

Hoskyns, John. "Whitehall and Westminster: An outsider's view". *Parliamentary Affairs* 36 (1983).

Hoskyns, John. "Conservatism Is Not Enough". *Political Quarterly* 55 (1984).

Howard, Ted and Martin O'Neill. "Beyond extraction: The political power of community wealth building". *Renewal* 26, no. 2, (2018): 46–53.

Howlett, Karen. "WTO rules against Ontario in green energy dispute". *Canada Globe and Mail,* 20 November 2012.

Hudson, Michael. *Killing the Host: How Financial Parasites and Debt Destroy the Global Economy*. New York: ISLET, 2015.

Institute for Government. *Previous Event: Tony Blair at the IfG*, https://www.instituteforgovernment.org.uk/events/tony-blair-ifg.

Institute for Government. "Civil service staff numbers". 12 September 2018, https://www.instituteforgovernment.org.uk/explainers/civil-service-staff-numbers.

Jackson, Tim. *System Dynamics: FALSTAFF,* https://timjackson.org.uk/ecological-economics/falstaff/.

Jenkins, Clive. *Power at the Top: A Critical Survey of the Nationalised Industries*. Westport, CT: Greenwood Press, 1976.

BIBLIOGRAPHY

Johnson, Christopher. *The Economy Under Mrs Thatcher 1979–1990*. London: Penguin, 1991.

Jones, Owen and Ellie Mae O'Hagan. *Agitpod*. "Episode 24—Sirio Canós Donnay" (Podcast).

Jónsson, Ásgeir and Hersir Sigurgeirsson. *The Icelandic Financial Crisis: A Study into the World's Smallest Currency Area and its Recovery from Total Banking Collapse*. London: Palgrave Macmillan, 2016.

Karitzis, Andreas. "The Dilemmas and Potentials of the Left: Learning from Syriza". *Socialist Register* (2016): 374–81.

Kay, John. *Other People's Money: Masters of the Universe or Servants of the People?* London: Profile Books, 2015.

Keen, Steve. "Manifesto", *Steve Keen's Debtwatch*, http://www.debtdeflation.com/blogs/manifesto/.

Kelf-Cohen, Reuben. *British Nationalisation 1945–1973*. London: Macmillan, 1973.

Kelly, Marjorie and Ted Howard. *The Making of a Democratic Economy: Building Prosperity for the Many, Not Just the Few*. San Francisco: Berrett-Koehler, 2019.

Kelly, Marjorie, Sarah McKinley, and Violeta Duncan. "Community wealth building: America's emerging asset-based approach to city economic development". *Renewal* 24, no. 2, (2016): 51–68.

Kentish, Benjamin. "Forty percent of homes sold under Right to Buy now in the hands of private landlords, new analysis reveals". *The Independent*, 8 December 2017.

Kerslake, Lord. *Rethinking the Treasury: The Kerslake Review of the Treasury*. London: Industry Forum, February 2017.

Keys, David, et al. *Thatcher's Britain: A Guide to the Ruins*. London: Pluto Press and New Socialist, 1983

Klein, Naomi. *The Shock Doctrine: The Rise of Disaster Capitalism*. New York: Picador, 2007.

Knai, Cecile et al. "Are the Public Health Responsibility Deal alcohol pledges likely to improve public health? An evidence synthesis". *Addiction* 110, no. 8, (Aug 2015): 1232–46.

Kouvelakis, Stathis. "Syriza's Rise and Fall". *New Left Review* 2, no. 97, (2016): 45–70.

Labour Party. *General Election Manifesto—New Labour: Because Britain Deserves Better*. London: Labour Party, 1997.

Labour Party. *Labour's Fiscal Credibility Rule*, 2017, http://labour.org.uk/wp-content/uploads/2017/10/Fiscal-Credibility-Rule.pdf.

Labour Party. *For the Many Not the Few*. May 2017, https://labour.org.uk/wp-content/uploads/2017/10/labour-manifesto-2017.pdf.

Labour Party. *Alternative Models of Ownership: Report to the Shadow Chancellor and the Shadow Secretary of State for Business, Energy and Industrial Strategy*. June 2017, https://labour.org.uk/wp-content/uploads/2017/10/Alternative-Models-of-Ownership.pdf.

Labour Party. *Labour Party Consultation Paper: Democratic Public Ownership*, https://labour.org.uk/wp-content/uploads/2018/09/Democratic-public-ownership-consulation.pdf.

Labour Party. *Our Town*, https://www.facebook.com/labourparty/videos/our-town/1737038089726749/.

Laclau, Ernesto and Chantal Mouffe. *Hegemony and Socialist Strategy: Towards a Radical Democratic Politics*. London: Verso, 1985.

Laidler, David. "Review: Dow and Savile's Critique of Monetary Policy—A Review Essay". *Journal of Economic Literature* 27, no. 3, (Sep. 1989): 1147–59.

Lakoff, George. *Don't Think Of An Elephant: Know Your Values And Frame the Debate*. Hartford: Chelsea Green, 1990.

Lapavitsas, Costas. *Crisis in the Eurozone*. London: Verso, 2012.

Lawrence, Mathew, Andrew Pendleton, and Sara Mahmoud. *Co-operatives Unleashed: Doubling the Size of the UK's Co-operative Sector.* New Economics Foundation, 3 July 2018.

Lilico, Andrew. "All that matters now is stopping Corbyn". *CapX*, 12 June 2017.

Local Government Association. *Case study: Govanhill, Glasgow.* 12 December 2016, https://www.local.gov.uk/govanhill-glasgow.

Lorenzo, Miguel. "Josep Oliu propone crear 'una especie de Podemos de derechas'". *El Periodico,* 25 June 2014.

Macfarlane, Laurie. "From PFI to privatisation, our national accounting rules encourage daft decisions. It's time to change them". *openDemocracy,* 18 January 2018.

Macfarlane, Laurie, ed. *New Thinking for the British Economy.* London: *openDemocracy,* 2018.

MacGregor, Graham A. et al. "Food and the responsibility deal: how the salt reduction strategy was derailed". *British Medical Journal* 350, (2015).

Machin, Howard and Vincent Wright, eds. *Economic Policy and Policy Making Under the Mitterrand Presidency 1981–1984.* New York: St. Martin's, 1985.

Marglin, Stephen A. and Juliet B. Schor, eds. *The Golden Age of Capitalism: Reinterpreting the Postwar Experience.* Oxford: Oxford University Press, 1990.

Mayer, Jane. *Dark Money: The Hidden History of the Billionaires Behind the Rise of the Radical Right.* New York: Anchor Books, 2017.

Mazzucato, Mariana. *The Value of Everything: Making and Taking in the Global Economy.* London: Allen Lane, 2018.

McCormick, Brian J. *Industrial Relations in the Coal Industry.* London, Macmillan, 1979.

McDonnell, John. "Governing from the Radical Left". Speech at The World Transformed, 25 September 2017.

McDonnell, John, ed. *Economics for The Many.* London: Verso, 2018.

McDonnell, John. *Speech to Labour Party Conference.* 24 September 2018, https://labour.org.uk/press/john-mcdonnells-full-speech-labour-conference-2018/.

McDonnell, John. *The Economic Policy of the Labour Party: Speech to the Marx Memorial Library.* 2 October 2018.

McEachern, Doug. *A Class Against Itself: Power and the Nationalisation of the British Steel Industry.* Cambridge: Cambridge University Press, 1980.

McLeay, Michael, Amar Radia and Ryland Thomas. "Money creation in the modern economy". *Bank of England Quarterly Bulletin* 2014 Q1, http://www.bankofengland.co.uk/publications/documents/quarterlybulletin/2014/qb14q1prereleasemoneycreation.pdf.

MacLean, Nancy. *Democracy in Chains: The Deep History of the Radical Right's Stealth Plan for America.* New York: Viking, 2017.

Macpherson, Sir Nicholas. "Speech to the Mile End Group by the Permanent Secretary to the Treasury: The Treasury View—a testament of experience". *HM Treasury,* 17 January 2014, https://www.gov.uk/government/speeches/speech-by-the-permanent-secretary-to-the-treasury-the-treasury-view-a-testament-of-experience.

Makin-Waite, Mike. *Communism and Democracy,* London: Lawrence & Wishart, 2017.

Marriage, Madison. "Why the UK's uber-wealthy voters fear a Corbyn-led government". *Financial Times,* 6 October 2018.

Maura, Eduardo. "Podemos: Politics by the people". *Red Pepper,* 22 February 2015.

Medhurst, John. *That Option No Longer Exists: Britain 1974–76.* London: Zero Books, 2014.

Meidner, Rudolf. *Employee Investment Funds: An Approach to Collective Capital Formation.* London: George Allen & Unwin, 1978.

BIBLIOGRAPHY

Meidner, Rudolf. "Why Did the Swedish Model Fail?" *Socialist Register* 29, (1993): 211–28.

Miller, Robert. "Corbyn is keeping us awake at night, say business chiefs". *The Times*, 23 August 2018.

Mills, Tom. "It Was a Fantasy: Centrist Political Commentators in the Age of Corbynism". *New Socialist*, 12 June 2017.

Millward, Robert. "The 1940s Nationalizations in Britain: Means to an End or Means of Production?" *Economic History Review* 50, no. 2, (1997): 210–12.

Millward, Robert, David Parker, Leslie Rosenthal, Michael T. Sumner and Neville Topham. *Public Sector Economics*. Longman: London, 1983.

Millward, Robert and John Singleton, eds. *The Political Economy of Nationalisation in Britain 1920–50*. Cambridge: Cambridge University Press, 1995.

Ministry of Reconstruction. *Employment Policy: Cmd. 6527.* London: The Stationery Office, 1944.

Mirowski, Philip. *Never Let a Serious Crisis Go to Waste: How Neoliberalism Survived the Financial Meltdown*. London: Verso, 2014.

Mirowski, Philip and Dieter Plehwe. *The Road from Mont Pèlerin: The Making of the Neoliberal Thought Collective*. Cambridge, MA: Harvard University Press, 2009.

Mishra, Pankaj. *Age of Anger: A History of the Present*. New York: Farrar, Straus and Giroux, 2017.

Mitchell, Jeanette et al. *In and Against the State*. London: London Edinburgh Weekend Return Group, 1979, https://libcom.org/library/against-state-1979.

Mitchell, William and Thomas Fazi. *Reclaiming the State: A Progressive Vision of Sovereignty for a Post-Neoliberal World*. London: Pluto Press, 2017.

Monbiot, George. "With Grenfell, we've seen what 'ripping up red tape' really looks like". *The Guardian*, 15 June 2017.

Morgan, Kenneth O. *Labour in Power 1945–1951*. Oxford: Oxford University Press, 1985.

Morris, Nigel. "Labour leadership race: Rivals turn on Jeremy Corbyn in row over Clause IV". *The Independent*, 9 August 2015.

Morrison, Herbert. *Socialisation and Transport*. London: Constable, 1933.

New Economics Foundation. *Agenda for Change: Building a New Economy Where People Really Take Control*. London: 2016.

Northcutt, Wayne. *Mitterrand: A Political Biography*. New York: Holmes & Meier, 1992.

Nunns, Alex. *The Candidate: Jeremy Corbyn's Improbable Path to Power*. London: O/R Books, 2018.

O'Donnell, Gus et al. *Report: Wellbeing and Policy*. London: Legatum Institute, 2014.

O'Neill, Jim. "I'm an ex-Tory Minister: Only Labour Grasps Britain's Desire for Change". *The Guardian*, 5 October 2018.

Osborne, Samuel. "Diane Abbott: Grenfell Tower fire 'direct consequence of deregulation, privatisation and outsourcing'", *The Independent*, 24 September 2017.

Ovenden, Kevin. *Syriza: Inside the Labyrinth*. London: Pluto Press, 2015.

Overbeek, Henk. *Global Capitalism and National Decline: The Thatcher Decade in Perspective*. London: Unwin Hyman, 1990.

Panitch, Leo and Colin Leys. *The End of Parliamentary Socialism: From New Left to New Labour*. London: Verso, 2001.

Parker, David. *The Official History of Privatisation, Volume I: The Formative Years 1970–1987*. Abingdon: Routledge, 2009.

Parker, David. *The Official History of Privatisation, Volume II: Popular Capitalism, 1987–1997*. Abingdon: Routledge, 2012.

Parker, George. "McDonnell strikes emollient tone with City leaders". *Financial Times*, 17 June 2018.

Pérez-Nievas, Santiago et al. "New Wine in Old Bottles? The Selection of Electoral Candidates in General Elections in Podemos", in Cordero and Coller, eds. *Democratizing Candidate Selection*. London: Palgrave Macmillan, 2018.

Performance and Innovation Unit. *Adding It Up: Improving Analysis and Modelling in Central Government*. London: The Stationery Office, 2000.

Peston, Robert. "Would Corbyn's 'QE for people' float or sink Britain?". BBC, 12 August 2015.

Pettifor, Ann. "Why business could prosper under a Corbyn government". *The Guardian*, 17 December 2017.

Phillips-Fein, Kim. *Invisible Hands: The Businessmen's Crusade Against the New Deal*. New York: W. W. Norton, 2009.

Pickard, Jim. "Labour plans for capital flight or run on pound if elected". *Financial Times*, 26 September 2017.

Piketty, Thomas. *The Economics of Inequality*. Cambridge, MA: Harvard University Press, 2015.

Pimlott, Ben, ed. *Labour's First Hundred Days*. Fabian Society tract, no. 519, April 1987.

Podemos. *Organisational Principles*, 2016, https://podemos.info/wp-content/uploads/2016/11/Organisational_Principles.pdf.

Polanyi, Karl. *The Great Transformation: The Political and Economic Origins of Our Time*. Boston: Beacon Press, 2001.

Pontusson, Jonas. *The Limits to Social Democracy: Investment Politics in Sweden*. Ithaca: Cornell University Press, 1992.

Powell, David. "Transforming the Treasury: The biggest and best idea of all". *openDemocracy*, 12 May 2014.

Powell, Lewis F., Jr. *Attack on the American Free Enterprise System*. U.S. Chamber of Commerce, 23 August 1971, http://law2.wlu.edu/powellarchives/page.asp?pageid=1251.

Pryke, Richard. "Labour and the City: The Predictable Crisis". *New Left Review* I, no. 39, (September–October 1966): 3–15.

Rhodes, R. A. W. "New Labour's Civil Service: Summing-up Joining-up". *The Political Quarterly* 71 (2000): 151–66.

Richards, Dave and Martin Smith. "The lessons of Tony Benn as a Cabinet Minister: Breaking the rules and paying the price". *LSE British Politics and Policy blog*, 19 March 2014, http://blogs.lse.ac.uk/politicsandpolicy/the-lessons-of-tony-benn-as-a-cabinet-minister-breaking-the-rules-and-paying-the-price/.

Ridley, Nicholas. *'My Style of Government': The Thatcher Years*. London: Fontana, 1992.

Roberts, Richard and David Kynaston. *City State: A Contemporary History of the City of London and How Money Triumphed*. London: Profile Books, 2002.

Rogow, Arnold A. *The Labour Government and British Industry 1945–1951*. Oxford: Basil Blackwell, 1955.

Ross, George, Stanley Hoffmann, and Sylvia Malzacher, eds. *The Mitterrand Experiment: Continuity and Change in Modern France*. Cambridge: Polity Press, 1987.

Russell, Bert. "Corbynism from (The Great) Below". *We Are Plan C*, 18 October 2017, https://www.weareplanc.org/blog/corbynism-from-the-great-below/.

Sabbagh, Dan. "Labour hopes new initiative will revive political education". *The Guardian*, 8 October 2018.

Sarkar, Ash. "This isn't just a culture war: We need a radical anti-fascist movement right now". *The Guardian*, 21 August 2018.

BIBLIOGRAPHY

Sassoon, Donald. *One Hundred Years of Socialism: The West European Left in the Twentieth Century*. New York: The New Press, 1996.

Secker, Graham, Matthew Garman, Krupa Patel, Lillian Huang, and Alix G. Guerrini. *Into Thin Air: 2018 European Equity Outlook*. Morgan Stanley & Co., 26 November 2017.

Seguín, Bécquer and Sebastiaan Faber. "Can Podemos Win in Spain?" *The Nation*, 14 January 2015.

Shaxson, Nicholas. *The Finance Curse: How Global Finance is Making Us All Poorer*. London: Bodley Head, 2018.

Shelley, Percy. "The Mask of Anarchy: Written on the Occasion of the Massacre at Manchester" *Poetical Works*, ed. Thomas Hutchinson. London. Oxford University Press, 1970.

Shinwell, Emanuel. *Conflict Without Malice: An Autobiography*. London: Odhams Press, 1955.

Short, Philip. *Mitterrand: A Study in Ambiguity*. London: Bodley Head, 2013.

Simon, Roger. *Gramsci's Political Thought: An Introduction*. London: Lawrence & Wishart, 1990.

Singer, Daniel. *Is Socialism Doomed? The Meaning of Mitterrand*. New York: Oxford University Press, 1988.

Sintomer, Yves. "From Deliberative to Radical Democracy? Sortition and Politics in the 21st Century". *Politics and Society* 46, no. 3, (2018).

Slobodian, Quinn. *Globalists: The End of Empire and the Birth of Neoliberalism*. London: Harvard University Press, 2018.

Sloman, Martyn. *Socialising Public Ownership*. London: Macmillan, 1978.

Smith, David. *The Rise and Fall of Monetarism: The Theory and Politics of an Economic Experiment*. London: Penguin, 1991.

Smucker, Jonathan. *Hegemony How-To: A Roadmap for Radicals*. AK Press, 2017.

Solidarity4All. *Solidarity is people's power: Towards an international campaign of solidarity to the Greek people*. Athens, 2013, https://www.solidarity4all.gr/sites/www.solidarity4all.gr/files/aggliko.pdf.

Solidarity4All. *Building Hope Against Fear and Devastation: Annual Report 2015*, https://issuu.com/solidarityforall/docs/report_2014.

Srnicek, Nick and Alex Williams. *Inventing the Future: Post-Capitalism and a World Without Work*. London: Verso, 2015.

Stedman Jones, Daniel. *Masters of the Universe: Hayek, Friedman, and the Birth of Neoliberal Politics*. Princeton: Princeton University Press, 2012.

Steil, Benn. *The Battle of Bretton Woods: John Maynard Keynes, Harry Dexter White, and the Making of a New World Order*. Princeton: Princeton University Press, 2014.

Stratford, Beth. "Falling house prices could be the reboot our economy desperately needs. But only if we prepare a soft landing". *openDemocracy*, 13 February 2018.

Syndicalist Workers' Federation. *How Labour Governed 1945–1951*. Direct Action Pamphlets no. 5.

Taylor, A. J. P. *English History 1914–1945*. Oxford: Oxford University Press, 1965.

Taylor, Nick. *American Made—The Enduring Legacy of the WPA: When FDR Put the Nation to Work*. New York: Bantam, 2009.

Terrill, Ross. *R. H. Tawney and His Times: Socialism as Fellowship*. Cambridge, MA: Harvard University Press, 1973.

Thatcher, Margaret. "Interview for *Sunday Times*". 3 May 1981, Margaret Thatcher Foundation, https://www.margaretthatcher.org/document/104475.

Thatcher, Margaret. *The Downing Street Years*. New York: HarperCollins, 1993.

Thompson, E. P. *The Making of the English Working Class*. London: Victor Gollancz, 1965.

Thompson, Noel. *Political Economy and the Labour Party*. London: Routledge, 2006.

Thompson, Willie. *The Long Death of British Labourism: Interpreting a Political Culture*. London: Pluto Press, 1993.

Tomlinson, Jim. *Democratic Socialism and Economic Policy: The Attlee Years, 1945–1951*. Cambridge: Cambridge University Press, 1997.

Traverso, Enzo. *Left-Wing Melancholia: Marxism, History, and Memory*. New York: Columbia University Press, 2016.

Tremlett, Giles. "The Podemos revolution: How a small group of radical academics changed European politics". *The Guardian*, 31 March 2015.

Turner, Adair. *Between Debt and the Devil: Money, Credit and Fixing Global Finance*. Princeton: Princeton University Press, 2016.

Turner, Graham. *Financing Investment: Final Report*. London: GFC Economist Ltd and Clearpoint Advisors Ltd, 2018.

UNISON. *Community and Voluntary Services in the Age of Austerity: UNISON Voices from the Frontline*. London: Unison, 2013.

Unterrainer, Tom, ed. *Corbyn's Campaign*. Nottingham: Spokesman, 2016.

Varoufakis, Yanis. *And the Weak Suffer What They Must? Europe, Austerity and the Threat to Global Stability*. London: Vintage, 2016.

Wainwright, Hilary. *A New Politics from the Left*. Cambridge: Polity, 2018.

Walker, David. "Babes in the Whitehall Wood". *The Independent*, 14 January 1997.

Waugh, Colin. *Plebs: The lost legacy of independent working-class political education*. Sheffield: Post-16 Educator, 2009.

Wells, Peter. "New Labour and Evidence-Based Policy Making: 1997–2007" *People, Place & Policy Online* 1, no. 1. (2007).

Westlake, Stian. "Is it time to break up the Treasury?" *Civil Service World*, 19 November 2015.

Wickham-Jones, Mark. *Economic Strategy and the Labour Party: Politics and Policy Making, 1970–83*. London: Palgrave Macmillan, 1996.

Wilks, Stephen. *The Political Power of the Business Corporation*. Cheltenham: Edward Elgar, 2013.

Williams, Raymond. *The Long Revolution*. Harmondsworth: Penguin, 1965.

Wilson, Harold. *The Labour Government 1964–70*. Penguin: Harmondsworth, 1971.

Wrack, Matt. "Deregulation and the Grenfell Tower fire". Fire Brigades Union blog, 20 June 2018, https://www.fbu.org.uk/blog/deregulation-and-grenfell-tower-fire.

Wren-Lewis, Simon. "A Labour run on Sterling?" *Mainly Macro*, 27 September 2017, https://mainlymacro.blogspot.com/2017/09/a-labour-run-on-sterling.html.

Younge, Gary. "Journalists' lack of curiosity about Corbyn was professional malpractice". *Prospect Magazine*, 16 June 2017.

Zeffmann, Henry. "Corbyn groomed for No. 10 by ex-head of Civil Service Lord Kerslake". *The Times,* 23 October 2017.

INDEX

INDEX

democratic economy, 9, 18–22, 29–33, 34, 39–44, 84, 87–88, 156, 166–67
Democratic Thought Collective, 170
democratised ownership. *See* public ownership
denationlisation, 60–61
departmental boards, 123–24
Department of Economic Affairs, 74–75
deregulated capitalism, 27
deregulation, 54–55, 86, 120–23
Desai, Radhika, 172, 182–83
devaluation, 75–77, 82–83
devolution, 136, 152
direct democracy, 142
disaster capitalism, 13
Donnay, Sirio Canós, 147
Don't Think of an Elephant (Lakoff), 162
Downing Street Policy Unit, 118
The Downing Street Years (Thatcher), 64
Drucker, Peter, 52

Eaton, George, 41, 109
economic alternatives. *See* alternative economics
economic models, 53, 127–31
. *See also* democratic economy; extractive economy
economic policies, 39–44, 63, 137
economic programmes, 33, 40, 46–47, 93–97
Economics for the Many (McDonnell), 91
The Economist (magazine), 33, 40–41, 61–62, 100, 196n22
"The education of Mr Attllee" (article), 107
efficiency of capital, 54
electoral politics, 14, 59, 145–46, 148–49
Elements of the Democratic Economy series, 195n18
Eley, Geoff, 11 13
elites, 25–28, 132, 149
Employee Stock Ownership Plans (ESOPs), 42
empowerment, 31, 131–33, 152–53, 155
EMS (European Monetary System), 80–83
energy companies, 8, 28, 39, 166–68, 182
Epstein, Gerald, 101
Erhard, Ludwig, 138
Ernst & Young, 52
ESOPs (Employee Stock Ownership Plans), 42
European Central Bank, 86, 97
European Commission, 97
European Economy Community, 80–81
European Monetary System (EMS), 80–83

exchange controls, 82, 101
exchange rates, 75, 93, 105
Exploring Economics network, 115, 130–31
extractive economy, 18, 25–29, 30–32, 167

Fabian Society, 49, 200n40
Farage, Nigel, 163
15M (*indignados*), 147, 151
Final Report of the Nationalised Industries Policy Group, 60–63, 65
finance capital, 3, 26, 55, 66–67, 87–88
financial crisis, 8, 84, 89, 102–3, 142
financial sector, 7–8, 54–55, 80, 84–88
. *See also* extractive economy
Financial Times (newspaper), 7, 95
Financial Transactions Tax, 88
Fiscal Credibility Rule, 90–91, 96–97, 138
floating signifiers, 162–64
flotation, 54–55
Focus on Enforcement, 122
folk politics, 144
Forging Democracy (Eley), 11–12
For the Many Not the Few (manifesto), 34, 42
France, 78–83, 106
franc fort policy, 82
free enterprise system, 58–59
free markets, 26–27
Freire, Paolo, 176–77
Fried, Bradley, 138
Friedman, Milton, 8, 17, 179, 183
full employment, 128

Gallas, Alexander, 54, 63
General Theory of Employment, Interest and Money (Keynes), 114
German Bundesbank, 137 38
Gimenez, Luis, 164
global capital markets, 81, 103 5
global economy, 103–5
global financial crisis, 96, 135, 143
global financial markets, 19, 94, 99–100, 184
Glover, Anne, 138
Glyn, Andrew, 101–2
González, Felipe, 79
Gorz, André, 33
Gowan, Peter, 43
Gramsci, Antonio, 11, 20, 143–44, 155, 162–64, 177, 179
grassroots movements, 137, 143–46, 150–51, 156, 158–60, 164

INDEX

INDEX

ABOUT THE AUTHORS

Christine Berry is a freelance researcher and writer focused on economic systems change. She is a fellow of the Next System Project, commissioning editor of *Renewal* journal, and co-chair of trustees at Rethinking Economics. She has previously worked as principal director of policy and government at the New Economics Foundation, as head of policy and research at responsible investment charity ShareAction, and in the UK parliament. She lives in Manchester with her husband Mark and son Rory.

Joe Guinan is vice president for theory, research, and policy at The Democracy Collaborative, a U.S.-based think-do tank working on the democratic economy, where he serves as executive director of the Next System Project. Born in Blackburn, Lancashire, he is a dual British-Irish citizen and a member of Labour International, a commissioning editor of *Renewal* journal, and a frequently cited expert on economic alternatives and system change. He lives in Washington, DC.